'Dillon and Craig help readers learn how to understan
of stories in public reasoning (*storylistening*) and show ho
the production of useful policy-relevant knowledge (*narrative evidence*). This book
makes a crucial contribution to the study of research, political debate, and public
policy.'

Paul Cairney, *University of Stirling, UK*

'Dillon and Craig have written a book of compelling value to policymakers. The
humanities must engage with public reasoning, but how can they better do so
in partnership with other forms of evidence? How can the insights that narratives provide enhance public reasoning? How can we listen better to stories to
balance their informative and democratising power against their potential to be
persuasive and manipulative? In answer, the authors present the framework of
storylistening.'

Sir Peter Gluckman, *Chair of the International Network for
Government Science Advice*

'This important new intervention makes a passionate and convincing case for
the power of narrative and storytelling in contemporary society, as well as for
the centrality of a public humanities in further understanding and facilitating
interdisciplinary conversations about some of the most pressing challenges facing
society today.'

Katy Shaw, *Northumbria University, UK*

'In this important and timely book, Dillon and Craig radically expand our notion of what constitutes the "evidence" that should inform policy-making: not
just scientific facts and statistical models, but stories too; not just *logos* but *mythos*.
They launch a powerful argument for why narrative literacy is as important for
wise and effective public decision-making as is scientific literacy or numeracy.'

Mike Hulme, *University of Cambridge, UK*

'In any domain of public policy, the prevailing stories shape ideas and decisions,
and therefore collective outcomes, but until now they have done so outside of a
formal framework for taking them seriously. In providing just that, *Storylistening*
is an essential contribution to understanding how change in society comes about.'

Diane Coyle, *University of Cambridge, UK*

'This book is brilliant, absolutely brilliant – timely, important, necessary. It is
compelling.'

Ben Davies, *University of Portsmouth, and
Secretary of University English, UK*

'This is a must-read book that highlights the absolute necessity to reimagine the power of stories in light of the rapid social and political changes cf the 21st century. It's a fascinating exploration of how policymakers can gather evidence from stories to inform their thinking.'

Tabitha Goldstaub, *Head of the UK Government's AI Council*

STORYLISTENING

Storylistening makes the case for the urgent need to take stories seriously in order to improve public reasoning. Dillon and Craig provide a theory and practice for gathering narrative evidence that will complement and strengthen, not distort, other forms of evidence, including that from science.

Focusing on the cognitive and the collective, Dillon and Craig show how stories offer alternative points of view, create and cohere collective identities, function as narrative models, and play a crucial role in anticipation. They explore these four functions in areas of public reasoning where decisions are strongly influenced by contentious knowledge and powerful imaginings: climate change, artificial intelligence, the economy, and nuclear weapons and power. Vivid performative readings of stories from *The Ballad of Tam-Lin* to *The Terminator* demonstrate the insights that storylistening can bring and the ways it might be practised.

The book provokes a reimagining of what a public humanities might look like, and shows how the structures and practices of public reasoning can evolve to better incorporate narrative evidence. *Storylistening* aims to create the conditions in which the important task of listening to stories is possible, expected, and becomes endemic.

Taking the reader through complex ideas from different disciplines in ways that do not require any prior knowledge, this book is an essential read for policymakers, political scientists, students of literary studies, and anyone interested in the public humanities and the value, importance, and operation of narratives.

Sarah Dillon is Professor of Literature and the Public Humanities in the Faculty of English at the University of Cambridge, UK.

Claire Craig is Provost of The Queen's College, Oxford, UK, and a former civil servant.

STORYLISTENING

Narrative Evidence and Public Reasoning

Sarah Dillon and Claire Craig

Routledge
Taylor & Francis Group

LONDON AND NEW YORK

First published 2021
by Routledge
2 Park Square, Milton Park, Abingdon, Oxon OX14 4RN

and by Routledge
605 Third Avenue, New York, NY 10158

Routledge is an imprint of the Taylor & Francis Group, an informa business

British Library Cataloguing-in-Publication Data
A catalogue record for this book is available from the British Library

Library of Congress Cataloging-in-Publication Data
Names: Dillon, Sarah, author. | Craig, Claire, (CBE) author.
Title: Storylistening: narrative evidence and public reasoning/
Sarah Dillon and Claire Craig.
Description: Abingdon, Oxon; New York: Routledge, 2022. |
Includes bibliographical references and index.
Identifiers: LCCN 2021027239 | ISBN 9780367406745 (hardback) |
ISBN 9780367406738 (paperback) | ISBN 9780367808426 (ebook)
Subjects: LCSH: Narration (Rhetoric)—Philosophy. |
Political science—Philosophy. | Justification (Theory of knowledge) | Reason.
Classification: LCC PN212 .D55 2022 | DDC 808/.036—dc23
LC record available at https://lccn.loc.gov/2021027239

ISBN: 978-0-367-40674-5 (hbk)
ISBN: 978-0-367-40673-8 (pbk)
ISBN: 978-0-367-80842-6 (ebk)

DOI: 10.4324/9780367808426

Typeset in Bembo
by codeMantra

For Gav and Chris

CONTENTS

FIGURES

AUTHOR NOTES

Sarah Dillon is Professor of Literature and the Public Humanities in the Faculty of English at the University of Cambridge. She is a scholar of contemporary literature, film, and philosophy, with a research focus on the epistemic function and value of stories, on interdisciplinarity, and on the engaged humanities. She is author of *The Palimpsest: Literature, Criticism, Theory* (2007), *Deconstruction, Feminism, Film* (2018), and many academic articles and book chapters. She is editor of *David Mitchell: Critical Essays* (2011), and co-editor of *Maggie Gee: Critical Essays* (2015) and *AI Narratives: A History of Imaginative Thinking About Intelligent Machines* (2020). In addition to her academic scholarship, Sarah is an established arts broadcaster on BBC Radio 3 and BBC Radio 4, having been selected as a 2013 BBC Radio 3 and AHRC New Generation Thinker. She has an intellectual and practical commitment to demonstrating the value and importance of the humanities across sectors, including in higher education, government, and wider culture and society.

Claire Craig is Provost of The Queen's College, Oxford and has extensive experience of providing scientific evidence to senior decision-makers in government and business. Originally a geophysicist, she became Director of the UK Government Office for Science, a member of the Prime Minister's Delivery Unit, and got her grounding in strategy at McKinsey & Co. She developed her interest in the power of stories initially through their roles in public reasoning about strategic futures and alongside the use of computational models of complex systems. Her 2018 pamphlet, *How Does Government Listen to Scientists?*, led her to become increasingly interested in the reasons behind the absence of systems and mechanisms to bring evidence about stories into public debate and decision-making explicitly, and the consequences of this absence.

ACKNOWLEDGEMENTS

The ideas for this book took root initially during discussions at the Royal Society, and our ambitions for the book have required ranging across disciplines and sectors. The description and evidence of the function of stories in particular has required extensive lateral movement across established disciplines, digging down deep enough to ensure solid knowledge and evidence was found, not so deep as to be subsumed into disciplinary commitments and demarcations, resurfacing to weave those findings with those mined in other quarters, all to the book's ends. We are deeply grateful to the following readers whose disciplinary expertise served to verify that we had mined the correct seams, not overlooked others, and treated the material extracted appropriately: Olivia Belton, Andrew Brown, Paul Cairney, Diane Coyle, Ben Davies, Jane Elliott, Keri Facer, Roman Frigg, Grace Halden, Veronica Hollinger, Mike Hulme, Genevieve Liveley, Raphael Lyne, Mary S. Morgan, Riel Miller, Susan Owens, Francesca Polletta, Jessica Pykett, Murray Shanahan, Michael Shapiro, Katy Shaw, Ted Shepherd, Will Slocombe, Sherryl Vint. All errors, misinterpretations, or omissions remain, of course, our own.

We also took on the challenge of seeking to address reflective practitioners: potential readers inside governments, and others seeking to create and use evidence to inform public reasoning, whose hinterlands might be generalist, issue-based, or academic. We are therefore equally grateful to the following readers, whose practitioner knowledge helped to ensure that exploration of the deeply fascinating academic matters and questions for further research was continually also brought back to insights presented in forms that might enable them to be tested and used by those who seek to influence and to make policy today: Laurent Bontoux, Ian Boyd, Ivan Collister, Peter Gluckman, Laura Smillie.

We are grateful to Polly Dodson, commissioning editor at Routledge, for believing in such an interdisciplinary and intersectoral project and giving it a home on her literature list. We thank the Routledge anonymous peer reviewers for their helpful feedback.

We thank all of the above for generously accommodating changes to the book's timetable caused by the impact of the COVID-19 pandemic in 2020 and 2021. Most of its stories are still being, and yet to be, written.

We have held many productive conversations that have informed the book, including with Syed Mustafa Ali, Olivia Belton, Ben Davies, Stephanie Dick, Rhona Jamieson, Susan Owens, Jonnie Penn, and Richard Staley. SD is particularly grateful to the community of global academics and practitioners who participated in the University of Cambridge Mellon Sawyer Seminar (2020–2021) – Histories of AI: A Genealogy of Power – from whom she learnt so much while writing the book. We are grateful to Mike Hulme and Kari de Pryck who gave their time to discuss their research on, and knowledge of, the Intergovernmental Panel on Climate Change (IPCC); to Ian Miles and Michael Burnam-Fink for correspondence on science fiction and Futures Studies; to Claire Wilkinson for reading suggestions on literature and economics; to Farah Mendlesohn and Edward F. James for so speedily tracking down a reference for us in their extensive SF library; and to Phoenix Alexander (Science Fiction Collections Librarian, Sydney Jones Library, University of Liverpool) for sourcing a copy of Philip Wylie's 'The Paradise Crater' for us, searching at length through his network of SF academics and archivists.

Our research assistants – Clementine Collett and Nathaniel Zetter – have been outstanding in their efficiency and geniality. Their work to support the research for, and the completion of, the manuscript has been invaluable and we are hugely grateful to have had their help. In particular, we thank Clemi for impressive cross-disciplinary literature reviews to assist with the production of the first sections of each chapter, and for her analysis of the IPCC. We thank Nathaniel for taking on the unenviable task of compiling such an extensive bibliography with ease and good humour, for carrying out a range of crucial research tasks on the home straight, and for working tirelessly alongside us to prepare the manuscript for submission.

Personal thanks from Sarah go, as always, to Gavin, Isaac, and Charlotte McHugh, for their unwavering love and support.

Personal thanks from Claire go to Chris Diacopoulos, for everything all the time, and to Susannah Wiltshire, particularly for sharing her joy in stories of so many kinds.

PROLOGUE

There's an enduring Scottish ballad in which the heroine (usually called Margaret or Janet) is pregnant with a child whose father, Tam Lin, has long been imprisoned by the Queen of Fairies. In order to return Tam Lin to the human world, Margaret has to pull him from his horse as he rides by as part of the fairy court and keep hold of him in her arms. The Queen, enraged, changes him into fire, a bear, a serpent and other terrifying forms and it is only by holding on through the worst the Queen can do that Margaret is rewarded by Tam Lin becoming human again, freed from enchantment. There are many folklore versions of similar stories, and many readings: for now, we would like you to see it as a story about stories and about this book. Stories, in their many shapes and forms, are part of human nature and humans are immersed in them: they are experienced as deeply individual and as integral to relationships between people; they provide explanations, meaning, and entertainment; people die for them, and people dismiss them as trivial; they enlighten and obscure; they enable judgement and reasoning and they seduce, persuade, and distort. We show that, by holding on, it is possible to listen to stories for the narrative evidence they provide, the cognitive value they possess, and the important ways in which they can enrich public reasoning.

For one of us (CC), the crystallising moment for this book was the realisation of 'three ways to read the Terminator', an enduring contemporary story. For a period of several years, scientific reports on machine learning, its capabilities and near-term implications, were accompanied in mainstream media by a near obligatory image of the red-eyed robot from *The Terminator* movie, with its implied story of malign, implacable, humanoid artificial intelligence. The scientists and decision-makers engaged in the debates, noticing this alignment, tended to take one of three views about it. One view was that it was irritating, because the story represented fiction that could be dismissed as irrelevant to the matters at hand. A second was that it was worrying, because it distorted public perception

DOI: 10.4324/9780367808426-1

by making human-level artificial intelligence seem closer than it is. Third (the least frequent) was that it was an interesting metaphor for general public anxieties about the links between unstoppable technologies and the malign powers of big business or big government, depending on one's political outlook. The contrast between the care and effort that went into considering and describing the science, and the near-complete lack of examination or awareness in public reasoning of the significance of the stories associated with it, was a driver for many of the questions that led to this book.

One of us (SD) reads the Terminator in a fourth way. The image of the Terminator robot has become detached from its originating text, developing a public resonance that does not fully correspond to the details of the original story. If one engages with *The Terminator* paying attention to the actual story and its main human protagonist, Sarah Connor, then the film can be read as a feminist parable. Connor transforms in the film from a helpless and hapless victim of male harassment at its opening, to defeating the Terminator (coded as a representative figure of male violence through his wearing of human clothes stolen from a male street thug), to a powerful self-sufficient survivor. Through the metonymic story of one woman's transformation, *The Terminator* tells a tale about systems of societal female oppression, feminist resistance, and freedom achieved. The contrast between the powerful public functioning of the Terminator image, and the possibility of this quite different (but not mutually exclusive) reading of the actual story from which it is taken was another prompt to questions that led to this book.

The 'four (or more) ways to read the Terminator' illustration shows one of the reasons stories are not taken seriously: they function in multiple ways. The same narrative content will have different effects depending on the storyteller, the storyimbibers, and the mode of telling. And it will vary across space and time. If it is possible to get a reading 'wrong', and if there are many possible readings, then it is perhaps easier to ignore the value gained from critically engaging with stories – in particular 'made up' ones – in the first place. Throughout this book, however, we take stories seriously. Stories cannot simply be dismissed as mere 'fiction'. For stories both operate in powerful ways in the world, and have cognitive value in providing knowledge about that world.

We start from the position that those who care about the quality of well-founded public reasoning are at an impasse. Contemporary circumstances have exposed the limits of the scope and power of scientific evidence, and the risks of ignoring or denying the power of stories to influence public opinion. However, there is no widely shared framework to enable rigorous reflection on stories in the context of public reasoning. At a time when it seems no longer possible – in some quarters even politically desirable – to maintain distinctions between true and false, fact and fiction, real and imagined, it may seem counterintuitive to assert the need to take stories seriously. It is not. On the contrary, it is now urgent to take stories seriously so that decision-makers, as well as wider publics, are able to more effectively understand their function and effects at individual and collective levels – we call this *narrative literacy*. More widespread narrative literacy would have the effect of reinforcing the importance of all forms of evidence, including scientific evidence.

Many sectors and disciplines take stories seriously within their sectoral and disciplinary boundaries, but nowhere are these various insights drawn together in ways that enable public reasoning. The result is that stories are neglected, dismissed as trivial, or feared as too dangerously powerful. Assumptions about what they might mean, or how and why they might matter, are left to intuition and instinct in a way that would be completely unacceptable for other forms of evidence. This book therefore draws together and builds on cross-disciplinary insights about the interactions between stories and human thought and actions. We focus on four cognitive functions of stories, in particular in relation to systems and collectives rather than individuals. Stories enable multiple points of view, increasing knowledge and understanding of a system of relevance to public reasoning. Stories create and consolidate collective identities, helping identify social groups, understand motivations and actions, and recognise social norms and how they are or might be changing. Stories are narrative models, functional tools that enable explanation and understanding. They also function as anticipatory narrative models, part of their wider role in anticipatory systems, imagining and testing a range of futures in order to enable better decision-making in the present. By outlining these functions – points of view, identities, modelling, anticipation – and demonstrating how stories operate in such ways in relation to key contemporary issues, we make a series of arguments that transcend disciplines and take forward the ways in which stories are understood in public reasoning. Overall, the book aims to create the conditions in which the task of critical listening to stories as part of public reasoning is possible, expected, and becomes endemic. In order to achieve this, we introduce a new framework that enables *storylistening*: the theory and practice of gathering narrative evidence to inform decision-making, especially in relation to public reasoning, as part of a pluralistic evidence base. *Narrative evidence* is the product of the expert act of both direct critical engagement with stories, and critical engagement with others' reading, viewing, or listening to stories.

The book's agenda as outlined here is situated of course within the wider context of an urgent need to reassess the value, power, and importance of stories in the West in light of the major social and political events of the twenty-first century – including the 2008 financial crisis, the rise of populism, the UK referendum on leaving the European Union, and the COVID-19 pandemic – as well as technological developments, such as the increased generation and spread of stories via social media and other digital platforms. But what you will find here is not a book about public reasoning and the telling of stories, that is, it is not a book about the rhetorical or persuasive power of stories, in governance or policymaking. This is not a book about misinformation, disinformation, or post-truth. It is not a book about politics and spin, nor about narrative manipulation. Storylistening, the framework we develop for taking stories seriously as a form of evidence, may well aid in contending with such phenomena – for instance, in our call for more widespread narrative literacy – but drawing out such connections is not our focus. It is not our intention to enable people to *tell* better stories, but to empower people to *listen* more critically and more carefully to existing ones.

This book therefore firmly steps into difficult intellectual territory. Because its prime aim is to provide insights to enable those engaged in public reasoning to consider the roles of stories more carefully, its structure starts from their interests. Starting from the point of public reasoning means that the avenues of enquiry cut across academic boundaries, which is one major challenge. Caring about how academic findings can be used in public reasoning means examining those findings in language that a (determined) layperson can understand, which is a second major challenge. The two helpfully align in so far as the only language common to disciplinary experts is the language of the public. It is inevitable that, as Adair Turner once said, 'any statement that is perfectly true is not useful, and any statement that is useful is not perfectly true' (quoted in Craig, 2019: viii). For this book, where we have stepped outside our areas of greatest personal expertise, we take responsibility and carry on, supported by the work and comments of others, and driven by the belief that the prize, that of making it easier to take stories seriously, is so big that it is worth the risks.

Another of the aims of this book is to provide a new shared framework for storylistening that will enable some disciplinary cross-fertilisation where that is useful, while recognising that disciplinary practices are deeply rooted and different, for fundamental and valuable reasons. If the framework provided here enables others to explore new questions in novel and perhaps more discipline-specific ways, then that will suffice. Looking further ahead, we believe that new technologies that bring new ways of observing how networks, societies, and individuals listen to stories will in turn require and enable academics to ask questions that they previously have not asked because there was no conceivable way of engaging with them with rigour. This book is also intended to stimulate some of those new questions. While the book has therefore had to chart a course through disciplinary specificities in pursuit of insights for public reasoning, the result is also a series of strong arguments for the ways in which the humanities disciplines as a whole might extend their imagining of themselves, and their structures and practices, in order to play a more active role in informing public reasoning.

INTRODUCTION

This book provides a sustained analysis of four cognitive and collective functions of stories – the provision of different points of view, the formation of collective identities, providing narrative models that enable surrogative reasoning about target systems, informing anticipation of the future – in order to provide a framework for storylistening, that is, the theory and practice of gathering narrative evidence to inform decision-making, especially in relation to public reasoning, as part of a pluralistic evidence base. To illustrate the four functions of stories, and to test their roles in public reasoning, we examine each function in relation to four policy areas where decisions are strongly influenced by contentious knowledge and powerful imaginings: climate change, artificial intelligence, the economy, and nuclear weapons and power. Based on this analysis and illustration, we identify both the benefits of storylistening to public reasoning, and what the most profound challenges might be for those concerned with public reasoning, and for those concerned with the humanities. We believe that the benefits are worth taking on these challenges, and we hope that both practitioners and academics will want to do so, knowing that the task will sometimes require structural evolution and sometimes benefit from new forms of scholarship. Overall, this book is written assertively, according to the logic 'if storylistening were to exist, this is how it would work and why it would be effective'. It is intended to prompt or provoke future practice and theory.

Many readers may wish now to dive straight into the book's first chapter. Please feel free to do so. For others, who are looking for or require a more sustained definition of terms and explanations of decisions made when constructing the book, we provide those in this Introduction. Here we explain how we are using the terms 'story', 'public reasoning', and 'evidence' and what is at stake in doing so, and we provide rationales for our choice of case studies and of the

DOI: 10.4324/9780367808426-2

stories we focus on in the performative readings. We end, as is conventional in academic books, with a summary of the book's structure and contents, to orient the reader from a high-level perspective, before diving in.

Definition of terms

This book draws on insights from a wide range of disciplines and practices. Each discipline and practice has its own precise language, sometimes using words that are not used beyond the discipline, sometimes using the same words as other disciplines but with different meanings, and sometimes using different words to denote overlapping but not identical concepts. We have also introduced a small number of new words, already deployed here and in the Prologue, in order to articulate and denote new ideas and concepts relating to storylistening. We have therefore created a glossary, to be found at the end of the book, in order to help the reader recognise why and how some words are used, and why some words that may be more familiar to them are not used or are used in unfamiliar ways. The reader is encouraged to refer frequently and at will to the Glossary, which does both descriptive and conceptual work. Here we focus in depth on just three terms that are fundamental to the book's aims: 'story', 'public reasoning', and 'evidence'.

Story

Wide-ranging reading reveals no consistency in the use of 'narrative' versus 'story' across disciplines and sectors. In some cases, narrative is used to describe the overall phenomena, with story denoting the way in which the narrative is constructed. In other cases, story is the overall phenomena, with narrative denoting the structuring elements of the story. In the face of this definitional inconsistency, we have chosen to use the noun 'story' rather than 'narrative' throughout this book, for a number of reasons which we now outline.

We adopt 'story' because it is the more widespread and popular name for a causal account of something happening that includes entities with agency. 'Story', in the sense in which we use it, includes both storycontent and how the story is told.[1] Generally, 'narrative' seems to be preferred over 'story' in contexts where there is a desire to take stories seriously and, implicitly or explicitly, make a case for doing so, so we are consciously going against the grain here.[2] We propose that 'narrative' tends to be used in such contexts because the word sounds more serious – thereby lending more gravitas to the topic of discussion – but also because using it circumvents to some extent complex questions around non-fiction and fiction, fact and fiction, and truth and untruth, whereas 'story' is more often associated with the latter category in each of these pairings. We use 'story' precisely because it retains a closer link than 'narrative' does to 'fiction' understood generically as the term referring to the body of made-up stories found across literature, film, television, on social media, in oral traditions and more. By using 'story', we are foregrounding that part of our case that some will find most surprising: that there is cognitive value in treating stories seriously when they are stories that are understood as 'fiction' in that sense, as well as when they are stories of the type that others might prefer to call 'narratives'. In doing so, we are not dispensing with distinctions between fact and fiction understood as truth and untruth, but making the case that storylistening enables better understanding of both truths and untruths about a system. Part of the challenge and task of storylistening at a collective level – and narrative literacy at an individual level – is identifying in what way a story is functioning, and therefore what specific value it has.

We do not deploy the terms 'fiction' and 'non-fiction' as generic categories in this book since stories move across both. We do, however, deploy a distinction where necessary between textual (embedded, embodied, and curated) and non-textual (transient and malleable) stories. We also do not dwell on a technical definition of a story's constitution. There is significant work offering definitions of narrative (Scholes and Kellogg, 1966; Genette, 1980; Jameson, 1981; Mitchell, 1981; Bruner, 1986; Somers, 1994; Lamarque, 2003; G.M. Wilson, 2003; Currie, 2010). But for the purposes of analysing the function of stories, we are inclined to agree with Raymond A. Mar and Keith Oatley (2008: 174) who conclude that 'the debate on what constitutes a useful categorical definition of a narrative may be a conceptual dead end'. Instead, we consider it more useful to attend not to how an archetypal story might be structured, but to specific stories, what they are about, the style and form in which they are told, how they function in relation to people (both individuals and collectives), and how they operate in the world.[3] As such, while bearing in mind the specificity of different forms of storytelling, we do not set up rigid distinctions between stories of different types (for example, literary or cinematic) or stories circulating via different media (for example, book, oral culture, social media).[4] The functions apply across such divides. That said, due to authorial expertise, our performative readings do primarily (although not exclusively) focus on textual stories (in particular literary and cinematic ones), but the understanding of that function in relation to non-textual stories is also foregrounded, often through pointing to the work of others. In the performative readings, we aim to demonstrate (although, for reasons of space, in perhaps less detail than a single disciplinary work would do) how form and function are inextricable. This is as true for a scientific paper as it is for a political speech, film, or novel, or for a story in whatever form it takes shape and moves through the world.

A premise on which the book is based is that stories are both affective and cognitive. This is another of the both/and rather than either/or movements that characterises many of our arguments. In storyimbibing, often the cognitive value is achieved in part because of the affective power of the story.[5] In storylistening, critically analysing the affective or persuasive power of the story is part of the task. While in no way therefore denying or negating the eudonic functions of storyimbibing and sharing – entertainment, escape, happiness, healing – nor the persuasive operations of storytelling, the functions on which we focus with regard to storylistening are those associated with the cognitive and the collective. That stories enable individuals to know things about the world and the beings that inhabit it, that they function as a source of sense-making (in particular in the face of complexity and uncertainty), is another premise of the book. Walter Benjamin (2019 [1936]: 51), in his famous essay 'The Storyteller', identifies 'an indispensable element of every real story. It serves, overtly or covertly, a useful function'.[6] The premise is well supported by existing work on the cognitive value of stories across disciplines.[7] Stories function as part of the informational context in which people think and act, make decisions, and formulate beliefs and judgements.[8] Research demonstrates that stories – textual and non-textual – influence social judgement, agenda-setting, and the perception of problem urgency and responsibility.[9] In *Storylistening*, we extend such work to consider the cognitive value of stories to public reasoning.

Perhaps surprisingly, there is more contestation around the issue of stories' cognitive value within the discipline devoted primarily to the study of textual stories – literary studies.[10] In closing this subsection, we turn our attention briefly to this discipline, in order to situate this book specifically in relation to its past, present, and possible futures. While we retain literary studies' demand that one must attend carefully to a story's form and genre, we move beyond a historical disciplinary trend that is suspicious of claims for stories' functional and cognitive value – a suspicion that is often accompanied by a belief that such a focus will neglect attending to the ways in which stories are told.[11] In *Uses of Literature* (2008), Rita Felski points to that history and argues instead for a renewed attention to literature's connectedness with, and embeddedness and action in, the social world. *Storylistening* can be situated as part of this turn in literary studies, marked by Felski's call for a change in the discipline's premises and practices. Separating literature off from other forms of storytelling, making claims for its difference and uniqueness, has restricted the ways in which it can be valued, and delimited the kinds of value it can be thought to have. Accordingly, in this book, we do not engage only with 'literary' stories, whatever they might be defined to be. We no more cut literary stories off from other kinds of stories than we cut them off from the world.

Felski (2008: 7) identifies that in many areas of literary studies there remains a deep mistrust of the idea that literature can have a use: 'What distinguishes literature, in this line of thought, is its obdurate resistance to all calculations of purpose and function'. In contrast, our focus is precisely on function, breaking the cognitive value of stories down into at least some of its constituent parts, in particular those functions most relevant to public reasoning. Such a move is necessary not least in order to make one possible case – in theory and practice – for the continued relevance of literary studies in the twenty-first century. In 2008, Felski noted that 'as teachers and scholars charged with advancing our discipline, we are sorely in need of more cogent and compelling justifications for what we do' (3). Over a decade later, that need remains. But the need for such justifications might be taken as an opportunity both to defend the discipline as it exists, and to expand what it is and does. This means expanding both its objects and methods of study, and making its borders more permeable to other disciplines within academia, and to sectors outside of it.

Public reasoning

We adopt Sheila Jasanoff's (2012: 5) definition of public reasoning as 'the institutional practices, discourses, techniques and instruments through which modern governments claim legitimacy in an era of limitless risks – physical, political and moral'. Attaining and maintaining well-founded public reasoning is key to the democratic legitimacy of states, to trust in decision-making, and to governmental accountability. We take it as axiomatic that well-founded public reasoning is informed by a pluralistic evidence base, of which we propose storylistening needs to form a part.[12] This definition of public reasoning moves away from other conceptual traditions regarding public reasoning that will perhaps be more familiar to academics in the humanities (summarised in Quong, 2018). Public reasoning as we deploy the term is located within institutions of power, such as the state, and constitutes the practical activity of such institutions when making decisions in the public interest. With Jasanoff (2012: 5), we do not use the term to denote the act of 'constructing principled arguments that obey universal rules of democratic deliberation' (Rawls, 1971). Nor do we use the term to refer to the activity of a public – here meaning a group of private people – reasoning collectively in opposition to public authorities (Habermas, 1989). Although we do address, in particular in Chapter 4, the need for the incorporation of deliberative democracy and citizen engagement in public reasoning, and the important role of storytelling and storylistening in those practices (Mair et al., 2019: 55; see also Fishkin and Luskin, 1999; Fishkin and Luskin, 2005; Lemos and Morehouse, 2005; Parkinson, 2006; Iandoli et al., 2009; Davies et al., 2011, Lampe et al., 2014).

The understanding of public reasoning as located outside of the institutions of government is aligned with a self-conception of the humanities' public role as that of challenging rather than supporting power structures and state operations (Brom, 2019). But, similarly to our position that narrative evidence is complementary to that derived from the sciences (and specific to certain objects of knowledge and not others), not a replacement for them, we also propose that the humanities might expand its self-conception to include considering (at least in some instances and areas) how it might play an active role in public reasoning as we understand it. The choice of whether to engage with today's institutions for public reasoning, and especially of whether to engage directly with governments, can appear to be simultaneously a choice about whether to surrender the ability to oppose or critique today's public goals and aims. However, as we go on to discuss throughout the book, there are many ways in which academics may take part in public reasoning and it is not always necessary to stay outside in order to retain the capacity to critique – indeed, in some cases, the 'difficult' message may be heard more clearly if it comes from an internal or unexpected source.

At least two adjustments would be required for the humanities to engage more fully in public reasoning as defined here (and we recognise that they are not insignificant ones). One would be a move away from the individualism that has traditionally dominated the humanities, towards a sense of how the knowledge it produces might be collected and synthesised (Brom, 2019). (This need to consider moves from the individual to the collective recurs across the book, on many levels.) Second, and a perhaps even more challenging trade-off, would be the need for individual humanities academics committed to influencing public reasoning as we understand it to operate publicly in more politically neutral ways (Lees, 2017).[13] In both instances, the role of the humanities in public reasoning is conceived of as different from, yet complementary to, the traditional role of the individual public intellectual.[14]

In another shift from the individual to the collective, we also move attention from the impact of stories on the single decision-maker to how to take stories seriously within institutional structures of decision-making. In proposing the incorporation of storylistening into public reasoning, we are not proposing that individual policymakers should imbibe more stories themselves (although we do propose that, like every citizen, they should be narratively literate). We therefore diverge from academic (Bechara and Damsio, 2005; Cosmides and Tooby, 2011; Scalise Sugiyama, 2011, 2016) and popular (Brown, 2020) claims for the importance of imbibing stories to the quality of the decisions made by an individual.

One final point to make regarding public reasoning concerns its relationship to terms such as policy and policymaking as used by scholars of public policy and by practitioners such as public officials, expert advisers, and politicians. We adopt Paul Cairney's (2020: 2) definition that public policy is 'the sum total of government action, from signals of intent to the final outcomes'. We also acknowledge Chris Whitty's (2015: 2) definition that anybody who makes decisions that have collective consequences is a policymaker. These definitions mean that policy and related terms refer to a wider landscape of public life than does public reasoning, given the latter's emphasis on institutional arrangements. With these definitions in mind, we hope that the insights and arguments made in this book might be of relevance to decision-makers and experts in a variety of settings and contexts. We focus here, however, on public reasoning in institutions that make decisions with regional, national, or multinational consequences and we draw largely on work located in the discourses of European and Anglophone jurisdictions, with some extension to global bodies such as the UN's Intergovernmental Panel on Climate Change (IPCC).

Evidence

The question of what constitutes good evidence for the purposes of public reasoning can be approached from a variety of disciplines and perspectives and we consider these first here, as a basis for the case we build throughout the book for the creation and use of narrative evidence. Placing the notion of evidence (see Glossary) in the context of the provision of scientific evidence in policy, the network of European academies providing advice to the European Commission (SAPEA, 2019: 15) draws on insights from the philosophy and sociology of science, the study of knowledge, and other traditions when it says 'what counts as "good" evidence varies with the questions' and that most practices 'are focussed on social values of legitimacy, trust, impartiality and credibility'. In their account of the characteristics of good systems for synthesising evidence for policymaking (discussed further in Chapter 3), the UK's Royal Society and Academy of Medical Sciences (2018) refer in addition to accessibility, meaning that the evidence is presented in a form that enables those outside the relevant fields to engage with it effectively. More succinctly, Justin Parkhurst (2017: 109) refers to Cash et al.'s (2003) model, developed within the environmental sciences, of effective scientific evidence needing to demonstrate *'credibility, salience* and *legitimacy'*.[15]

Discussions about the characteristics of good evidence have in common a desire to acknowledge the need for academic evidence to be robust as judged by the standards of the most relevant academic discipline(s), while also acknowledging that there are wider judgements to be made about the relationship between the types of evidence available within academic frameworks, and the evidence that might in principle be most valuable to furthering well-founded public reasoning or policymaking. These dimensions can be in tension if, for example, there is evidence that is perceived as particularly strong in the sense of being methodologically rigorous on its own terms (perhaps because it is based on methods, such as randomised control trials, which are extremely successful within their own contexts) but which, by its exclusive or over-weighted adoption, might diminish the breadth or depth of the public reasoning that could take place if a wider range of forms of evidence were to be regarded as sufficiently credible to inform debate. Such consideration of the judgements involved in turn points to the need to consider carefully the systems for creating and using evidence, a shift referred to by Parkhurst (2017: 147–174) as 'from evidence-based policy to the good governance of evidence'.

Even though academic systems for assessing the quality of research are, to a greater or lesser extent, international, the systems for creating and using evidence vary across geographies and often by topic. Jasanoff's work describes different national cultures of rationality, what she calls *civic epistemologies*, which means that democracies can differ significantly in how they deliberate in the public interest, including how and what evidence they draw into that process.[16] Each nation needs to reflect its constitutional and broader societal arrangements and engrained modes of public reasoning, so the structure of formal systems to provide evidence varies significantly between them. In practice, this involves different detailed arrangements, funding, and incentives across institutions such as government departments, including their research arms, regulators and agencies, the publicly and privately funded research bases, and boundary organisations such as national academies and sector-specific bodies.[17]

Most of the institutional structures and initiatives to incorporate evidence in public reasoning relevant to our case studies focus on science and technology, but it is increasingly recognised that they need to incorporate all aspects of economics, social sciences, and – as with public reasoning more generally – the humanities (Shah, 2020). We are not arguing that the existing mechanisms in any country or setting are perfect, nor that the details of what works for the sciences would work for the humanities. For instance, recent work to map out how the social sciences are incorporated into the structures of public reasoning (Cooper, 2016) suggests that the modes and structures in which it does so, and might do so better, are different to those of the sciences more generally. Similar work is needed with regard to the methods and structures that might best facilitate the inclusion of the humanities. In this book, by considering the potential forms of narrative evidence available within the context of our case studies, we hope to open up ways for this particular form of humanities' knowledge to become an integral part of public reasoning. Within this, we note here that our definitions of good evidence encompass the fact that narrative evidence itself is not a single type, as we go on to tease out in more detail. For example, narrative evidence that draws on listening to stories functioning as models of the world, where the storycontent and legitimacy of the narrative matter (as discussed in Chapter 3), will be different from narrative evidence that draws on listening to stories functioning through narrative networks, where the storycontent may be irrelevant or even wholly false – as assessed by other forms of evidence – but attending to the narrative networks may provide important narrative evidence about collective identities (as discussed in Chapter 2). In the context of significant concerns about post-truth, deceit, and misinformation in public reasoning, which might otherwise lead to the neglect of some valid forms of evidence, we argue that it is increasingly important to have frameworks that, by making such careful distinctions, allow for stories to be taken seriously.

Rationales

During the course of planning this book, we had to make certain decisions on inclusion and focus. The rationales for such decisions were both intellectual, and influenced by our own areas of expertise. They necessarily mean, of course, that much is omitted, but we explain our choices here.

Case study selection

The case studies we address are the evolution of evidence and policy on climate change, the development of artificial intelligence technologies, the application of economic theory to economic policymaking, and the history of nuclear war and nuclear energy. These are clearly extremely broad topics so we are not in the least attempting to be comprehensive in our accounts of any of them, but to interrogate aspects within them to test and illustrate the arguments we are presenting. The case studies were selected because they each exemplify different and significant aspects of the ways in which storylistening might inform public reasoning. Debates on the application of AI are driven initially by the emergent properties of the science and technologies to apply it. Climate change represents the big, distributed, systemic risk of our times, with several decades of expert and popular reflection on the relationship between the initial findings from the physical sciences and the evolution of policy on local to global scales. Nuclear science provides largely historic illustrations of engagement with relatively narrowly defined risks (of nuclear war, or of catastrophic nuclear power site failure) with immediate consequences when they crystallise. Finally, the economics case study provides material from an area where expertise has often been well embedded in public reasoning and which therefore prompts different questions and opportunities for the provision of narrative evidence.

This selection also serves as something of a limit or test case for the role of the humanities in public reasoning. It is perhaps not too difficult to make a case for the role of the humanities in policy areas that might be grouped under the heading of social injustice (Lees, 2017). Such an approach takes advantage of existing foci within the humanities disciplines – for instance on gender, race, class, etc. – from a predominantly left-leaning political perspective. It is more challenging, and we believe more interesting, to examine the role the humanities might play in policy issues that have traditionally been more firmly the terrain of evidence and advice from the sciences.

Story selection for performative readings

Within academia, textual stories considered within a single scholarly work will often cohere according to established disciplinary criteria such as the same national literature, period, genre, medium, or topic. This is not always the case, for instance in comparative literary studies, but it is predominantly so. The organising principle for the textual stories engaged with in the performative readings in this book does not fully align with these traditional criteria. They range across media and, albeit to a lesser extent, across national literatures and periods. They are predominantly (but not exclusively) Anglophone stories, from the mid-twentieth century onwards, often drawn from the genre of science fiction. This focus – of language, period, and genre – is in part a consequence of the authors' expertise. But there are also stronger rationales.

Given the UK system of public reasoning is our primary context, it makes sense to engage with stories in English that might most readily inform that system. Within that category, though, we have attended to stories that bring in a range of perspectives, and a diverse range of authors, including Indigenous stories. We anticipate that the arguments made here – about public reasoning and about storylistening – could be adopted and adapted in different national contexts, taking into account differences in systems and structures of decision-making (as discussed above), as well as differences in stories and cultural heritage more broadly. We hope that that work will be done by those with the expertise to do it. At the same time, we recognise that our case studies have global not just national significance, and that public reasoning ought to take that into consideration. Storylistening, especially in multilateral institutions, therefore needs to be informed by expertise across a range of languages and stories; what we are trying to do here is create the knowledge and structures through which the narrative evidence from that wider range of stories can have access to power.

We focus primarily on what might loosely be termed contemporary stories because of another premise that grounds the book – that stories are in dialogue with their context of creation, production, and dissemination. They therefore have an intimate and informative relationship with the dominant concerns of their historical moment, rendering contemporary stories of particular cognitive value to contemporaneous public reasoning. Again (both/and not either/or), this is not to dismiss the significance of historical stories and historical knowledge more broadly, but to make a claim for the complementary importance of the contemporary.[18]

Across our four case studies, but particularly with respect to the AI and climate change case studies, science fiction stories have lent themselves most readily to textual performative readings. This is because the AI case study is primarily about the creation and application of new science and the climate change study is primarily about collective anticipations of uncertain futures, topics with which SF has traditionally engaged most strongly. This prompts the need for wider reflection on how 'mainstream' textual stories might evolve to also engage with such topics – for instance, by more fully incorporating them as background elements of stories, not necessarily as plot drivers or thematic foci (see, for instance, discussion of the *albert* report 'Subtitles to Save the World' [2019] in Chapter 4). In addition, there is a need for wider reflection on how other genres that already have structurally established plot drivers (such as comedy, romance, detective fiction, and so on) might enable engagement with such topics without the need to depend plot-wise on catastrophe, apocalypse, or other dystopian extremes (see, for instance, our discussion of Jane Harper's *The Lost Man* in Chapter 3). Note that this genre and textual focus in our performative readings definitely does not mean that storylistening needs only to attend to SF nor, more broadly, only to textual stories – our readings are singular illustrations of how storylistening works, not acts of comprehensive storylistening. In practice, that comprehensive act needs to take into account the full range of non-textual and textual stories (irrespective of genre) of relevance to a policy issue.

Ranging across stories, and across genre and medium, is integral to effective storylistening. It is not sufficient only to take seriously stories already designated as serious according to some a priori criteria, for instance that of traditional literary canon formation. Stories big and small, labelled as fact and fiction, realistic or fantastical, low-brow or high-brow, can all function powerfully and cognitively. Storylistening needs to attend to that functioning in order to produce narrative evidence drawn from the most relevant stories to the issue in question, irrespective of prior designations of what might be deemed proper to take seriously.[19] To predetermine in advance what stories might be worth or not worth listening to is an act of mislistening that risks judging the importance of a story in relation to criteria – for instance the notion of the aesthetic quality that might determine the idea of 'great literature' – which may not be the correct or most appropriate criteria for the task at hand. We therefore take a democratic approach in this book, selecting stories for our performative readings according to the criteria of how well they illustrate a specific story function in relation to a specific case study.

Structure and contents

In the first section of each chapter, we synthesise the leading edge of academic evidence for each function and present new arguments arising from such synthesis, where necessary. In all four chapters, part of the work of this first section is to demonstrate how the functions apply to both non-textual and textual stories – that is, where existing research often focuses on 'narratives' (excluding 'fiction') we show how the functions apply equally to 'narratives' and to stories such as those found in novels, films, and more. In general, each function category tends to align strongly with one or two deeply embedded disciplinary approaches to studying stories: English and Psychology in Chapter 1; Sociology, Cultural Studies, and Anthropology in Chapter 2; Philosophy, and History and Philosophy of Science in Chapter 3; and Futures Studies in Chapter 4. In addition, over the course of the book we engage with the study of stories in a range of other disciplines, including Communication Studies, Geography, Political Science, Policy Studies, Science Communication, Science and Technology Studies (STS), Marketing, and Business Studies. Due to their interdisciplinarity, and in order to effect a robust synthesis, the first sections of each chapter are heavily referenced.

It is in the nature of the role of stories that, to varying extents, all of the functions of stories are relevant to each of the case studies, so the case studies cut across the function chapters. In the second section of each chapter, we complement the policy case studies with performative readings of example stories, thereby bringing both our core areas of expertise (policy practice and narrative analysis) to bear. The readings further illustrate the roles of the story functions in relation to the case studies and, importantly, begin to show how storylistening can be put into practice. To avoid continued density of referencing, extensive reference to existing academic literature on the example stories is not included (in distinction to what would be expected in an exclusively literary studies disciplinary work). Just as all the functions pertain to each case study (although to greater and lesser degrees), many of our example stories can be functioning in more than one way (although again to greater or lesser degrees). One of the tasks of storylistening is to identify the most relevant stories to a policy issue, and to identify correctly the relevant mode(s) in which they are functioning.

In the third section of each chapter, we draw out the consequences for public reasoning, and for the humanities, of that chapter's arguments and analyses, to prompt future theory and practice. We consider the benefits of storylistening in relation to the function the chapter is focusing on, and identify what might be the most profound challenges, for both public reasoning and the humanities. These are challenges that we believe practitioners and academics will want to take into account, some of which will require structural evolution, others of which would benefit from new forms of research. The third section of each chapter is based on the weight of evidence in the first and second sections, but it is assertive, that is, as we note above, it is written according to the logic 'if storylistening were to exist, this is how it would work and why it would be effective'. We intend that these sections in particular will prompt or provoke future theory and practice. These are the sections on which exclusively policy-oriented readers might productively focus.

Turning to the contents of each chapter, Chapter 1 opens by shifting attention from stories' potential empathetic function (focused primarily on individual storyimbibers) to exploring how stories provide access to different points of view, both within a system and on a system. We discuss the lack of evidence for the narrative-empathy-altruism hypothesis (NEAH) – the idea that reading makes one empathise and therefore act in better ways – and propose instead the idea that an individual understands others, and how one functions in relation to them, by understanding their point of view, that is their situatedness in space and time, their story. Importantly, this understanding does not depend on imagining feelings, or on similarity or proximity. Our interest is not understanding the point of view of the single other, but in what evidence such different points of view might provide about the parts of the world relevant to public reasoning. To explore this we move from examining the attempted deployment of the NEAH in storytelling about climate change, to considering how storylistening can provide narrative evidence about different points of view (human and non-human) on the Earth system, and how these points of view can inform reasoning about it. We consider the problems of persistent anthropomorphisation in AI stories, and identify stories more useful to public reasoning around automated decision-making (stories about distributed intelligence) and artificial general intelligence (AGI) (stories imagining radically different alien intelligence).[20] We explore the mobilisation of empathy in relation to an identifiable victim and how storylistening must contend with the power of affective stories, in particular looking at different deployments and depictions of the figure of the child, and how different points of view found in stories can require triangulation by experts to create narrative evidence of value to storylistening. We show how storylistening (in particular in relation to points of view) can help decision-makers with the challenges of framing, scaling, and narrative deficits. Storylistening in relation to this function is particularly important to public reasoning because of the otherwise overwhelming tendency to notice, to value, and hence to attempt to model or account for those things or humans with which the dominant publics and decision-makers of the time feel most empathy and proximity. Like all forms of evidence gathering, storylistening calls on the knowledge of experts – in the final section of Chapter 1, we consider the opportunities and challenges faced by academics working in the humanities who might wish to inform public reasoning based on their expertise.

Moving beyond empathy as the only proposed function of stories on which claims about their value to public reasoning might be based clears the way for an exploration of the three further functions of stories, explored in the subsequent chapters, that together with points of view collectively build a robust case for the importance of storylistening to comprehensive public reasoning. In Chapter 2, we explore how persistently and consistently, across all parts of society and in relation to diverse identities and issues, stories function to create and consolidate collective identities, and to store and transmit social knowledge. Storylistening that takes into account this function of stories can help decision-makers identify social groups, understand motivations and actions, and recognise social norms and how they are or might be changing. After establishing the cross-discipli-nary evidence base that stories function in this way, we provide examples of stories doing so in relation to our four case studies, exploring *both* how stories shared within groups convey social norms and other information relevant to group coherence, influencing behaviour, *and* how stories provide insight into the nature of collective identities, how they are formed and maintained, through their modelling of such identities in the storycontent. (We then explore this rep-resentational function at more length in Chapter 3.) We consider how stories can provide insight into collective identity systems; the connection between Indige-nous knowledge, communities, stories, and climate change; how certain stories (for instance of apocalypse) can create narrative lock-in; and how storycontent and storysharing can define research collectives. In the final section, we show how storylistening can help identify publics, and understand narrative networks and norms, while acknowledging the challenges of such an enterprise, both ethi-cal and methodological. We draw attention to the need for narrative literacy, and highlight the dangers of, and potential deficits resulting from, narrative lock-in.

It is worth noting here that, at the very least, one of this book's aims is to give the storylistener a starting point to begin to develop their narrative literacy. If it does no more than prevent the easy adoption of a single mode of listening, dismissive or other, then that is a start. But more than this, we make the case for storylisteners to take it for granted that stories do matter, and to have some idea about the kinds of questions that would help them know how much, and how, in a particular context. Storylistening requires both basic narrative literacy on the part of the decision-maker, and the advice of narrative experts who are highly skilled in analysing and interpreting the functioning of stories.

Part of the work of Chapter 2 is to demonstrate how stories can function as models of collective identity systems; in Chapter 3, we provide the theoretical and practical basis for understanding how stories can function as models more generally. We explore this modelling function in relation to our case studies by considering what steps storylistening has to take to gather evidence from narrative models and how such models might complement other types of model relevant to the reasoning. These steps include identifying the relevant story, identifying its target system, identifying the modelling mode (mimetic or anticipatory), and determining mimetic legitimacy. We also consider how stories navigate between the global and the local, the general and the particular, one of a number of factors we explore in this chapter that demonstrate why narrative models are important as complements to, but in no way replacements of, scientific models. Finally, we draw out the consequences for both decision-makers and humanities academics of understanding stories as narrative models, including identifying the need for a pluralistic evidence base, synthesis that sets out the leading edge of knowledge within and across disciplines, in a comprehensive but accessible way, interdisciplinary working, and investment in building long-term relationships.

In Chapter 4, the final of the four function chapters, we turn to the future. The role of stories in anticipation is of fundamental importance to public reasoning because all decision-making depends on how the future is imagined, and what futures are imagined, despite the fact that the future can never be known. We consider Futures Studies' (FS) methods and techniques for anticipating the future and the place and role of stories within and across them, as well as make the case for the value to storylistening of narrative futures methods, including attention to anticipatory narrative models. Informed by the role of stories across futures techniques, as well as from stories themselves as anticipatory narrative models, storylistening can contribute narrative evidence to the work of anticipating the future, in order to enhance the quality of current decisions in particular by bridging from imagined future scenarios to present action. This chapter's performative readings demonstrate the role of stories as mimetic narrative models of the theory and practice of FS itself, enabling surrogative reasoning about its aims and effectiveness that might inform how and in what ways it is incorporated into public reasoning. We present the importance for storylistening of a move from looking to individual stories for predictions to thinking about collective narrative anticipation, of particular use for detecting weak signals, and we introduce the idea of treating stories as data. We then move to exploring how stories can expand FS's predominantly linear conception of time, and how their narrative structures and techniques can facilitate understanding of the expansive space-time sweep of latent futures. Stories can make explicit the structures of power implicit in FS's commitment to 'our' ability to shape the future when it is left uninterrogated who is included in and excluded from that empowered collective, and we offer examples of initiatives deploying narrative methods to encourage civic engagement and expand whose stories of the future influence public reasoning. We then explore how stories function in the context of a move in futures practice from focusing on end-states to thinking about pathways, risk, and adaptation. Finally, we consider the ways in which the structures of public reasoning might evolve to enable and incorporate storylistening, as well as how the humanities might evolve to better inform public reasoning, a process which might involve both stronger and more widespread performance of its current practices, as well as change and adaptation. We note how, for anticipation, the task of producing and listening to new stories is central, as is creating the spaces out of which such stories can emerge. We conclude by introducing the idea of individual and collective narrative responsibility.

Our exploration of four cognitive and collective functions of stories, and their illustration in relation to the four case studies through the chapters' performative

readings, together make the case for storylistening, providing both a robust theoretical basis for it, as well as demonstrations of how it can, and why it should,
work in practice. In the Epilogue, we conclude with a summary of our arguments, and an outline of the steps that could be taken now, across public reasoning, in order to start putting storylistening into practice. We argue that the
persuasive power of storytelling should not deter decision-makers from *listening*
to stories, attending to their functions, and recognising the role storylistening
can play in creating a comprehensive, pluralistic evidence base.

Notes

1 This usage is different to that within the field of narratology in literary studies where,
   put basically, the story is the events that are told and the discourse is the way in
   which they are told. This distinction is found in Russian formalism in the difference
   between *sjužet* and *fabula* (Erlich, 1955); in French narratology in the difference between *récit* and *histoire* (Genette, 1972); and in anglophone theory in Chatman's (1980)
   distinction between *story* and *discourse*.
2 There are many examples of this use of 'narrative' throughout the book's bibliography. Just a selection of recent examples from different areas might include Mair et al.
   (2019), Shiller (2019), and Morgan, Hajek, and Berry ([forthcoming]).
3 Michael Bamberg (2016: 1296) notes that such an approach in fact complicates any
   abstract definition of a story: 'While investigations of story form and story content
   have relatively clear textually defined units of analysis, an analytic perspective that
   aims to investigate what stories are used for complexifies the definition of the unit
   that is actually analyzed'.
4 We do not engage in detail in the book with stories circulating via social media, but
   we propose that our arguments can usefully apply generally to stories of all types and
   media. Our arguments regarding narrative literacy and storylistening – in particular
   our delineation of the cognitive value of stories and how to properly understand that
   value, and the functions and effects of stories more broadly – could usefully feed ideas
   about the place and role of stories into the fields of media and digital society research
   (see, for instance, the papers collected in van Dijck and Rieder, 2019).
5 We use the verb 'imbibe' – and the noun 'storyimbiber' – to distinguish individual
   engagement with stories from the collective, expert-informed, act of storylistening.
   Imbibing (meaning to absorb, assimilate, or take into one's mind) covers the different ways in which people receive stories in different media, as well as acts of story
   engagement such as embellishment, co-creation, or sharing, not denoted under the
   more limited term 'reading'.
6 See White (2017) for an account of the continued relevance of Benjamin's essay in the
   digital information age.
7 See, for example, Mink (1978), Robinson and Hawpe (1986), Somers (1994), Swirski
   (2006), Brooks (2014), Morgan (2017), and Christensen et al. (2018).
8 See, for example, Gregory et al. (1982), Pennington and Hastie (1988), Prentice et al.
   (1997), Strange and Leung (1999), and Wheeler et al. (1999).
9 See, for example, Simon (1987), Iyengar and Kinder (1987), Iyengar (1990, 1991), and
   Gibson and Zillmann (1994).
10 'Literary studies' is used here to name a now expansive field that studies, in addition
   to traditional literary texts (drama, poetry, short stories, the novel), stories in other
   narrative media such as film, video games, graphic novels and more, and contains a
   variety of methods and approaches. See Poovey (2008: 1) for an important historical
   approach to investigating the 'the *function* of the discipline, and, by extension, [...]
   the functions that Literary writing played during the last two centuries'. Poovey

understands function in terms of value and shows how nineteenth-century writers were at pains to identify a special function for literary writing that moved it away from its function, at the end of the seventeenth century, 'to help people understand the new credit economy and the market model of value that it promoted' (1–2) and towards instead 'a special kind of value – one not defined by the market' (2).

11 Felski (2008: 83) disputes Marjorie Perloff's (2004: 17) assertion, for example, that 'if the main purpose of a literary text is to convey knowledge or formulate truth, questions of form and genre take a back seat'.

12 The 2019 European Commission Report 'Understanding Our Political Nature' notes: 'The linkages between the use of evidence, its quality and relevance to the multi-actor policy process and the increase in quality and efficiency of resulting policies are well established' (Mair et al., 2019: 62). See also Davies (2008), Aravind and Chung (2010), Whitty (2015), and Castellani et al. (2016).

13 As Brom (2019: 6) warns:

> The consequence of engagement in public sphere scholarship is individual political engagement. For the societal position of the humanities as such, individual political engagement might – perceived as activism – even have negative consequences, creating an image of left-wing scholars who are unable to engage professionally with societal problems and who "sell" their political opinions cloaked in academic garb.

14 We discuss these ideas further in 'The Humanities Expert' in Chapter 1, and in 'Evolving the Humanities' in Chapter 4.

15 For more discussion see, for example, Cartwright (2007), Cartwright and Hardie (2012), Douglas (2015), Felt et al. (2017), and Newman (2017).

16 See Jasanoff (2007) where the concept is introduced, and Jasanoff (n.d.) for the following definition, and references to further relevant papers: 'Civic epistemologies are the stylized, culturally specific ways in which publics expect the state's expertise, knowledge, and reasoning to be produced, tested, and put to use in decisionmaking'. See also Jasanoff (2011).

17 As Jasanoff (2012: 7) notes, one must attend to 'the circumstances of knowledge production', as well as

> the institutions and practices that condition receptivity toward public knowledge claims of any kind – in short, the dominant forms of a nation's civic epistemology. Such public knowledge ways consist of established commitments to particular forms of evidence garnering, argument, and demonstrations of reasonableness.

In an article aimed at practitioners and potential practitioners, the former Chief Scientific Adviser to the New Zealand government, Sir Peter Gluckman (2014: 165), says that 'different approaches suit different purposes and are the product of a country's culture, history, political and social structures and approaches to civic reason'. For an evidence synthesis of effective practice in boundary organisations at the 'knowledge-policy interface' see Topp et al. (2018).

18 This is a position corroborated by emerging work on the relevance of the humanities to policymaking: 'While historians have many lessons from the past to impart, AHRC may consider helping researchers of contemporary issues or issues with implications for the present to bring their work before policymakers' (Lees, 2017: 42).

19 Janice Radway (1984) justified her then groundbreaking study of American women readers of romance novels, for instance, in a similar way. She notes that 'while "elite" literature might be taken as evidence for the beliefs of a particular section of the American population, assertions based upon it could not easily be extrapolated to wholly different classes or ethnic groups' (Radway, 1984: 3). She continues, 'if accurate statements were to be made about more "ordinary" Americans, the popular literature produced for and consumed by large numbers ought to become the primary focus of culturally oriented scholarship' (Radway, 1984: 3). Although she did

not discover it until after her research, Radway's approach is aligned with that of the Birmingham Centre for Contemporary Cultural Studies in the UK, founded in 1964, which committed to studying mass culture and its political significance, combining literary criticism with anthropology, history, and sociology, in a move that disrupted the established conventions of academic practice.

20 AGI is the hypothetical (since not yet technically achieved) intelligence of a machine that has the same intellectual capacities as a human being. It is sometimes also called 'strong AI', although this often includes attributing human-level consciousness as well as intelligence. See Goertzel (2011) on the coinage of the term.

1

POINTS OF VIEW

Introduction

On 15 September 2001, the front cover of *The Guardian* featured a response by Ian McEwan to the 9/11 terrorist attacks on the USA. 'Among their crimes', McEwan (2001: n.p.) wrote, 'was a failure of the imagination':

> If the hijackers had been able to imagine themselves into the thoughts and feelings of the passengers, they would have been unable to proceed. It is hard to be cruel once you permit yourself to enter the mind of your victim. Imagining what it is like to be someone other than yourself is at the core of our humanity. It is the essence of compassion, and it is the beginning of morality.

McEwan here holds with what has been called the empathy-altruism hypothesis (EAH) (Batson et al., 1991; Batson et al., 2015). This hypothesis proposes that increased empathy with fellow human beings leads to increased prosocial behaviour – that is, behaviour that supports the common good, not just one's own interests. The narrative-empathy-altruism hypothesis (NEAH) proposes that stories function to produce the empathy that leads to the prosocial behaviour. This is one of the most widely held, and longstanding arguments for the functioning, and therefore the value, of stories. Its validity, or lack thereof, is, as Andreea Deciu Ritivoi (2016: 52) identifies, a question of importance 'not just for narrative theory but also for political thought'.

The dominance of the NEAH has led most scholarly and public discussion to focus on empathy as the most important, in some cases in fact the *only*, function of stories that might make them relevant to public reasoning. Whether or not the NEAH actually holds, faith in it remains strong and many storytellers and storyimbibers are committed to its principles. We therefore begin this book with attention to empathy in order to expose the problems with, and limits of, the

DOI: 10.4324/9780367808426-3

evidence that stories in fact function in this way. We do so in order to clear the ground for proposing a different function of stories that is of more robust value to public reasoning – that of providing multiple points of view (POV). The gain here for public reasoning is not the insight stories may give into the emotional state of others, nor (posited) emotional or even intellectual changes in the storyimbiber. Rather, the gain is the increased knowledge and understanding of a system of relevance to public reasoning that is obtained by having multiple perspectives on it, derived through storylistening.

Gathering multiple points of view on a system has two potential consequences of value to public reasoning: either, it changes the boundaries of the system (what is included or excluded); or, it changes what is brought most sharply into focus or foregrounded within it. Increased understanding of individuals in this context is of value to the extent that individuals are part of collectives, and understanding collective identities is crucial to effective public reasoning. This latter is the subject of the following chapter. When stories function to offer insight into collective identities, they are providing information about groups of individuals that are part of the system. In the POV function, stories' useful information is not about the holder of that point of view, but about the systems that holder is observing, the object of their perspective. Increased understanding of a single individual is less important to public reasoning in either instance, except when such individuals are charismatic actors with strong influence on or within systems, meaning that they are of interest as agents within that system, or where the individual story is determined to have metonymic legitimacy (that is, represents a whole).

Because of its deep-rooted prevalence, we use the first section of this chapter to set out the limits of the NEAH by assessing the rhetorical claims and empirical evidence presented in support of it, before explaining the POV function. In the second section, our performative readings in relation to the book's case studies illustrate how the POV function works in practice, as well as further addressing the challenges empathy poses to storylistening and public reasoning. In the final section, we draw out the important consequences for public reasoning, and for the humanities, of a practice of storylistening that accounts for the limitations of empathy and navigates the relationship between stories, points of view, systems, and decision-making. In sum, this chapter begins our work of presenting a framework of the useful functions of stories for public reasoning, a framework that moves beyond the dominance of the empathy argument in order to provide a more robust and comprehensive case for the importance of storylistening that produces narrative evidence for the purposes of public reasoning.

Function description and evidence

The narrative-empathy-altruism hypothesis (NEAH)

The term 'empathy' has been used across sectors and across academic disciplines. As such, its meaning is shifting, contextual, and often contradictory. In her overview of the term, its features and effect, Amy Coplan (2011: 42) concludes that 'there is no clear and agreed upon answer to the question of what empathy is'.[1] Most often in relation to the NEAH, empathy is understood as the imagining of, or even entering into, the feelings of another, so this will be our working definition. This aligns with Paul Bloom's (2017) category of affective or emotional empathy, which evidence distinguishes from cognitive empathy or theory of mind (Zaki and Ochsner, 2012; Jordan et al., 2016). We address the latter at the end of this section when discussing the POV function. If users of the term differ in their understanding of its meaning, there is much stronger consensus that empathy is universally 'a good thing'. Michael Fischer's (2017: 432) informal survey of the use of the term in recent opinion pieces in *The New York Times* and the *Chronicle of Higher Education* reveals empathy to have achieved the status of a modern panacea, hailed as the essential foundation of moral judgement and action, an evolutionary survival tool, a fundamental way of resolving conflict non-violently, as well as 'the key to successful fund-raising, classroom teaching, university administration, doctor-patient communication and drug addiction treatment' and even 'a reason for the decline of fighting in the National Hockey League'.

The term 'empathy' entered the English language in 1909 as Edward B. Titchener's (1909: 21) translation of the German psychological term *Einfühlung* (coined by Robert Vischer and expanded upon by Theodor Lipps). From its earliest English language use, empathy has been associated with stories, and with reading (Keen, 2006: 209).[2] However, the NEAH has a far longer history in Western thought, stemming back at least to Aristotle's theory of tragic drama, through Adam Smith's (2010) concept of 'sympathy' in *The Theory of Moral Sentiments* (1759), to its most committed contemporary presentation in the work of philosopher Martha Nussbaum. In *Poetic Justice* (1995) and *Cultivating Humanity* (1997), Nussbaum argues for the importance of reading for the cultivation of a compassionate imagination essential to public reasoning, and crucial for responsible and effective democratic citizenship:

> Narrative imagination is an essential preparation for moral interaction. Habits of empathy and conjecture conduce to a certain type of citizenship and a certain form of community: one that cultivates a sympathetic responsiveness to another's needs, and understands the way circumstances shape those needs.
>
> *(Nussbaum, 1997: 90)*

For Nussbaum (1995: 5), 'the ability to imagine what it is like to live the life of another person who might, given changes in circumstance, be oneself or one of one's loved ones' is nurtured through engagement with stories. Such engagement, she believes, 'constructs empathy and compassion in ways highly relevant to citizenship' (10).

Problems with the NEAH

Advocacy of the NEAH is often impassioned, persuasive, and integral to wider defences of the public value of literature, literary studies and humanistic education.

But the position is flawed, vulnerable to both rhetorical and empirical critique. Proponents of the NEAH tend to focus on only one type of story – for Nussbaum it is the nineteenth-century realist novel. Their arguments, if they hold at all, therefore only hold for one type of story and cannot be generalised to, and in fact might be undone by, engagement with other types of story. Dramatist Berthold Brecht's (2001) theory and practice of the alienation effect in order to provoke a social and critical response in theatre audiences through radical defamiliarisation, as well as Darko Suvin's (1979) theory of science fiction as achieving its political aims through a process of cognitive estrangement, both offer counter-theories to the NEAH and offer competing accounts of how different types of stories produce social or political effects in their storyimbibers.

Other critiques of the NEAH allow that literature might produce empathy, but question the (limited) focus or effects of that empathy. Susan Keen (2007) identifies that a thorough theory of reader empathy must be derived from engagement with a diverse range of stories and their readers. She suggests that such a theory might emphasise the importance of empathy in readerly engagement while dissociating this from any moral or prosocial effects. Anna Lindhé (2016) proposes a paradox of narrative empathy. She claims that while enlisting empathy for certain characters, stories necessarily also ensure de-empathising for other characters. The paradox is that empathy (for one Other) is therefore produced at the cost of reduced empathy (for a different Other). Paul Bloom (2016) calls this empathy's spotlight effect, focusing attention on the individual rather than the collective. Also engaging only with nineteenth-century realist fiction, Lindhé does not go further in her critique, for instance to address the challenge to the NEAH of stories that might develop empathy for evil, or distinctly anti-social characters (consider the television series *Dexter*, for instance, or Vladimir Nabokov's *Lolita*). The NEAH depends on the assumption that the storyimbiber empathises with the character that is suffering, but many stories depend for their narrative power on drawing the imbiber into feelings of evil, or at least morally suspect, characters.[3] Even if a story does not so strongly privilege the perspective of the evil character, different storyimbibers might empathise more naturally with different characters, for instance those inflicting the suffering, not those receiving it.

The NEAH depends on a perhaps unconscious, definitely uninterrogated, assumption regarding the proper moral position of the empathiser, and the proper subject of empathy. For example, a storyimbiber might empathise with the wealthy business owner in a story, struggling to maintain her business, rather than the workers she uses in order to do so. It is not inconceivable, for instance, to argue that Ian McEwan demonstrates a failure of the imagination himself when he is not able to imagine the feelings of the terrorists, convinced of the righteousness of their actions in response to sustained American aggression against Muslims worldwide. Such an extension of empathy is not to condone such actions, but to understand their motivations and contend with the possibility that the attackers' actions, from their perspective, could equally be motivated by empathy, just for previous Muslim victims rather the people shortly to become their own. Empathy is not always directed at a universally agreed upon sufferer, nor does it guarantee actions universally accepted as prosocial.[4]

Empathy, if indeed it is an effect of imbibing stories, is therefore not unequivocally a moral good. Narrative empathy might in fact be a form of hypocritical moral absolution, an indulgence in feeling with the suffering of the other which serves to exempt the storyimbiber from any form of social or political action in response (Williams, 1983; Wood, 2002). Empathy can be criticised for always being in the interests of the empathiser rather than the empathised (Shuman, 2005). Even if there is an intention to act, excessive empathy might in fact paralyse prosocial behaviour, or lead to the avoidance of situations in which empathy might be triggered (Klimecki et al., 2014).

Empathy, as most often construed, also depends on the idea of similarity – one can imagine oneself in another's shoes, one can imagine their suffering being one's own suffering. But this dependence on similarity, or familiarity, to produce an empathetic response inhibits engagement with others that are radically different, whose lives are so different from one's own that their circumstances are never likely to be one's own. The argument here is that empathy is a response to a human universality. But the similarity and the universality conditions of empathy have also been subject to strong critique, for impeding an empathetic response to strangers (Hoffman, 1996), and for ensuring we only empathise with those like us, which in fact reinforces ingroups and outgroups (Chow, 1995; Hoffman, 2000; Kruger, 2003; Slovic, 2007a; Hein et al., 2010; Ritivoi, 2016; Bloom, 2017). Feminist and postcolonial critiques challenge the idea of universality.[5] Key for the investigations of this book is the case that while empathy might well be beneficial in the context of intimate individual relationships (for example, between family and friends), it is not helpful at the collective level of public reasoning (Scarry, 1996; Prinz, 2011). Strong arguments have been made that empathy is actually dangerous at a public, collective level, creating a fantasy of being able to imagine the feelings of those different from oneself – usually focused on the individual – which elides broader understanding of the political and other structures that cause or consolidate suffering (Delgado, 1996; Berlant, 2004; Hammond and Kim, 2014). This leads to favouring 'generous imaginings' (Scarry, 1996: 99) as the route to effect change, rather than significant structural and constitutional adjustments. A recent US study suggests that empathetic concern, rather than reducing intergroup conflict and partisan polarisation, is associated with higher levels of affective polarisation and greater partisan bias (Simas et al., 2020).

With regard to public reasoning, empathy is particularly problematic in respect of the challenge of scaling, that is, the question of the effectiveness or accuracy of navigating from the singular to the general. Here it is important to consider the role of anecdotes in relation to empathy. As a result of what psychologists have called the identifiable victim effect (Schelling, 1968; Jenni and Loewenstein, 1997; Kogut and Ritov, 2005a; Koopman and Hakemulder, 2015), human beings are more likely to respond empathetically to the story of a single individual, with accounts of suffering on a larger scale risking 'psychic numbing' (Lifton, 1967; Slovic, 2007b). However, an empathetic response to a story of singular suffering can distort decision-making in favour of one individual which may in fact be counter to a collective or more equitable good (Batson et al., 1995a, 1995b; Kogut and Ritov, 2005a, 2005b; Batson, 2014). Empathy for the one can imperil justice for the many. Empathy can therefore inhibit robust public reasoning aimed at developing policies for the collective good (Keen, 2007; Nussbaum, 2013; Ritivoi, 2016). Combining the critiques of similarity, of scaling, and of proximity, Hannah Arendt (1973) identifies empathy's role – in her terminology, 'compassion' – in disabling political action. For Arendt, empathy causes an emotional overload which is eased by attention to the immediate suffering of one individual but which does not create the foundations for rational analysis and decision-making that would lead to action to address wider suffering, beyond that which is immediately present.[6]

Empirical studies of the NEAH

Turning to empirical studies, the evidence in both cases – that empathy causes prosocial behaviour, and that storyimbibing causes empathy – is inconclusive. In the first instance, while there is a body of research that suggests a link between empathy and prosocial behaviour (Eisenberg and Miller, 1987; Batson, 1991; Batson and Shaw, 1991; Davis, 1996; Penner et al., 2005; Dovidio et al., 2006; Stocks et al., 2009), there is also empirical evidence against the hypothesis (Piliavin and Piliavin, 1973; Krebs, 1975; Hornstein, 1978; Hoffman, 1981; Piliavin et al., 1981, 1982; Karylowski, 1982; Schroeder et al., 1995). Nancy Eisenberg and Janet Strayer (1987: 10–11) conclude that 'the relationship between empathy and prosocial behaviour is neither direct nor inevitable'. Similarly, studies of the relationship between reading stories and empathy have proved at best a correlation between a lifetime's reading and an increased empathetic response, but without proving causation – that is, it may be that people who read a lot are already naturally more empathetic, rather than that long-term reading develops empathy. Nor has direct causation been proven between an immediate reading experience and an immediate or short-term increase in empathy (Oatley, 1999; Coplan, 2004; Mar et al., 2006a, 2006b, 2009; Johnson, 2012; Fong et al., 2013; Kidd and Castano, 2013; Koopman, 2015; Koopman and Hakemulder, 2015). A number of these studies have not proven replicable (Djikic et al., 2013 did not replicate Johnson, 2012; Panero et al., 2016 did not replicate Kidd and Castano, 2013). Other studies suggest that the effect of stories on empathy can be both positive and negative: Bal and Veltkamp (2013) observe that while high transportation into the story leads to high empathy, no transportation can in fact lead to lower empathy; Djikic et al. (2013: 42) found that people high in Openness in fact had their cognitive empathy reduced after reading. Recent research also challenges the emphasis of previous studies on the importance of 'literariness' or high-brow literature in creating empathetic effects, paralleling the criticism of the focus on the literary, and in particular on canonical fiction, in dominant rhetorical defences of the NEAH: Kuzmičová et al. (2017) failed to confirm the hypothesis that literary texts prompt more empathy than popular ones. Many such studies also tend to simply assume the validity of the EAH, focusing their attention only on whether narrative engagement causes empathy and assuming that, if it does so, this is a good thing.

A significant amount of the work published as empirical research contains a strong rhetorical component, proposing and defending the NEAH without in fact proving it. Despite the lack of conclusive evidence of a causal relationship between reading, empathy, and prosocial behaviour, this holy trinity tenaciously remains the primary focus of empirical research into theories of reading. Such work might in fact be viewed as being founded upon the same belief in this relationship which grounds the rhetorical accounts alike. The idea that reading makes one more empathetic and therefore a better person is an article of faith without conclusive empirical foundation. It is therefore not a proven function of stories, even as it is the most dominant proposal for their significance, and their relationship to public reasoning. Once aware of this, a decision-maker can be careful of falling foul of the many pitfalls of what might be renamed the narrative-empathy-altruism fallacy. Storylistening needs to be conscious of these pitfalls and of the potential political dangers of empathetic response. Empathy might be an important element of storyimbibing, but not an important function of stories in relation to public reasoning. Empathy centres more often on the similar and the individual than the different and the collective, skewing decision-making where this is not acknowledged, and presenting challenges of legitimate scaling where it is. Empathy is not always directed at a universally agreed upon sufferer, nor does it guarantee actions that might be universally agreed to be prosocial, nor in fact does it guarantee any action at all. Storylistening needs to be sensitive to how empathy can misfunction, and attend instead to the more relevant functions of stories to public reasoning, as presented in this book, for instance, their role in providing multiple points of view on a system or systems.

From empathy to points of view

The NEAH fosters a focus on empathy as the most important function of stories in relation to public reasoning. This is because entering into another's thoughts and feelings is held to lead to better (meaning prosocial) behaviour and decision-making. The NEAH focuses primarily on the relationship between stories (usually written ones), empathising with other human individuals, and storyimbibers acting well, and empathetic response depends on similarity and proximity. Its structure and mode of operation is represented in Figure 1.1, in which the charismatic characters are usually taken to be human.

Figure 1.2a represents our proposal, that is, that stories can function to enable the storyimbiber to access multiple points of view on a system, without

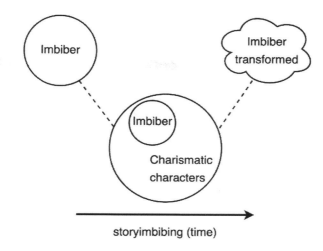

FIGURE 1.1   Representation of the Narrative-Empathy-Altruism Hypothesis (NEAH).

needing to be similar or proximate to the character holding that point of view. Here, points of view are revealed through story in relation to multiple characters, which collectively provide the storyimbiber with a more complete picture of the system. They may increase knowledge or understanding of the characters as well, but this is not the focus or reward of the POV function. In Figure 1.2a, Ca, Cb, Cc, C*n* might be an individual human, a collective of humans, or another actor whose point of view on a system can be imagined through story, for instance a mountain, as in Aldo Leopold's 'Thinking Like a Mountain' (1949) or, as we discuss among the performative readings in the next section, a tree.

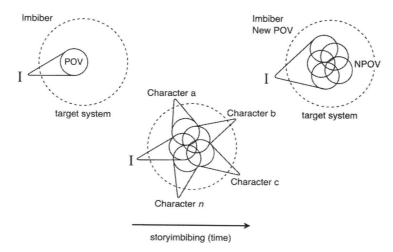

FIGURE 1.2 (a)   Representation of Points of View – Part A: Storyimbibing.

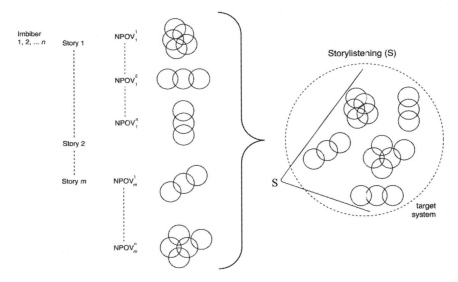

FIGURE 1.2 (b) Representation of Points of View – Part B: Storylistening.

Even if the NEAH were without the flaws already discussed in this section, there is little evidence that it makes sense to scale this up to arguing for a key empathetic function of stories in informing public reasoning in the interests of the collective good. For in this instance the concern has to be with human and non-human collectives, gaining multiple perspectives, and creating a fuller picture of a policy or other target system, in order to make effective decisions.[7] In this context, the POV function can be effectively scaled up, demonstrating how storylistening can play a role in gathering evidence about multiple points of view as they are contained and conveyed in stories, thereby creating a fuller picture of a system and enabling better decision-making. This is illustrated in Figure 1.2b.

When moving from empathy to POV, it might be supposed that research on cognitive empathy or Theory of Mind (ToM) would provide useful evidence in which to ground the POV function case, since ToM or cognitive empathy is also referred to as perspective-taking, and is one of two theories of social cognition that account for the way in which people are able to interact effectively with other people and in social situations. (The other is simulation theory [ST].) But ToM, like affective or emotional empathy, depends on the idea of mentalising, that is, understanding one's own and other's mental states. According to ToM and ST, social cognition is possible because either (1) one is able to understand that others have minds, to which one can attribute mental states based on one's own experience (ToM: Leslie, 1987; Gopnik and Meltzoff, 1993); or (2) one simulates in one's own mind the situation, or the mental state of the person, that one encounters, and hence deduces motivation and how to act accordingly (ST: Gordon, 1986; Goldman, 1989). Both theories have been contested on the basis that infants demonstrate social cognition before they are able to mentalise (that is, understand their own, or others', mental states). In the course of standard development, this ability occurs in children around the age of three or four. But developmental research shows that infants prior to that age are more than capable of social cognition, including interpreting the intentions of others. They do so not through mentalising, but through embodied perception, for instance reading the movements, facial expressions, and gestures of others. Such evidence calls into question the validity of ToM and ST as explanations of social cognition, that is, of how one effectively understands and interacts with others.[8]

In place of ToM and ST, Shaun Gallagher and Daniel Hutto (2008) propose a combination of three processes that are sufficient to account for effective social cognition: (1) intersubjective perceptual processes, (2) pragmatically contextualised comprehension, and (3) narrative competence. Processes (1) and (2) do not involve stories, but are explained briefly here in order to contextualise the role of stories. The first process – intersubjective perception – holds that one understands other people's intentions because of their expressive behaviours and embodied actions. This is a perceptual, non-mentalising mode of understanding others, and can be seen in the behaviour of newborns (Bermúdez, 1996; Gallagher, 1996; Gallagher and Meltzoff, 1996; Gallagher, 2008). The second process – contextual comprehension – holds that one's primary interaction with others is not cognitive but perceptual, adding that we perceive others as agents whose actions are embedded and meaningful in pragmatic physical and intersubjective contexts (Gallagher, 2008). The third process – narrative competence – is of particular relevance for our purposes, since it holds that human beings make sense of another's motivations and actions through effectively understanding stories (Gallagher, 2006; Gallagher and Hutto, 2008). Engagement with stories from an early age provides the training for understanding the motivations and actions of others, and human beings are able to understand those actions by framing them in narrative ways (Dunn, 1988; Hutto, 2007b). Importantly, doing so does not require any mentalising inference, any access to their inner life through ToM or simulation or empathy. Rather, the situatedness of the other in body, time and space, and therefore their point of view, is perceived through understanding their story (MacIntyre, 1981; Dilthey, 1988; Galafassi et al., 2018).

Two strands of empirical research provide further support for this account of how one effectively understands and operates with others. The first is the body of work that evidences a relationship, stronger than mere correlation, between narrative abilities and social cognition (Astington, 1990; Feldman et al., 1990; Dunn, 1991; Lewis, 1994; Lewis et al., 1994; Peterson and McCabe, 1994; Nelson, 2007). The second is work that demonstrates a parallel between the structure of narratives and the operations individuals use to make sense of them on the one hand, and the structure of the agency system in human psychology and the strategies used to understand and anticipate the behaviour of goal-directed agents on the other (Csibra et al., 2003; Scalise Sugiyama, 2005, 2016). Effective social interaction and behaviour is achieved not by imagining or entering into the feelings or thoughts of others, but by understanding their point of view through story, either their own story, or one's own narrative framing of their behaviour.

Adaptations are needed to this account of social cognition in order to develop a robust case for how stories can inform public reasoning through providing multiple points of view. For even Gallagher and Hutto's non-mentalising ac- count of social cognition focuses primarily on individual-individual interaction and behaviour, and on the role of stories in facilitating interaction with other human beings, but not with non-human others and the environment. In order to shift from stories' role in effective individual social interaction with other people to stories' role in effective public reasoning about systems, changes have to be made. The major changes are the plural number of actors whose points of view are taken into account, the importance of those multiple perspectives to building a fuller picture of a system (rather than to gain knowledge of individuals), and the externality of storylistening to the actors and the system.

Performative readings

In this section, we explore how the NEAH functions, and misfunctions, in re- lation to the book's case studies, and demonstrate how the POV function works in practice. We examine how the NEAH is mobilised in storytelling about cli- mate change and question how effective this is. We then explore how storyl- istening can provide different points of view (human and non-human) on the Earth system. We consider the problems of persistent anthropomorphisation in AI stories, and identify stories more useful to public reasoning around auto- mated decision-making (stories about distributed intelligence) and AGI (stories imagining radically different alien intelligence). We explore the mobilisation of empathy in relation to an identifiable victim and how storylistening must contend with the power of affective stories, in particular looking at different mobilisations and depictions of the figure of the child. And we show how differ- ent points of view found in stories can require triangulation by experts to create narrative evidence of value to storylistening.

Climate change and the Earth system

As discussed above, one of the limits of the NEAH is that it depends on proxim- ity and similarity – storyimbibers are more likely to engage empathetically with 'others' (real or imagined) who are in fact adjacent to them. The NEAH does not contend with how one understands and acts prosocially in relation to those oth- ers radically different to oneself, both human and non-human. In other words, what might induce someone to treat other people and things as they would wish to be treated themselves, while at the same time never believing that they are like them? Such challenges and questions are pertinent to climate change, a phenom- enon that is systemic, and which imbricates both the human and the non-human, the animate and the inanimate. The NEAH is mobilised most often in story*telling* regarding climate change, rather than in story*listening*. For example, a complex phenomenon, in this instance the Earth system, is anthropomorphised in order that single individuals might empathise with the suffering of the Earth (rendered as another single individual) and therefore be induced to treat it properly and behave in environmentally friendly ways. Storytelling in this mode reduces the radical other to the human and the proximate in the hopes of leveraging empathy. The opening of Pope Francis' 2015 encyclical on climate change, Laudato Si', exemplifies this point, mobilising as it does the personification of the Earth found in Saint Francis of Assisi's *Canticle of the Creatures*. The encyclical begins:

1   'Laudato si', mi' Signore' – 'Praise be to you, my Lord'. In the words of this beautiful canticle, Saint Francis of Assisi reminds us that our common home is like a sister with whom we share our life and a beautiful mother who opens her arms to embrace us. 'Praise be to you, my Lord, through our Sister, Mother Earth, who sustains and governs us, and who produces various fruit with coloured flowers and herbs'.

2   This sister now cries out to us because of the harm we have inflicted on her by our irresponsible use and abuse of the goods with which God has endowed her. We have come to see ourselves as her lords and masters, entitled to plunder her at will. The violence present in our hearts, wounded by sin, is also reflected in the symptoms of sickness evident in the soil, in the water, in the air, and in all forms of life. This is why the earth herself, burdened and laid waste, is among the most abandoned and maltreated of our poor; she 'groans in travail' (*Rom* 8:22). (Francis, 2015: n.p.)

In these two paragraphs the Earth is transfigured – it is no longer a planet, nor even a complex system, but a human being, and one directly proximate to the listener – their mother or sister. In transfiguring the Earth in such a way, the Pope aims to enable the listener to feel empathy for the suffering of the Earth by analogy with how they would feel empathy for the suffering of a family member. They are able to do so because the Earth is both attributed human emotions and feelings, and cast in a character universally proximate to any human being – a sibling or parent. The Earth can now feel pain, suffer, be violated; human beings are culpable now for treating another human being (personified Earth) in this way, another example of their original sin, and humankind's drive to power and domination. Humans are rhetorically induced to cease such behaviour, and treat the Earth as one would one's sibling or parent.

As the discussion in the first section of this chapter has shown, it is far from certain that such narrative anthropomorphisation creates empathy that mobilises prosocial behaviour. But at least in relation to climate change, anthropomorphisation through storytelling can be viewed as contributing to a shift in perception of the status of the natural environment – from a primarily Western view of nature as a property from which to extract wealth, to a perspective which understands human and non-human to constitute together the complex world system. This perspective can be found in Gaia theory (Lovelock, 1979, 1988, 1991, 2006; Margulis, 1998; Crist and Rinker, 2009), and is aligned with Indigenous knowledge, for instance in the rich Inuit concept of *Sila* which links life, climate, and wisdom (Qitsualik, 1998; Martin, 2012; Todd, 2016). It requires an 'ethical relationality' (Donald, 2009: 6) with others, human and non-human, that does not imagine difference can be transcended through an act of imagined sameness, but rather foregrounds and navigates the different social, cultural, and historical contexts in which a person is embedded and which define their point of view on the world.

This perspective moves away from 'generous imaginings' towards attention to the legal and other structures of governance within which we think and act (Todd, 2016). Prosocial behaviour towards the environment from this perspective can be mobilised through attributing legal personhood to the natural world, granting it rights that can be enshrined and defended in the constitution and in law (Leopold, 1949; Stone, 1972; Pierce, 2013; Hillebrecht and Berros, 2017; *The Rights of Nature*, 2018; Mauch, 2019; Greene, n.d.), rather than attributing feelings to the inanimate in the hope that it can then be empathised with.[9] Storytelling and storylistening can play a role in this further extension of rights to that which has previously been 'rightless' – in humankind's past, this has included women, enslaved peoples, children, and other minorities. What is involved here is not empathy, but a change of perspective, an understanding through story of the point of view of the radical other, and a consequent acknowledgement of their rights irrespective of whether one can or cannot imagine or enter into their thoughts or feelings, or even contend that they might have such. Decision-making regarding climate change might be informed by storylistening to stories that dispense with the attempt to evoke empathy and instead provoke such a disruptive change of perspective. This storylistening would reveal multiple points of view and help build a fuller picture of the systemic imbrication of the environment and the species, including humankind, that inhabit it.

Despite opening with the strategy of the NEAH effected through anthropomorphisation, the final lines of the Pope's second paragraph do shift to an acknowledgement that the 'natural' world is not in fact an object separate to and independent of humankind, but is in fact part of a complex system in which humans and their environment are radically imbricated in the effects they have on each other:

> We have forgotten that we ourselves are dust of the earth (cf. *Gen* 2:7); our very bodies are made up of her elements, we breathe her air and we receive life and refreshment from her waters.
> *Nothing in this world is indifferent to us*
>
> *(Francis, 2015: n.p.)*

These lines persist in anthropomorphising the Earth through the use of the gendered third-person pronoun 'she', but at the same time they effect an anti-anthropomorphism. Rather than the Earth being made human, humans are reminded that they are not separate from the Earth. Instead of rendering the natural world human and thus attempting to leverage empathy with it in order to induce humans to treat it properly, these lines challenge the boundaries put around the category of 'the human', inserting it into the complex system of which it is in fact a part, both as an individual and collective body. Some of 'us' (the Pope's 'we') may have forgotten this, but storylistening can attend to, for example, Indigenous stories and knowledge which have not suffered from such amnesia. For example, Nalo Hopkinson's novel *Midnight Robber* (2000) provides a sophisticated exploration of different configurations of human and non-human animal and environment, as its protagonist Tan-Tan moves from a high-tech society, to a colony of those banished from that society, to living with the Indigenous inhabitants of the planet to which they have been banished.[10] With its dominant narrative intercut with folk tales, the novel also performatively demonstrates the importance of storytelling to establish and convey social knowledge.

As explained in the first section of this chapter, stories can provide access to different points of view on a system – human and non-human – thereby creating a fuller picture of that system. In relation to non-human actors, this process is often achieved in experimental artistic forms that veer more towards the lyrical than the narrative, for instance Australian poet Les Murray's (1993) animal poetry – consider 'Pigs' or 'Shoal' – or the immersive, experiential shipping industry film *Leviathan* (2013). But it can also be rendered and explored in more narrative-driven stories. For example, Ursula Le Guin's (2015) short story 'Direction of the Road' (1974) is narrated by a tree. The tree's point of view conflicts with at least lay human understanding of the physical world – the tree considers itself to be mobile and agential, the changes in its size and shape a result of its own carefully managed movement towards or away from the human beings passing along the road. Its careful management is made more and more difficult by the increased speed of human travel with the advent of the motor car. The tree struggles to keep up with humankind's increasingly rapid but illusory pursuit of progress and eventually resents that it becomes symbolic of the death of the human species – a result of its unavoidable clashes with these rapidly moving humans – rather than being recognised as alive and, importantly, mortal, not eternal. Imagining the tree's point of view through story might lead to consideration of the rights of trees but, perhaps even more importantly for public reasoning, the tree's point of view (imagined through story) offers a different perspective on the target system. Where an initial framing might be about how to maximise movement and speed and reduce accidents, and would take for granted the perspective of the car driver, taking the story of the tree seriously would mean expanding the system it was necessary to consider, to include stationary and slow-moving animate and inanimate entities adjacent to the road, which might include pedestrians as well as hedgerows, for example. It would foreground the consequences of increasing speed for static or slow-moving parts of the landscape. In cities it might be part of the shift to regarding cities as 'systems of systems', in which delivering social and economic goals requires careful design of all forms of infrastructure, shaping each city's morphology and metabolism and the spaces through which people and things move (Government Office for Science, 2016). In this mode of operation, the function does not necessarily lead to discussion of rights, but it provides an opportunity to test and develop the conception of the system that is the subject of public reasoning, and hence what evidence, as well as which agents, might be needed to inform the reasoning.

AI and anthropomorphisation

The above example from the Pope's encyclical reveals a close connection, when dealing with the non-human, between empathy and anthropomorphisation. Turning to our AI case study, persistent anthropomorphisation in stories about intelligent machines can serve to elicit empathy with similar effects to the anthropomorphisation of nature. That is, anthropomorphisation leads to a consideration of the need to extend rights to the non-human. The revolutionary droid L3-37 (played by Phoebe Waller-Bridge) in *Solo: A Star Wars Story* (2018) plays out this logic – L3-37 is sentient, intelligent, and capable of independent thought and emotion. There is no question in her mind that she and other droids deserve equal rights to humans. Throughout the film she engages in acts of activism in pursuit of that equality, whether in her attempt to rouse the droids being made to fight each other for human entertainment to anger and revolt, or in freeing enslaved robot workers in the mines of Kessel. However, whereas the extension of legal rights to the natural world serves an urgent purpose in addressing the climate crisis, the current extension of legal rights to purported 'AI' is a distracting hoax. In 2017, Hanson Robotics' humanoid robot, Sophia, created by an artist who previously worked as a sculptor and researcher in Disney's Imagineering Lab, was awarded Saudi Arabian citizenship and was named the world's first United Nations Innovation Champion. Sophia is neither sentient, nor capable of independent thought, yet it has more rights than some human citizens of Saudi Arabia and a deeply ironic official role to work with the UNDP to safeguard human rights and equality. Extensive imaginative exploration in stories of the question of attribution of rights to intelligent machines would be relevant *if and when* sentient artificial general intelligence were ever actually achieved. But public reasoning now should not be wholly distracted by a line of thought that is irrelevant to the technical realities and social challenges of the increasing contemporary prevalence of automated decision-making (Royal Society, 2017, 2018; Russell, 2019).

Anthropomorphism, including the attribution of feelings to AI to mobilise empathy, leads to reasoning about personhood and rights. However, non-humanoid and distributed AI – for instance in the form of automated decision-making – includes far more sinister present and future prospects in terms of its actions and effects in the world, and presents a different challenge to how humans might control and manage that action. Important, then, are stories that explore the consequences and effects of the structural imbrication of the human and machine, in particular within the context of governance and decision-making, and stories that recognise and explore the networked, distributed, nature and effects of automated decision-making technologies. Robert A. Heinlein's *The Moon Is a Harsh Mistress* (1966) is an example of the former, which while still making the central supercomputer, Holmes IV, a sentient character for storytelling purposes, positions the computer in relationship to, and as a part of, the system of governance of lunar civilisation, both its strict regulation and its use as part of the resistance movement. Examples of the latter include E. M. Forster's *The Machine Stops* ([1909] 2011), Isaac Asimov's 'The Evitable Conflict' (1950), Paul W. Fairman's *I, Machine* (1968), and the popular television series *Person of Interest* (2011–2016).[11]

Alien points of view

If there remains a benefit to public discussion of the potential consequences of the creation of sentient AGI, such discussion would be better informed by stories that are not premised on the fact that such consciousness would be human-like, but which rather explore the possible nature and effects of encounters with radically different forms of intelligence and consciousness. In this respect, stories about encounters with alien life forms are more useful here than those of anthropomorphised machines. Consider, for instance, Naomi Mitchison's (1985) *Memoirs of a Spacewoman* (1962), narrated by Mary, a specialist in 'communication', who travels to worlds in different galaxies to seek out knowledge about their inhabitants according to a code of strict non-interference which is hard in practice to observe. This interference is also inevitably bidirectional. Early on in her story, Mary focuses on the way in which encounters with other forms of life, intelligence, and consciousness necessarily change the human in that encounter: 'I suppose one of the things which one finds it hardest to take is that one must develop a stable personality and yet that inevitably it will be altered by the other forms of life with which one will be in communication, and that these biophysical alterations must be accepted' (Mitchison, 1985: 18). 'In spite of books, films, contacts of all kinds', these inevitable alterations are still unanticipated: 'the impact of other worlds on this apparently immovable stability comes as a surprise' (19).

On her first space exploration to the world of lambda 771, Mary attempts to communicate with the native species which is descended from radial form, their biological make-up necessarily determining the nature of their psychology and consciousness: 'the radial pattern which had developed out of the budding spiral had remained throughout evolution and completely dominated all mental and physical processes' (20). This encounter makes Mary realise 'how much we ourselves are constructed bi-laterally on either-or principles' (20). The more time she spends with the radiates, the less she herself thinks in terms of either-or. The story provokes reflection on the nature of the consciousness, action, mathematics, art, and governance that necessarily emerges from binary logic, and asks what different forms might emerge 'if alternative means, not one of two, but one, two, three or four out of five' (27). In this story what is of value is not just a different point of view, but a different sort of looking; seeing the world in a different way is what produces the different point of view.

A similar exploration of the effects of forms of embodiment on forms of consciousness, and of the changing effects – on both individuals and framings of systems – of an encounter with radical otherness, occurs in Ted Chiang's (2015) short story 'Story of Your Life' (1998) (on which the 2016 film *Arrival* was based). The narrator, Louise, is a linguist tasked with establishing communication with alien life forms that have just appeared on Earth. As she starts to decode their written and verbal languages – which constitute separate languages – she realises that their perception of the physical world is entirely different to human perception, the former being teleological, the latter causal:

> When the ancestors of humans and heptapods first acquired the spark of consciousness, they both perceived the same physical world, but they parsed their perceptions differently; the worldviews that ultimately arose were the end result of that divergence. Humans had developed a sequential mode of awareness, while heptapods had developed a simultaneous mode of awareness. We experienced events in an order, and perceived their relationship as cause and effect. They experienced all events at once, and perceived a purpose underlying them all.
>
> *(Chiang, 2015: 159)*

This different perception alters the nature of their speech, their writing, their mathematics, and probably much more that the humans do not discover before the aliens leave as abruptly as they arrived. Louise's encounter with them has left her changed, however, which is revealed cleverly through the structure of the narrative. Louise's encounter with the aliens is understood by the reader to be the present of the narrative – the moment in time from which Louise is narrating. That account is intercut with what the reader assumes to be memories of the conception, life, and death of her daughter. At the end of the story, however, the reader realises that the encounter with the aliens is in the past – the physicist she works with during that time becomes her husband and her daughter's father – and what are perceived to be memories or flashbacks no longer make sense as such, but rather as some form of anticipation. In this story, Chiang challenges the reader's conception of linear temporality in storytelling, and of firm locations of the narrator in specific moments in time which then determine past and present, cause and effect, in relation to them. The narrative construction of the story therefore performs the shift in perspective from human to heptapod that Louise herself has undergone. Different points of view are located then not just in different spaces, but also in different times, and are affected by different understandings of time and space. (We discuss this further in Chapter 4.)

Stories such as these explore the effects of imagined encounters with alien forms of consciousness not through establishing empathy with the alien, but through demonstrating the potentially radical effects of taking into account different points of view on individual perception and on perception of a system or environment. They also alert the storyimbiber and storylistener to the way in which different forms of human embodiment, as well as the technologies and systems to which those bodies are subject, encode and determine consciousness, behaviour, decision-making, and point of view. Another of Le Guin's (2015) short stories, 'Vaster than Empires and More Slow' (1971), combines an encounter with a radically different form of sentience with a critical interrogation of the idealisation of empathy as an unmitigated good. A group of ten interplanetary travellers seeking to explore alien worlds, known as an Extreme Survey crew, travel to and land on World 4470. One of the group members, Mr Osden, has an enhanced power of empathy, 'properly speaking, of wide-range bioempathetic receptivity' (Le Guin, 2015: 172). He has been included in the mission as this skill will enable him to sense any sentient life forms on the new planet. But his presence among the crew is deeply disruptive. Experiencing their fear of him, Osden is neither compassionate nor sympathetic to them, but rather angry and oppositional: 'Can't you understand that I don't give a damn for all of you?' (172). His empathy makes him vulnerable:

> He was wholly at their mercy. If they disliked him he had to be hateful; if they mocked him he became grotesque; if they listened to him he was the storyteller. He was helplessly obedient to the demands of their emotions, reactions, moods.
>
> *(191)*

His access to their feelings does not lead to prosocial behaviour but to quite the opposite – he becomes aggressive as a form of self-defence: 'He's evil', another crew member, Porlock, declares, 'He'll end up shattering this team, sabotaging it, one way or another. Mark my words. He's not fit to live with other people!' (177). With the crew convinced that there are no sentient life forms on the planet, Osden is sent out to an isolated part of the vast forest in order to conduct a species count. On his return – after Porlock attempts to murder him – Osden reports that there is sentience on the planet after all, the forest, and its empathetic capacity has created a paralysing feedback loop of fear between Osden, lying wounded on the forest floor after Porlock's attack, and the trees:

> I felt the fear. It kept growing. As if they'd finally *known* I was there, lying on them, under them, among them, the thing they feared, and yet part of their fear itself. I couldn't stop sending the fear back, and it kept growing, and I couldn't move, I couldn't get away. I would pass out, I think, and then the fear would bring me to again, and I still couldn't move. Any more than they can.
>
> *(188)*

The sentience of the trees is not located in a single tree, as it is not located in 'one axon, or one detached glial cell' (Le Guin, 2015: 192); the sentience is located in connectivity – 'sentience or intelligence isn't a thing, you can't find it in, or analyze it out from, the cells of a brain. It's a function of the connected cells. It is, in a sense, the connection: the connectedness' (192). The crew come to realise, however inconceivable they find the idea, that the biosphere of the planet might be 'one network of communications, sensitive, irrational, immortal, isolated' (196).

The story ends rather mystically with Osden, determined to see if he can communicate with the forest, surrendering himself over to it, and remaining there when the others leave. One of the crew members, Tomiko, views this as an act of extreme empathy, where the division between the self and the other is entirely removed: 'He had given up his self to the alien, an unreserved surrender, that left no place for evil. He has learned the love of the Other, and thereby given his whole self' (201). But, she notes, 'this is not the vocabulary of reason' (201). In locating alien sentience in a distributed planetary intelligence, Le Guin's story brings together the climate and AI case studies discussed in this section, and interrogates whether empathy is an unmitigated good. In addition, if, as its ending implies, the ultimate end-point of empathy is an erosion of the division between self and other, and that erosion is beyond reason, then in relation to public reasoning the story prompts thought about the need to manage ethical relations to others that acknowledge their points of view and incorporate them into one's understanding of the system about which one is making decisions, without becoming absolutely absorbed in or identified with their position.

Nuclear attack and the identifiable victim

Storylistening must take into account the affective power, and therefore increased prominence and circulation, of stories that attempt to mobilise an empathetic response to an identifiable victim. Two British nuclear films from the second half of the twentieth century provide an instructive illustration here: *The War Game* (1965), written and directed by Peter Watkins, and *Threads* (1984), written by Barry Hines and directed by Mick Jackson. The films share many similarities – both are imaginative docu-dramas, both unflinchingly portray the potential effects of a domestic nuclear strike, both were commissioned by the BBC. There are also notable differences, however, in both their history and form. Watkins made *The War Game* while working in the BBC's Documentary Department but, in the end, the BBC decided not to broadcast the film on television in a controversial decision that led to Watkins accusing the BBC of having betrayed him. The decision also prompted a parliamentary question from West Fife MP William Hamilton to the Secretary of State for the Home department regarding government interference in the BBC's programming decisions (Chapman, 2006: 84). Both the government and the BBC stated that the BBC's decision not to broadcast 'was not the result of outside pressure of any kind' (House of Commons, 1965). According to their public statement, the BBC decided not to show *The War Game* because it was 'too horrifying for the medium of broadcasting' (Chapman, 2006: 75). A couple of decades later, *Threads* was commissioned by the then Director-General of the BBC, Alisdair Milne (after he watched *The War Game*). It was first screened in 1984, and repeated in 1985 as part of a week of programmes marking the fortieth anniversary of the bombings of Hiroshima and Nagasaki (during which *The War Game* was in fact broadcast for the first time [Binnion, 2003]). *Threads* is equally, if not more, horrifying than *The War Game*, yet it was not censored.

There are strong historical arguments that this was a result of the different historical contexts of production and reception between the 1960s and 1980s.[12] The relationship between the government and the BBC had changed, with BBC programming of the 1970s and 1980s being far more politically engaged, and the BBC's relationship with Margaret Thatcher's government being far more oppositional. (Indeed, Thatcher's government succeeded in engineering the removal of Milne as D.G. in 1986 [Milne, 2015].) The 1960s was influenced (even in the UK) by the peaceful atom movement, attempts by government not to further agitate the anti-nuclear movement, and developments to reduce risk, such as the 1963 Partial Test Ban Treaty and the Doomsday Clock being moved backwards. The focus was therefore on presenting a 'safe' atomic world and future. In the UK especially, details of the ramifications of the Windscale fire of 10 October 1957 in the North-West of England were still slowly leaking to the public. The year 1963 was therefore a fragile moment with regard to nuclear power, public perception, and policy, into which the broadcast of *The War Game* would have been viewed by government as a deeply destabilising intrusion.

In contrast, *Threads* was produced after many well-reported nuclear incidents (in industry as well as military usage – the Three Mile Island accident in the USA being a major one), after whistleblowing, and after the commercial and critical success of *The China Syndrome* (which we discuss in Chapter 3) and other nuclear television and film content. Public exposure through stories to nuclear knowledge and nuclear incidents was therefore greater and more involved in the 1980s than in the 1960s. The general audience (broadly speaking) was more critically engaged and educated on nuclear debate. In 1984 the Doomsday Clock read 3 minutes to midnight, with a statement from the *Bulletin* noting that 1984 saw humanity stand 'at the threshold of a period of confrontation' and citing 'the great upsurge of public concern about the nuclear arms race' (The Editors, 1984: 2). And by the 1980s, nuclear stories were highly saleable.

In addition to these arguments, however, there is a case to be made that *Threads* was broadcast when *The War Game* was not due to differences internal to the films, which we consider now. *The War Game* combines voice over with face-to-face interviews with ordinary people (staged but presented as real), and 'real-life' reportage footage (again, carefully staged), intercut with statements from government documents and figures, and fictional interviews with establishment figures based on genuine quotations. It does so in order to present a pseudo-documentary account of the impact of an imagined Soviet nuclear strike on Britain, and highlight the contrast between official statements and the actual experience. Although images of some of the same people recur, *The War Game* does not weave in a story focused on a particular character or characters. There is therefore no attempt to elicit an empathetic engagement from the viewer through dwelling on the experiences and feelings of specific characters for the duration of the film. Rather, the film starkly juxtaposes two points of view – that of official figures on nuclear weapons (through the quotes and expert interviews), and that of the accounts of the actual effects of a nuclear attack (through the footage and lay interviews) – in order to expose the insufficiency or inaccuracy of the former in relation to the latter. After first viewing the film, Huw Wheldon, Controller of Programmes, was disappointed as he had expected from the script that 'the varying points of view about the deterrent would be presented with equal force – and this had not been done' (Chapman, 2006: 83). Wheldon is correct – varying points of view are most definitely presented, but very much in order to discredit the official one – but this does not align with the official reason for censoring the film, that it was too horrifying. Perhaps more revealing is Wheldon's other comment, that 'as it stood the film was not a sufficiently brilliant overall statement to override other considerations, or to enable him to recommend it to the D.G. with complete conviction' (Chapman, 2006: 83). It might be suggested that what Wheldon was responding to here was the way in which the horror of the film is too unrelenting and too unindividuated – that is, without a specific identifiable victim, the film numbs the viewer rather than drawing them into the experience of a single individual. Without this affect, the film is not able to cloak or disguise its explicit polemic and politics, to smuggle them through. The result is that it was prevented from informing the public (through television broadcast) and, perhaps, contributing to public reasoning through its representation of different points of view.

Threads also contains different points of view on nuclear defence and attack. Although it focuses primarily on the effects of such an attack, it does also follow the local officials tasked with response to it, representing them sympathetically (they sacrifice being with their families to their civic responsibilities) but as ineffective, trapped in a bunker under the town hall, well-meaning but unprepared and impotent. The film is therefore less critical of the establishment than *The War Game*. In addition, the film weaves an individual story into its more documentary elements – including voice over and informative surtitles – that of Ruth, who conceives at the outset of the film, and whose pregnancy spans the attack and its immediate aftereffects, changing the world beyond recognition so that her preparations for marriage and a first home are replaced with death, desolation, and giving birth alone in a barn. Through Ruth, *Threads* also follows the effects of the attack further into the future than *The War Game*, ending with her death, and then briefly following her now teenage daughter's struggle for survival, and her rape, pregnancy, and childbirth. In anchoring the film in the story of a specific individual, *Threads* is more powerfully affective than *The War Game*, if in fact less informative about contrasting perspectives on nuclear armament. Its powerful affect contributed to its immediate popular success (it received the highest ratings on BBC Two of the week it was screened) and its lasting impact in the memory of those who have watched it.

In this example, more potential for empathy – via an identifiable victim – creates a more affective and perhaps effective story. That story is then distributed more widely and has a stronger impact on public perception, despite *The War Game* being more interesting in offering multiple points of view out of which to build a fuller picture of the nuclear issue. The capacity of a story to provoke empathy may determine its availability, and therefore its capacity to influence public reasoning. Storylistening therefore needs to take careful account of the power of affective storytelling, and of factors such as power, money, and distribution choices, which may enable charismatic stories to become more widespread. Storylistening must also attend carefully to stories that are less affective, less popular, but equally, or in some cases more, important in terms of offering multiple points of view of value to building fuller pictures of policy systems and enabling more effective decision-making.

The child

Threads is characteristic of nuclear and other stories that mobilise the emotive figure of the Child, with the loss of children often functioning as a powerful symbol of the future that is threatened or lost.[13] In Lynne Littman's film *Testament* (1983) (based on Carol Amen's short story 'The Last Testament' [1981]), for instance, the sparse plot follows a family of five living in the fictional town of Hamelin, California as they move from the normal, noisy business of family life through the after-effects of proximate nuclear attacks. The father never returns from work on the day of the strikes, and the viewer is told that tens of thousands of the town's adults die, but the focus is not on them. It remains unrelentingly focused on the death of children. In particular, those in the nuclear family on which the story centres, or in its orbit. First a neighbouring newborn dies, then slowly the mother's children die, one after another, in harrowing detail – her youngest son, then her daughter (her eldest child), as well as her neighbour's orphaned son who she has taken in. The film intercuts this plot with the production and performance of that year's primary school play, a heavily symbolic dramatic rendition of the Pied Piper of Hamelin legend in which the child Mayor despairs at the disappearance of the children – 'Oh my son, he's gone, he's dead. Oh what have we done?' – only to be reassured by the lame boy left behind that, 'Your children are not dead. They will return. They are just waiting until the world deserves them'. There is no doubt that the viewer is meant to be as moved to tears by this as the women in the audience on whom the camera lingers in turn.

In *Testament*, the mother stops short of killing herself and her remaining son and another fostered orphan, despite knowing that their deaths are just a matter of time. Infanticide and suicide are not avoided in the film *On the Beach* (1959) (based on Nevil Shute's 1957 novel of the same name) in which suicide pills or injections are in fact provided by the Australian government. *Threads*, *Testament*, and *On the Beach* are part of a body of nuclear films (others include *Ladybug, Ladybug* [1963] and *The Children* [1980]) that evoke the powerful affect of the loss of children and transfer that horror onto the envisioned effects of, and damage caused by, nuclear weapons, both to those children and the future that is now lost or irrevocably changed. In contrast to this use of the child in such films, the child was actually used as a vehicle for early selling of nuclear power by the nuclear industry, and by both industry and government to inform public opinion. Consider for instance the pro-atomic energy film *Atomic Energy as a Force for Good* (1955) – intended to educate the population about the safety of nuclear power plants, and other beneficial uses of radiation, for instance in the treatment of cancer – in which the protagonist's granddaughter is dying from terminal brain cancer.

The powerful figure of the child is therefore mobilised in nuclear stories, whether it be the child whose future is lost or threatened, or the child whose future could be saved or secured. This former trend remains visible in more contemporary nuclear and climate stories, for instance in Cormac McCarthy's *The Road* (2006), possibly a nuclear and/or climate change story, and in Maggie Gee's climate novel *The Ice People* (1998). Both of these stories centre on a father's drive to stay alive in post-apocalyptic or crisis conditions, in order to protect, and try to secure a future for, his son.[14] In his documentary on climate change, *An Inconvenient Truth* (2006), Al Gore tells the story of the near loss of his six-year-old son in an attempt to establish a connection between the emotions people would feel at the loss of a child and the emotions they ought to feel about the loss of the planet. Gore attempts to move the viewer through mapping the empathetic and affective response to a potential individual loss onto a communal loss.[15]

In the context of empathy, storylistening needs to be particularly careful of stories that mobilise the figure of the child, since there is powerful affect located there that heightens the identifiable victim effect and can skew public reasoning. That said, there are stories that mobilise the figure of the child not empathetically, but to provide a different point of view on, and thereby draw attention to, systemic problems. Such stories can and are useful in informing public reasoning. One such example is Ladj Ly's 2019 film *Les Misérables*.

Les Misérables shares with its namesake, Victor Hugo's novel, a desire to draw attention to the economically disadvantaged citizens of Paris. The film so appalled French President Emmanuel Macron that he encouraged his ministers to watch it, and launched an investigation into how to improve living conditions in the Paris suburb, Montfermeil, which the film depicts (*JDD*, 2019). In interview, Ly finds Macron's ignorance about conditions in the suburb unfathomable: 'How could he not have known the extent of the problems I show in the film? It's not like it's news. It's been like this for ever' (Jeffries, 2020). Ly's film has successfully made those problems visible in an example of a story directly impacting on public reasoning. The film is so effective because it eschews playing on empathy in favour of playing with point of view, enabling insight into the suburbs and their economic problems through a range of perspectives – Macron was reportedly 'upset by the accuracy' of the film (by implication, not because of empathy with its characters). *Les Misérables* repeatedly signals that it is a film about how things are seen, with a drone playing a key role in the plot and providing an aerial point of view on some of its main events. The drone is piloted by a child called Buzz, who also features in the final riot scene where he observes the events in the stairwell through a spy hole in his front door. This is a story about what is seen and what is not seen, about how things are seen and who is doing that seeing, about whose points of view are visible and whose are not (Ly is committed to providing points of view not present in mainstream media or discourse), and about how all of these things determine how the system is understood.[16]

Ly does not romanticise or demonise the children in the film, which is particularly restrained in the detail with which they are portrayed. The viewer is not given access to their feelings, to their inner life. In particular, Issa, the other main child character, remains inscrutable. When he is wounded by the police in a bungled arrest – which notably damages his eyes, and therefore his capacity to see – the film does not attempt to mobilise empathy for him, with only a brief shot of him sitting alone within the waste grounds of the suburb fleetingly intimating his feelings of desolation, abuse, and abandonment. In fact, the film ends with Issa leading a violent youth uprising against the police unit that violated him. The figure of the child in this film is not a passive victim motivating empathy but a powerful and aggressive force of retribution. In moving between the perspectives of the children, the different residents, the suburb's major, and the three very different policemen – enabling only just enough access to each to move the story along – the film does not allow the viewer to enter fully into the thoughts and feelings of any, nor to settle into too easy categories of right and wrong. 'I haven't shown all the cops as racists', says Ly, 'And I'm certainly not showing the boys who riot as innocent victims. Reality is more mixed up' (Jeffries, 2020). The film's ending is particularly effective in maintaining this balance, freezing Issa and the policemen in a moment of unenacted but potentially fatal violence, both at once victim and aggressor. The film therefore reveals all of its characters to be imbricated in the same system and demonstrates that what is required is systemic change, not empathy nor 'generous imaginings'. *Les Misérables* is an example of a breakthrough story that is useful to public reasoning because it gives access to the points of view of a group of people that together provide a very different picture of a set of systemic conditions, points of view that can otherwise remain hidden from decision-makers.

Another of Le Guin's (2015) short stories is also instructive regarding the question of stories, empathy, and the figure of the child. 'The Ones Who Walk Away from Omelas' (1973) features a seemingly perfect city, except that the wealth, health, and happiness of its citizens is only possible if one child is always sacrificed for the greater good, imprisoned in filth and squalor at the heart of the city. All citizens know the child is there, many visit her or him in their youth. The visit often prompts empathy in the short term, but most then rationalise the sacrifice of the child, justifying their inaction regarding saving him or her since it is in the interests of the greater social good. Those who are not able to do so leave the city. For the former, empathy does not lead to prosocial action in terms of the child, although it might be argued it does so for the greater good of society.

Those who leave effect no action on the circumstances of the city. 'Omelas' presents the trade-offs made in public reasoning, the fact that all economic structures, systems of governance, and decision-making have beneficiaries and casualties. Public reasoning means making decisions that will always have differential effects. The story describes this problem, without resolving it, but can still be used to encourage explicit reflection on this characteristic of public reasoning. The story is also helpful in indicating that to manage this characteristic requires framing debates such that both values and numbers play a part – the question as to whether a small number of people should suffer for more to gain, for instance, perhaps depends on the degree of suffering and gain, and the matters of principle that frame the decision-making.

Forty-five years after Le Guin's story appeared, N. K. Jemisin published a response, 'The Ones Who Stay and Fight' (2018). Jemisin's story is written from an anti-establishment perspective and refuses the idea that some must inevitably suffer:

> *It's possible.* Everyone – even the poor, the lazy, even the undesirable – can matter. Do you see how just the idea of this provokes utter rage in some? That is the infection defending itself…because if enough of us believe a thing is possible, then it becomes so.
>
> *(Jemisin, 2018: 12)*

These final lines can be understood as normative not descriptive – that is, they are not necessarily describing the way things are, but how they should be; they point to a politically motivating aspiration, and they are domain specific. They do not mean that collective belief and action can change things like the laws of nature, but that such unity can create enough momentum to change social structures, policies, and norms. Such a belief is necessary to mobilise action and activism in sites otherwise disenfranchised from, or peripheral to, formal centres of power. These lines are descriptive to the extent that they provide knowledge about the political beliefs about where power can be located, how it can be wielded, and how change can be effected, held by a certain collective identity of activists and those campaigning for social justice. They provide insight into the point of view of a certain stakeholder community and its perspective on policy systems.

In Jemisin's story there is a third option to ignoring the child or leaving the city – stay and fight. As is much of her work, Jemisin's story is a call for social justice, for the rights of all – in particular those whose lives have not been historically valued in the dominant systems – to rectify the fact that, as the citizens of Um-Helat come to realise, 'once, value was ascribed to some people, and not others. That once, humanity was acknowledged for some, and not others' (9). Attending to Le Guin and Jemisin's stories together can inform public reasoning by building of fuller systemic picture through different points of view: Le Guin's story is sensitive to the challenges of decision-making; Jemisin's story raises awareness of the casualties of the judgements that are made about who is predominantly considered to be of value and who is not during that process, and provides insight into the beliefs and values of communities working outside of government to attempt to rectify that. Narrative experts presenting such stories to storylistening decision-makers must put their own ideological positions aside in order present a range of stories to the decision-maker so that the multiple points of view to which they provide access can be used to build as full a picture of the system as possible, and thereby enable better decisions.

Consequences

This section draws out the implications of the previous two sections for incorporating expert-informed storylistening into public reasoning, in particular because of the otherwise overwhelming tendency to notice and to value those things or humans with which the dominant publics and decision-makers of the time feel most empathy and proximity. Here we elaborate on how storylistening can aid with the challenges of framing, scaling, and narrative deficits, and we consider what it might mean to be a humanities expert informing public reasoning.

Framing and points of view

Stories' compelling powers, when scaled up from individual listeners to collective decision-makers, lock in particular framings that may lead public reasoning to false resolutions, or cause the omission of consideration of ways forward that were available at the time but not noticed by anyone. It is easy for story-imbibers to be so enthralled by the story that they accept a limited or even false framing of the policy issue, assuming that the story says more than it necessarily does about the matter at hand, that it says it more completely, and/or that it provides the most relevant, the most widely shared, or even the only point of view for considering the matter.[17] Whereas lock-in at the individual level may have to do with a range of attributes in the story, the teller, and the imbiber, lock-in in public reasoning may be enhanced by the embedding of some mediated version of these individual selections. So, for example, the framing determines which data, or which experiments, or whose experiences are considered to count as evidence, or are sought out to be included (Drukman and Lupia, 2017). In some instances, it can even determine the only story it is possible to tell in public. As we go on to discuss in Chapter 4, where framing influences the selection or availability of evidence (and the reverse), this in turn may close off versions of potential futures that could properly inform public reasoning when part of pluralistic accounts.

In public reasoning, framing involves determining what parts of the wider potential system are assumed to matter, including which types of people or other entities, and foregrounding particular types of relationship between them (Cairney, 2015, 2016).[18] The European Commission states that the importance of framing, narratives, and metaphor 'cannot be underestimated' in political decision-making (Mair et al., 2019: 45). Sheila Jasanoff (2012: 179) concurs, but notes that

> few policy cultures have adopted systematic methods for revising the initial framing of issues. Frame analysis thus remains a critically important, though neglected, tool of policy-making that would benefit from greater public input.[19]

Storylistening can form part of a systematic method for effective frame analysis through enabling decision-makers to consciously navigate challenges of scaling, lock-in, values, multiple points of view, and narrative deficits.

Escaping the empathy trap and understanding the value of listening to stories from, or containing, a range of perspectives drives an essential step for the policymaker, which is to ensure arrangements to collect as many potentially relevant points of view as possible. In most cases, this starts with realistic human-based stories: 'people like us'. Then, in increasing degrees of challenge both to find and to interpret, come stories about people 'not-much-like-us', but still relevant to the policy issue at hand. Then come stories about non-human entities, animals, plants, rivers, trees, complicated systems such as forests, corporations, or cities, and, of course, entirely speculative intelligences such as artificial, magical, or alien ones. Obtaining such multiple points of view will inform surrogative reasoning about the relevant system, which we discuss in Chapter 3.

By not seeking multiple points of view and by imposing normative perspectives on the policy issue, narrow or unreflective framing weakens the moral basis of the public reasoning by disproportionately foregrounding or giving influence to the norms of some groups over others. It also weakens the evidential basis of the public reasoning by allowing relevant parts of the policy area concerned, and potential evidence about it, to be neglected. Frame analysis informed by effective storylistening serves to decentre, or to test the robustness of the evidence for, the dominant point of view, drawing on multiple points of view, human and non-human, to create a fuller picture of the relevant system. It also challenges public reasoning to consider the points of view of all human beings – and to understand how and in what ways they are relevant – as well as the other forms of life which are necessarily affected by the decisions humans make (Facer, 2019). As we go on to discuss in detail throughout this book, to consider a wide range of narrative evidence provided through storylistening is not to consider all that evidence as being of the same type and, in all cases, it needs to form part of a pluralistic evidence base. For example, stories that show the point of view of human collectives who see the system in ways that are at odds with other forms of evidence are still providing evidence, but the evidence is about the people and what influences them, not about – for example – the reality of the efficacy of a vaccine or the laws of physics underpinning climate modelling.

Scale-up and metonymic legitimacy

A major challenge arises from a story's relationship to the distributed, longer term, systemic matters that are the proper concern of public reasoning. This is the challenge of scaling – of knowing when, and when not, to navigate from the singular to the general. Empathy can distort public reasoning by motivating decision-making that will affect a large number of people based on the power of one charismatic story about a single individual. We call this the challenge of determining *metonymic legitimacy* – that is, storylistening must determine to what extent a single story is legitimately representative of a whole issue (or, as explored in the following chapter, collective identity), and to identify when it is not. The strong empathetic power of a single story can make determining metonymic legitimacy difficult but, again, that does not mean that charismatic stories should be ignored, nor that they might not be important and effective. Empathy-evoking charismatic stories – like anthropomorphisation, or those focused on loss – are commonly deployed in story*telling* that aims to focus attention on, or shift public perception on, a policy issue. Story*listening* must be attentive to the consequences of such stories for decision-making. A metonymically legitimate charismatic story can serve an important function in drawing attention to a policy issue (a complicated or complex system of some kind) and in framing that matter in an affective way. For instance, a charismatic story, like a charismatic megafauna (consider the image of an emaciated polar bear on an isolated ice floe), can powerfully motivate a useful empathetic response if, in the case of the polar bear for instance, the image draws attention to the loss of ice and reasons for it, rather than only to the plight of the polar bear. In the latter instance, the story of the polar bear is effective in using the focus on an individual to draw attention to a system.[20] What a charismatic story does not do, when functioning in the empathetic mode, is convey any social knowledge or theory of that system.

Determining metonymic legitimacy requires expert knowledge, and a pluralistic evidence base. The expert can draw attention to a range of stories, not just a single story. The narrative evidence produced by storylistening to that range of stories can be taken into consideration alongside other forms of evidence and help determine to what extent the individual story is representative of a larger system. If it is representative, the particular can be used to draw attention to and highlight a system or collective that might not otherwise be attended to. If it is not, then the dangers of falsely reasoning on the basis of a single case can be avoided.

Narrative deficits

Narrative deficits are areas in which there is a falling short either in terms of the ability or willingness to take stories seriously, or because there is in fact an (actual or perceived) absence of stories. It is, of course, harder to notice what is not there than that what is, particularly with stories, as it is in their very nature to be attractive and so to draw attention towards themselves and away from the spaces around them. And, like William Gibson's unevenly distributed but very present futures ('Survey', 2001: 6), if you look hard enough at any time and in any place, all the stories that can be conceived are probably being conceived somewhere by someone, it is just that some non-dominant ones are not being listened to very much. So the stories that dominate popular understanding and imagination, and those that are closest to hand for decision-makers in the public, private, and civic spheres, are never a comprehensive set. One important implication of taking stories seriously is that it leads to greater awareness of these absences.

Storylistening must attend to these narrative deficits, for instance taking into account the stories that do not get told because they are not powerfully affective, such as stories not of individual victims of policies but of collective suffering averted because of them (Bloom, 2016, 2017). Public reasoning can be usefully informed by storylistening that identifies narrative deficits around collective beneficiaries, improved statistical shifts, and increased numbers of non-victims. For example, economic stories focusing on an individual suffering or success may have a benefit if the individual story legitimately represents a whole (see our discussion of scale-up and metonymic legitimacy in this section). However, the Western economic systems that are associated with that suffering or success have also been associated with many more collective benefits and costs: collective benefits such as individuals' increased healthy life expectancy, reduced female and infant mortality, higher levels of education, and less inequality between the sexes; collective costs such as continued inequality, and social injustices in particular around labour and environmental impacts. These parts of the system in particular suffer from narrative deficits because they do not lend themselves easily to charismatic storytelling. They involve good news without tension, large numbers of people rather than individuals, distributed effects over more than a person's lifetime, and complexity of cause and effect.

Narrative deficits can therefore arise through some phenomena being more or less storyable, through different voices not being heard, and, of course, intentionally through narrative misdirection or obfuscation. Of importance to storylistening is being able to identify narrative deficits, whatever their source, and knowing why it is worth doing so. In addition to identifying the deficits, we discuss in Chapter 4 the need for individual and collective narrative responsibility to ensure the identification and production of stories that fill that absence. If left unnoticed and unfilled, such deficits can distort policy framings by determining which elements of the system are most noticed and which are unseen, leading to less effective decision-making and unintended public outcomes. Elements of the system to which less attention is paid are not only likely to be neglected during debate, but also less likely to be paid attention to for the gathering of data, or the formulation of research questions across disciplines.

The humanities expert

Like other forms of evidence gathering, storylistening calls on the knowledge of experts. In the case of storylistening, narrative experts can provide evidence about how dominant stories are functioning, and draw attention to relevant but non-dominant stories. Experts from the sciences have played advisory roles in relation to evidence gathering for some time and the knowledge that has amassed during this time regarding the contribution of science expertise to public reasoning can be applied to humanities expertise. Of course, given the profound differences in the modes of creation of different forms of knowledge, few learnings will transfer directly, and some may not transfer at all. But in some cases it should be possible for humanities academics to learn from the practice of and scholarship in science advice, and so to leapfrog decades of (sometimes painful!) learning by scientists and policymakers.

In *The Honest Broker: Making Sense of Science and Politics* (2007), Roger A. Pielke, Jr. outlines four idealised types of engagement that scientists can adopt (depending on their view of science and of democracy) when considering the range of roles they may choose to play if they wish (or do not wish) their research to inform public reasoning in some way. These are the pure scientist – focusing on research with ostensibly no regard for its utility; the science arbiter – a responsive role, providing expert advice when approached by a policymaker with a specific request; the issue advocate – who has a desired policy outcome in mind; and the honest broker of policy alternatives – one who 'engages in decision-making by clarifying and, at times, seeking to expand, the range of choices available to decision-makers' (Pielke, 2007: 17).[21] Pielke also identifies a fifth type, called the stealth advocate, representing experts who attempt to ignore or disguise their intentions by over-emphasising the apolitical or independent nature of their advice, with related risks to the overall quality of the public reasoning. Pielke's framework has proved helpful for practitioners seeking to provide or use scientific evidence.[22] For our purposes, the types it sets out offer a useful starting point for considering the opportunities and challenges faced by academics working in the humanities who might seek to inform public reasoning.[23]

Humanities academics have traditionally inhabited the role of pure academic, or of issue advocate. Extending consideration of Pielke's types from scientists to experts (including humanities academics) more generally would show that avoiding the move into stealth advocacy requires the expert to be explicit about their values, beliefs, and intentions.[24] As already noted in the Introduction, explicit recognition of personal values and beliefs in the context of one's research or scholarship, although challenging in all disciplines, can be a particular challenge in the humanities. For example, personal values often explicitly inform the humanities academic's motivations and direction of research, meaning they clearly prioritise some academic questions over others.[25] However, where humanities academics are able to be explicit about their personal values and beliefs, they can operate openly as issue advocates intending to influence policy in a particular direction. This role may include taking part in political activism. As Pielke (2015: n.p.) notes, 'the defining characteristic of this role is a desire to reduce the scope of available choice, often to a single preferred outcome among many possible outcomes'; he continues, 'issue advocacy is fundamental to a healthy democracy and is a noble calling'. But issue advocacy is not the only possible role a humanities academic can play in public reasoning – some humanities academics can also function as humanities arbiters and honest brokers.

The science arbiter 'supports a decision maker by providing answers to questions that can be addressed empirically, that is to say, using the tools of science' (Pielke, 2015), often playing this role as a member of expert advisory committees. The humanities arbiter can support a decision-maker by providing answers to questions that can be addressed through the tools of the humanities, also as a member of expert advisory committees. In literary studies, these tools include robust research methods (as recognised by sub-field); depth and breadth of knowledge of the existing critical literature and the situation of one's research in relation to it; sensitive, detailed, and acute close reading; archival research, or identification by other means of new relevant material; the construction of coherent and compelling arguments substantiated by evidence gathered; peer review; and ongoing engagement, rejection, refinement, and deployment of arguments and ideas across a field, over time, leading to cumulative knowledge as well as evolution and novelty. Routine effective, explicit, academic, and public description and communication of the methods and structures guaranteeing rigour in the humanities would enable the role of humanities arbiter to be filled more regularly, enable humanities academics to be more easily incorporated into the structures of expert advisory committees, and give decision-makers more confidence to ask humanities experts questions, and more confidence in the robustness of their answers. It would build well-founded confidence in humanities expertise on the part of decision-makers and publics, further legitimate humanities expertise externally, enable its more widespread incorporation into public reasoning, and potentially contribute to developments and advancements within and across its disciplines.[26]

To function as an honest broker rather than an issue advocate, the humanities academic must deploy their expertise to serve the public good regardless of whether they, as citizens, are aligned in terms of politics or values with the policymaker of the day. Indeed, it may be more important to be the expert in the room with a policymaker whose values or politics are different precisely because they (the policymaker) may otherwise be paying insufficient attention to forms of knowledge or points of view that they assume are only presented to promote the expert's preferred outcome. Those the academic might most seek to inform may be precisely those with whom both sides feel they have least in common. The policymaker, in turn, may place higher confidence on synthesised insights that come from a given field of research, where it is clear that the academics themselves adopt different political leanings or sets of values.

Again drawing on the experience of scientific advisers, Ian Boyd (2013a: n.p.) argues that effective engagement with government

> means sticking to the evidence and describing clearly what it does and does not say; expressing the balance of risk associated with one or other policy option and avoiding suggesting that policies are either right or wrong; and being willing to make the voice of science heard by engaging with the mechanisms already available through science advisory committees, by working with embedded advisers [...], and by being the voice of reason, rather than dissent, in the public arena.

The same criteria for effective engagement would apply to the humanities honest broker, although the humanities would need to work with government and others to explore how existing advisory structures could best evolve to include them fully.[27]

Pielke (2015) suggests that the arbiter and broker roles are best performed by individuals acting as part of committees (a point we pick up in discussion of evidence synthesis in Chapter 3), and argues that when an academic is in the role of the honest broker,

> what is important is the commitment to clarify the scope of possible action so as to empower the decision maker. Sometimes honest brokers are unnecessary in a political setting, for instance, when advocacy groups collectively cover the scope of available choice. But sometimes policy making would benefit from greater clarity on choice, or even the invention of choices previously unseen.

The fuller incorporation into public reasoning of storylistening, and of humanities experts functioning as both humanities arbiters and honest brokers, can contribute to making visible a wider range of policy options.

One final point to make regarding expert knowledge pertains to the importance of recognising the limits of expertise, the need for competency in assessing one's own competence and that of others. This means an expert knowing their strengths and boundaries, complemented by the policymaker's ability to know when and how to call on expertise. While an academic's views within their own domain should be treated by those outside it with the utmost respect, the same person's views on what is proper public policy on the matter are no more significant than any other citizen's. Being expert in, say, twentieth-century French literature or nuclear physics, makes an academic precisely that, and they may be able to help with public reasoning but, unless they are also expert in other relevant areas, their expertise does not validate their views on a policy question such as, say, whether and how to achieve a net zero carbon target. Kenneth Wheare (1955: 15) recognised such limits in his early work on expert committees: 'Most people are expert in a few things; everyone is a layman in regard to most things'. Those concerned about well-founded public reasoning need also to pay attention to the relationship between expertise, access, and authority. In practice, expertise leading to status in one domain or sphere does lead to status more generally and hence, at the very least, to preferential access to power. It also sometimes leads to a halo effect in which the expert's views on matters outside their domain are given more weight than if the same view were expressed by someone perceived differently. Incorporating multiple points of view into public reasoning via storylistening can help to mitigate against this effect.

In this chapter, we have moved beyond empathy as the only function of stories on which claims about their value to public reasoning might be based, and we have introduced the POV function to explore how stories are of use to public reasoning in providing multiple points of view on a relevant system. In the next three chapters, we explore three further cognitive and collective functions of stories: their role in the creation and consolidation of collective identities, helping identify social groups and understand motivations and actions; stories as narrative models, functional tools that enable explanation and understanding; and the role of stories in anticipatory systems, imagining and testing a range of futures in order to enable better decision-making in the present. In doing this, we further develop the implications of storylistening for the humanities and for public reasoning, as well as emphasise the decision-maker's need for curated expertise from others, across different types of story, tellers, and publics (Jasanoff, 2006; Owens, 2015; Brom, 2019).

Notes

1 See also Batson (2009) who identifies eight definitions of the term.
2 See Keen (2006: 208–210) for a detailed but succinct exploration of the question 'What is empathy?'. See also Cooke (2017) for a brief history of the concept and arguments against its value.
3 Eric Leake (2014) calls this 'difficult empathy' but argues for its benefits. See also Keen (2007: 131–136), 'Feeling with Villains'.
4 Paul Bloom (2017: 27) notes that 'empathy is often used by those who wish to generate animus toward outgroups'. See also Bloom (2016) and Bennett and Weisskopf (2003).
5 Although see Hassan (1998) for an unusual postcolonial navigation of universality.
6 See Keen (2007: 145–168), 'Contesting Empathy', for an excellent overview of critiques of empathy.
7 In 'Do You Speak Lion?' (2016), arguing for plurality of perspectives on conservation challenges systems, Bill Adams quotes Wittgenstein's (1953: 16) 'if a lion could speak, we could not understand it', but in the context of an example of an intervention that failed because it did not anticipate learned behaviour by elephants.
8 For a comprehensive and sustained critique of ToM and ST, see Gallagher (2001, 2004, 2007a, 2007b) and Hutto (2004, 2005, 2006, 2007a, 2007b, 2008).
9 Boaventura de Sousa Santos (2016: 25), referring to his involvement in the enshrinement of the rights of nature in the Constitution of Ecuador, notes that 'the concept of the rights of nature is a legal and cultural hybrid because the concept of rights comes from the West'; in the Ecuadorian context, 'the rights of nature is a mix of the Western concept of rights with the Quechua concept of nature. This is a de-colonial form of hybridity'.
10 An excerpt from *Midnight Robber* is included in Grace L. Dillon's *Walking the Clouds: An Anthology of Indigenous Science Fiction* (2012) which provides an excellent introduction to the genre, as well as directing the reader to key stories, such as those by

Gerald Vizenor. The opening of Vizenor's *Bearheart: The Heirship Chronicles* (1990) (a revised version of his first novel, *Darkness in St Louis: Bearheart* [1978]) provides a rich evocation of the interrelation of bear, river, crow, cedar wood, and human in the worldview and embodied existence of its Indigenous protagonist, Proude Cedarfair.

11 See Slocombe (2020) for detailed exploration of these stories.

12 Our thanks to Grace Halden for sharing her detailed knowledge of the historical context, and for her knowledge of nuclear stories more generally which informed this chapter's discussion.

13 See Sheldon (2016) for a wide-ranging exploration of the figure of the child in literature, science, and culture, in particular in relation to catastrophe and climate change.

14 See Lee Edelman (2004) for a strong critique of what he names 'reproductive futurism', that is, the dependence of all American politics on a belief that the future will give meaning to the present, and the investment of this faith in the future in the emblematic figure of the Child. See Dillon (2015) for a detailed engagement with, and critique of, Edelman's theory via a reading of Gee's *The Ice People*.

15 For an account of loss and empathy as useful in contending with climate change, see also Bradon Smith (2014). In the context of species extinctions, Ursula Heise (2016) discusses ways in which stories of loss and anticipation in connection to humans' relations with plants, animals, and other living and inanimate aspects of the Earth influence today's academic and public directions. She argues that that sense of loss is linked to memory, which is imaginings about the past, and that it tends to lead to wanting to recreate in the future an imagined better past. She points out the attractiveness of group narratives of loss and custodianship in which seeing one's life as about preventing the loss of an existing species is potentially more attractive to more people than imagining a future in which that species does not exist but other new ones might.

16 Discussing an earlier short film that he shot during and after the 2005 Paris riots, called *365 days in Clich-Montfermeil*, Ly observes: 'I wanted the insider's perspective on what happened during the riots rather than the one the media portrayed, so I put it online. This was before YouTube, so it was quite revolutionary' (Jeffries, 2020).

17 For an example of some of the extensive literature on this point in the context of climate change, see, for example, Hulme (2009), Howe (2014), and Rapley et al. (2014). For a clear account of the differences between stories and framings, see Cairney (2020: 67)

18 Cairney (2018: 200) puts it bluntly: 'Policymakers have to ignore most policy problems and most ways to understand and solve them'.

19 See, for example, Cairney (2016: 33) and Craig (2019).

20 For discussion of the relationships between charismatic animals, the understanding of ecosystems, and conservation objectives, see, for example, Heise (2008), Ducarme, Luque, and Courchamp (2013), Krause and Robinson (2017), and Thompson and Rog (2019).

21 See Pielke (2015) for a high-level overview.

22 The framework is not, of course, without its critics. See, for instance, Jasanoff (2008), who focuses on its limitations in representing the insights of Science and Technology Studies (STS) scholarship in particular. For an example of wider discussions about democracy and science that indirectly challenge the simplifications of the framework, see Turner (2014).

23 For other overviews of the craft and science of providing scientific advice, see Cairney and Oliver's (2020) summary of advice to academics seeking to influence policy, as well as Gluckman (2014) and Fischoff (2015).

24 In a recent rhetorical piece drawing on extensive research in science communication, Blastland et al. (2020: n.p.) endorse the need for academics to be cognisant of, and transparent about, their own values and motivations: 'There is a continuum from "informing" to "persuading" – and researchers should choose their position on it consciously'; they caution that researchers should not 'assume that they are apolitical,

unbiased and utterly objective – all of us have values, beliefs and temptations. Even if we choose to be an "honest broker", the first person we need to be honest with is ourselves'. In the context of their case for scientific evidence communication intended to inform but not persuade, they focus on only one function of storytelling – persuasion – which they argue operates to the detriment of proper communication of, and engagement with, the scientific evidence. They do not consider other functions of stories, such as those explored in this book, and thus what value stories themselves might have as a source of evidence.

25 In making our arguments in this section on the role of the humanities expert, we are aware that we are touching on a large and contentious cross-disciplinary field of debate (with a long history) regarding (put crudely) objectivity and subjectivity in relation to the sciences and the humanities. We do not enter that fray here, since our intention is to offer a practical starting point for how a humanities academic might engage in public reasoning; *Storylistening* as a whole presents our case for the cognitive value of the narrative evidence that a narrative expert might provide in such engagement. We acknowledge here, though, the extensive research in Science and Technology Studies (STS) into the social construction of science and technology (see, e.g., Latour and Woolgar, 1986 [as well as the wider body of Latour's work]; Galison and Stump, 1996; Hacking, 1999; Longino, 2002; Jasanoff and Kim, 2015), as well as criticisms thereof (e.g. Gross and Levitt, 1994). (For recent reflections on STS in relation to 'post-truth', see Sismondo, 2017; Collins et al., 2017; Jasanoff and Simmet, 2017; and Latour interviewed in Kofman [2018]). Such work is connected to the role of objectivity and subjectivity in policy, which shows that both the belief systems of the decision-maker and their policy goals determine how they engage with the science presented (Sabatier and Jenkins-Smith, 1993; Stone, 2011) – evidence is deployed strategically in line with existing beliefs and values. Even more widely, it is connected to experimental work demonstrating how biased assimilation means people more generally process new information in ways that confirm their established understandings of world and self (e.g. Taber and Lodge, 2006; Kahan et al., 2007; Stroud, 2008).

26 Panels assessing humanities publications in the most recent Research Excellence Framework exercise in the UK (REF 2014) were instructed to do so according to the criteria of originality, rigour, and significance, but no explicit definitions of any of these terms in relation to humanities scholarship were provided. Focusing on rigour as the key concept determining research quality may in itself be another compromise necessary to facilitate the humanities-policy interface, since Ochsner et al. (2016) demonstrate that rigour is just one category, and not the predominant one, that humanities scholars use to describe and assess research quality in their disciplines.

27 Elsewhere, Boyd (2013b: n.p.) notes, 'it is not their [scientists'] job to make politicians' decisions for them – when scientists start providing opinions about whether policies are right or wrong they risk becoming politicised. A politicised scientist cannot also be an independent scientist' and Douglas (2015: 296) says that 'While science is neither apolitical nor value-free, it can (and should) be pursued with integrity. Detecting science with integrity and defining the legitimate roles values play in such science opens the space for genuine deliberation and a way forward out of an ideological stalemate'. (It is noticeable that Douglas discusses the distinctions between science, values, and religion but, like most such discussions, does not consider the humanities' relationship with them.) Cairney and Kwiatkowski's (2017: 2) observation pertains here, too, that effective engagement 'involves showing simple respect and seeking ways to secure their [policymakers'] trust, rather than feeling egotistically pleased about "speaking truth to power" without discernible progress. Effective engagement requires preparation, diplomacy, and good judgement as much as good evidence'. See also Collins (2014), and work on the role of experts in various decision-making settings such as that cited in Sutherland and Burgman (2015: 318) who, among other things, observe that 'people who are less self-assured and assertive, and who integrate information from diverse sources tend to make better judgements'.

2

IDENTITIES

Introduction

It is said that in 1862, on or around Thanksgiving, Harriet Beecher Stowe, author of the bestselling novel *Uncle Tom's Cabin* (1852), was introduced to President Abraham Lincoln who greeted her with the following words: 'So you're the little woman who wrote the book that made this great war!' (Weinstein, 2004: 1). The quotation is apocryphal, a part of Stowe family lore, as well as that of Stowe biographers, literary critics, and historians (Vollaro, 2009). But in one sense it does not matter whether the event actually happened, because the anecdote functions to powerfully convey the very real social, cultural, and political impact of Stowe's novel. Appearing first in serialisation in the anti-slavery periodical *The National Era* (June 1851-April 1852), *Uncle Tom's Cabin* was published in book form in 1852, selling 300,000 copies in the USA in the first year.[1] Its narrative contents were spread through sales, as well as through its movement across different forms, being taken up by the equivalent of the television and movie industries of the nineteenth century – theatre – in hundreds of dramatic adaptations, and then actual movie adaptations from the turn of the century. The story spread even further through songs, poems, and what we would now think of as merchandising (ranging from themed jigsaw puzzles to drinks and snacks) (Kaufman, 2006). *Uncle Tom's Cabin* cohered the abolitionist movement and conveyed their concerns, and social knowledge about the brutality of slavery, to a wider American public (Douglas, 1986).[2] It also prompted a backlash from pro-slavery groups and ignited American sectionalism. In his account of *The Civil War in American Culture*, Will Kaufman (2006: 20) concludes that Beecher, and the audiences who 'received, emulated, and challenged' her story, 'performed much of the groundwork that prepared the cultural battlefields of the war and […] its aftermath'.

DOI: 10.4324/9780367808426-4

Uncle Tom's Cabin is an example of a charismatic story that, through its sto-rycontents and storysharing (across different media), cohered collective identi-ties and conveyed social knowledge, with powerful cultural and political effects. Below, we consider a number of other historical examples of charismatic stories functioning in this way in relation to our case studies, but in the chapter as a whole we show how this function of stories is not restricted to such famous examples. Persistently and consistently, across all parts of society and in rela-tion to diverse identities and issues, stories function to create and consolidate collective identities, and to store and transmit social knowledge. Storylistening should be informed by narrative evidence regarding this role of stories, which can help identify social groups, understand motivations and actions, and rec-ognise social norms and how they are or might be changing. Following the structure established in the previous chapter, in the first section here we present the cross-disciplinary evidence base that stories function in this way. In the sec-ond section, we provide examples of stories doing so in relation to our four case studies. We explore *both* how stories shared within groups convey social norms and other information relevant to group coherence, constituting identities and influencing behaviour, *and* how stories provide insight into the nature of collec-tive identities, how they are formed and maintained, through their modelling of such identities in the storycontent (a representational function which we explore at more length in Chapter 3).

Moving beyond historical examples we consider in the second section how stories can provide insight into collective identity systems; the connection between Indigenous knowledge, communities, stories, and climate change; how certain sto-ries (for instance of apocalypse) can create narrative lock-in; and how storycontent and storysharing can define research collectives. In the final section, we draw out the consequences of the first two sections for the practice of storylistening, consider-ing how it can help identify publics, and understand narrative networks and norms, while acknowledging the challenges of such an enterprise, both ethical and meth-odological. We draw attention to the need for narrative literacy, and highlight the dangers of, and potential deficits resulting from, narrative lock-in.[3]

Function description and evidence

Stories play a fundamental role in individual and collective identity formation. Forming an individual or collective sense of self is a temporal, spatial, and rela-tional process (Somers, 1994). Each of these axes must be navigated in order to differentiate and integrate a sense of self (Bamberg, 2011) and stories are the tools by which humans effect this navigation. Stories function in this way because they are able to meet two mutually necessary but also potentially conflictual needs: the need to create cause and effect coherence over time, and the need to allow for the shifting multiplicity of individual and collective identities which are inherently relational and complicatedly networked. The function of stories in this respect is ontological, that is, stories constitute identities, as individuals and as collectives. (We examine the representational and anticipatory functions of stories in the subsequent two chapters.) Stories also influence behaviour, for they constitute the identities that are the preconditions for our actions: 'people act, or do not act, in part according to how they understand their place in any number of given stories – however fragmentary, contradictory, or partial' (Somers, 1994: 618). As a species we are, in Walter R. Fisher's (1984: 6) terms, *homo narrans.*

Stories and individual identities

Evidence that stories function in this way is strong and diverse, ranging across disciplines and methodologies. With regard to story and individual identity, it includes 'life story' scholarship, which investigates how, through the development of a life story, individuals establish for themselves and others their present identity, how it came to be, and their projected identity in the future (Bertaux, 1981; Bertaux and Kohli, 1984; Freeman, 1984; Polanyi, 1985; Linde, 1986; Lieblich and Josselson, 1994; Plummer, 2001; Ghorashi, 2008). What has been called narrative identity, established through autobiographical reasoning, thereby provides selves with meaning and coherence (Ricoeur, 1979, 1984–1988; Singer, 2004; McAdams and McLean, 2013; Habermas and Köber, 2014). In addition to the role of 'big story' in narrative identity formation, 'little stories' play a role.[4] Identities are forged and tested through everyday storytelling and storyimbibing interactions, in local conversations and dialogues (Georgakopoulou, 2007; Schiffrin et al., 2010; Bamberg, 2011). Identities are constructed through stories, with individuals using stories to process their experiences over time and integrate them, to construct a coherent narrative identity. Stories influence action both through this role in individual identity formation, and because individuals act based on assumptions, recollections, and anticipations acquired from the dominant cultural, social, or other public narratives available to them (Somers, 1994).

Stories and collective identities

Stories have also been demonstrated to play a role in the creation and consolidation of collective identities, for instance familial (Langellier and Peterson, 2004, 2006; Huisman, 2014), national (Eder, 2009), political (Bearman and Stovel, 2000), class (Somers, 1992), gender (Tuchman et al., 1978; Bamberg, 2004), and organisational (Boje, 1991; O'Barr and Conley, 1992; Stutts and Barker, 1999; Coupland, 2001; Cunliffe, 2001; Samra-Fredericks, 2003; Brown, 2006). Collective identities can be examined through their associated narrative networks (an idea explored further below specifically with regard to its consequences for public reasoning) in which the production, circulation, and reception of stories are in a constant process of defining, and being defined by, the collective identity. From a network perspective, a single individual is a node in a multiplicity of collective identities.[5] As such, any individual is, in line with the original meaning of 'node', a point of entanglement, where any number of collective identities converge. The take-up and adaptation of shared stories functions as a form of boundary construction – a social process fundamental to identity production – delimiting the possibilities of social interaction and action (Tilly, 2002: 11). Collective identities can also be embedded within other collective identities with which their storytelling, and thereby collective identity, does or does not align, for instance different groups within the same institution (Humphreys and Brown, 2002; Brown, 2006). Attending to the narrative basis of collective identity formation is particularly important in a global, digital age in which social networks are as often established through mediation as through co-presence (Eder, 2009).

Collective identities are reciprocally formed and expressed through cultural expressions such as clothes, rituals, idioms, but also through stories (Polletta and Jasper, 2001). Stories often function in this way not as extended narratives but in compressed form, as what Chabay et al. (2019: 3) call a concise affective narrative expression (CANE): 'a characteristic piece extracted from the complete narrative as a memorable, easily communicable, and affective verbal or visual representation of the core message'. CANEs are easily transmitted and serve to cohere collective identities – and mobilise action – if to the individual or collective storyimbibers they are plausible, relevant, affective, motivational, and acceptably normative (Chabay et al., 2019: 6–7). Attending to stories, and the collective identities they play a role in constituting, offers insight into why collectives of actors manifest at a particular moment, what their motivations are, what drives their strategic choices, and the social effects of collective action (Polletta and Jasper, 2001; Tilly, 2002; Chabay et al., 2019). Such attention must examine *both* story form and content, *and* the story as social object; that is, *both* the meaning contained within stories and how that meaning is constructed, *and* the contexts of a story's production, circulation, and reception.[6]

The case made, and literature surveyed so far, with regard to the identity formation function of stories pertains almost exclusively to stories and storytelling in non-textual forms. But the same case applies equally to textual stories. The literature, film, and television with which people engage contributes to individual identity formation, and the circulation, exchange, and reception of such stories can define, and be defined by, collective identities. Storylistening that considers the identity formation function of textual stories – through both their form and content, and in their manifestation as social objects of exchange – will generate insight into collective identities, their manifestation, motivation, strategies, and effects. Work on the history of the book demonstrates how the historical study of reading can identify 'distinctive traits of communities of readers' (Cavallo and Chartier, 1999: 2) and how research into the reading practices of historically and geographically situated readers can serve to 'reconstruct the communities of which they were members' (Pawley, 2002: 144; see also: Darnton, 1982; Kaestle et al., 1991; Long, 1993; Chartier, 1995; Wiegand, 1998). Ethnographies of reading (Gubrium and Holstein, 2008; Rosen, 2015) and viewing from empirical reception studies (Radway, 1984; Morley and Brunsdon, 1999; Griswold, 2000) and studies of participatory culture (Jenkins, 1992; Jenkins et al., 2013) reveal the uses and functions of stories within specific communities or collectives.[7] Media and communication studies demonstrate the ways in which stories function to inform societal and individual self-perception through the nature of their representations of specific social identities (Gerbner and Gross, 1976; Brookes and Hérbert, 2006). Storyimbibing and storysharing are understood here as forms of behaviour influenced by, and influencing, individual and collective identity.

Stories can form an intersection between entertainment, literary and popular culture, and civic discourse (Jenkins et al., 2013: ch. 4). If the collective identities constituted by shared story engagement are conceived as publics, then it is necessary to value them as 'active, critically engaged and politically significant' (Livingstone, 2005: 18) (rather than as disconnected, passive consumers) and attend to them as one would to any other public, with valuable insights gained from doing so. For instance, segmenting publics by narrative network (rather than categories such as race, class, age) yields different collective identity categories. These new categories can help decision-makers to understand behaviour which may not make sense based on essentialist, categorical, or structural models of stable identity and predictable action, but may be explicable by attending to the nature and effects of those networked narrative identities (Steinmetz, 1992; Somers, 1994; Cornell, 2000).

Power and normativity

Storylistening in relation to collective identities must also acknowledge the imbrication of stories and power. Storylistening to the stories that constitute individual and collective identity, and influence political and other action, involves attention to questions such as the following: what stories are being told? Who is telling them? Who is listening to them? Why? How are they shared or circulated? Where and by whom are they accepted, and where and by whom are they contested? In what ways do they conflict with other stories in circulation?[8] Stories, those created and those circulated, are sites of power, whether that be hegemonic or resistive, reactionary or progressive. In *It Was Like a Fever: Storytelling in Protest and Politics*, Francesca Polletta (2006: 7) demonstrates that tracing 'the careers of particular stories' exposes 'not only the political processes by which they come to be tellable or authoritative but also the dynamics by which newly legitimated stories produce new modes of action and new terrains of contention'. Stories can function to sustain inequalities between different collective and individual identities, or to challenge inequalities; to reinforce authority and the status quo, or to effect conflict or change. In relation to social norms, ethics, and codes, a single story (because containing multiple meanings and subject to interpretation) can even serve both a conservative and a progressive function at once. A story can therefore function to suppress the evolution of societal knowledge but, even at the same time, it can also function to disrupt societal norms and introduce new practices and ideas (Leach et al., 2010; Lynam and Walker, 2016).

Stories play a role in the creation and maintenance of collective identities because of their effectiveness in storing and transmitting social knowledge. But they are not a neutral form of information conveyance and acquisition within and between collective identities – they are normative. That is, they can be used to disseminate or enforce social norms, for instance by the behaviours they represent and then condone or condemn (MacIntyre, 1981; Ochs and Capps, 2001; Polletta et al., 2011). This role is seen for instance in the trickster genre across forager societies, which represents antisocial behaviour and its consequences, or in monster stories used to enforce childhood compliance (Biesele, 1993; Scalise Sugiyama, 2011, 2016). Ethnographic research has evidenced this function in storytelling in insurance firms, to convey information about the normative duties of employees (Linde, 2001), in stories about what it means to be a member of a family (Stone, 1988), and in stories instructing American men regarding patriarchal fatherhood (Ochs and Taylor, 1995). Stories can therefore serve an important function in ensuring societal cohesion and cooperation (Boyd, 2009). Due to this function, they can be used in education, to teach social norms, and promote certain kinds of behaviour (Mahasneh et al., 2017). They can also be used to challenge and change dominant social norms, for example by exposing people to the norms of minority groups, thereby increasing understanding of groups with which one does not otherwise have direct familiarity, in some cases leading to greater societal cohesion (Litcher and Johnson, 1969; Katz and Zalk, 1978; Galinsky and Moskowitz, 2000; Paluck, 2009). Storytelling can also function to create shared concepts between different collective identities, operating as a key part of diverse knowledge co-creation processes (Galafassi et al., 2018).

Performative readings

In line with the general move in this book from understanding how stories function in relation to individuals to understanding how they function in relation to collectives, the case study examples explored here focus on the role of stories in the formation and maintenance of a range of different collective identities: researchers, institutions, marginalised groups, national identities, emergent collectives, and partisan and generational identities.[9] With regard to storylistening and public reasoning, we are concerned with networks of storyimbibers and offer illustrations of the links between shared stories and shared identities, where these are particularly relevant to public reasoning. We explore how the circulation and content of salient charismatic stories can create new collective identities, as well as examine how storycontent can model and provide insight into complicated and often conflicting collective identity systems. We consider how stories can create communal cohesion and actions towards positive futures, as well as how stories – for example, extreme stories of apocalypse – can cause narrative lock-in, re-enforcing boundaries between collectives and leading to social inaction and narrative deficits. We identify the way in which the sharing and circulation of stories define collective research identities, within a specific research area (AI) and within institutions (the IPCC), influencing the research questions pursued, and the forms of knowledge considered useful or legitimate.

As noted in the previous section, with regard to stories, collective identities, and social knowledge, storylistening must take into account both stories as social objects in circulation, and storycontent: the performative readings in this section that address storycontent are, therefore, combined with examples of more empirical or sociologically informed work of the type that is required in order to effectively attend to stories as social objects. We propose the need for more such work, and for further consideration of the relations between the roles of stories in the formation of collective identities, and the roles of such identities in the creation and operation of sites of collective influence and power as considered in policy studies (Cairney, 2020), in the final section of this chapter.

Historical examples

There are documented historical examples of a single textual story mobilising the creation of a new collective identity through and around it. Such examples offer interesting case studies of particular charismatic stories and serve an important role in drawing attention to the collective identity formation, social knowledge exchange, and action-influencing function of stories; hence, we begin by considering some of them here, in relation to our economics case study. However, such prominent examples should not draw storylistening's attention away from the need for narrative evidence regarding the way in which stories consistently function in this way across a range of different collective identities of relevance to policy issues.

There are two prominent examples of charismatic stories in relation to economics, from either side of the political-economic divide. On the left is Edward Bellamy's novel, *Looking Backward: 2000–1887* (1888). *Looking Backward* was published at the end of two decades of economic turmoil in the USA – including the Long Depression (1873–1879), recessions, the rise of organised labour, and industrial action. There was a need for new ideas about economics – and other structures of power and organisation – that might address and improve manifold social problems. Bellamy offered these ideas in a story. The protagonist, Julian West, falls asleep at the end of the nineteenth century, only to wake up in the year 2000, during which time the USA has been transformed into a socialist utopia, to which his guide Doctor Leete introduces him (and the reader). In his foreword to the 1960 edition of *Looking Backward*, Erich Fromm (1960: 1) describes its galvanising effect not just on select individuals, but on a new community of thought and action: 'It is one of the few books ever published that created almost immediately on its appearance a political mass movement'. John Hope Franklin (1938: 754) details the role the book played in creating and sustaining the Nationalist movement, with 158 'Bellamy clubs' existing across 27 states and the District of Columbia two years after the book's publication: 'the textbook of the movement was a novel'. Further stories were deployed both for (Albert Ross' *Speaking of Ellen* [1889] and Laurence Gronlund's *Our Destiny* [1890]) and against (Arthur Vinton's *Looking Further Backward* [1890] and J. W. Roberts' *Looking Within* [1893]) the force of Nationalism organised and propelled by Bellamy's novel. On the right, the stories of Ayn Rand, in particular in her novels *The Fountainhead* (1943) and *Atlas Shrugged* (1957), have played a fundamental role in shaping and sustaining American conservatism and libertarianism. Like Bellamy's novel, Rand's stories have influenced individual readers, from Ronald Reagan to Donald Trump, but have also contributed to shaping collective identities and actions, from White House economic policies to the Tea Party movement (Burns, 2009; Chait, 2009; Heller, 2009).

While famous and salient examples such as these require study and attention, storylistening should be cognisant of how stories consistently and persistently create such effects. Less visible stories intersect with the creation and agency of groups decentred from the central site of power in any given society. For instance, while beginning her discussion with Rachel Carson's best-seller *Silent Spring* (1962), Shelley Streeby (2018: 14) discusses a range of what she calls 'cultural texts' that have been fundamental to the formation of environmental social movements – shared stories circulating within and consolidating collective networks. Storylistening to narrative evidence from research such as Streeby's demonstrates how collective stories, and the identities they form and maintain, can be linked to activism, to the desire for social change, as well as to the consolidation and perpetuation of social norms.

In *Narrative Economics* (2019), Robert Shiller traces a number of popular economic stories that, often aided by association with charismatic individuals,[10] have gone viral, influencing individual and collective economic beliefs and actions.[11] Without using the term, Shiller is arguing for storylistening here, that is, making the case that economists should incorporate evidence of the role such stories play in economic events into their explanations of those events. He argues that this will enable economists to better forecast and anticipate the future. (We attend to the relationship between stories and anticipation in Chapter 4.) Shiller (2019: xv) observes, as we do above in relation to the apocryphal story of Lincoln and Stowe's encounter, that such economic stories influence belief, actions, and therefore the economic system, irrespective of their veracity. Shiller's focus is on popular non-textual stories spread orally, through the news and through social media. His examples include the Bitcoin narrative, which has so successfully cohered an anarchic and cosmopolitan collective identity that transcends nation state divisions, as well as nine other dominant narrative constellations that have influenced, and are influenced by, economic behaviour. Shiller does not include attention to textual stories, and the different media they circulate through, but his work represents a move away from the focus of mainstream economics which George A. Akerlof and Dennis J. Snower (2016: 68) argue 'ignores the role of narratives in generating and maintaining identities since it assumes that preferences are located exclusively in the individual; the influence of social groups on individual preferences is ignored'.

It should also be noted, before we move on, that the historical examples explored here were written with the explicit intention to mobilise collectives and action. Although he originally stated that he had no serious intentions to catalyse social reform with *Looking Backward* (Bellamy, 1889), later Bellamy ([1894] 1937: 223) provided a different account of his motivations:

> I sat down to my desk with the definite purpose of trying to reason out a method of economic organization by which the republic might guarantee the livelihood and material welfare of its citizens on a basis of equality corresponding to and supplementing their political equality.

Rand wrote her book explicitly as propaganda, inspired by the expert propagandists of her native Russia: 'She used to say, "I was educated by the best propagandists of all"' (Ha, 2017: n.p.).

Stories are of course not value-neutral, and storytelling is often deployed to convey social norms or challenge them, to promote and justify certain types of behaviour, or to offer alternative visions of collective identity and action. In the following section, however, we consider stories that are more significant to storylistening for their modelling of collective identities, than for their mobilising of them.

Modelling collective identity systems

Large collective identities, such as national identity, are naturally not homogeneous, but rather contain within them a range of other, often conflicting, collective identities that overlap, in the sense that any individual is also naturally part of many collective identities. Which collective identities matter most for the purposes of public reasoning depends on the matter under consideration. Storylistening can contribute to making decisions informed by a more nuanced understanding of the relevant collective identities, their intersection, interaction, and the tensions between them. In this respect, stories can function as models of these collective identity systems (a function we explore at more length in Chapter 3). Here we look at two examples of stories functioning as collective identity models in relation to climate change: Dave Eggers' *Zeitoun* (2009), and Barbara Kingsolver's *Flight Behaviour* (2012).

Zeitoun is a narrative nonfiction account exposing some of the effects on New Orleans and its residents of Hurricane Katrina, through telling the story of Abdulrahman and Kathy Zeitoun. Eggers wrote the story with the full support of the Zeitoun family, who he interviewed for the book, and facts in their story such as dates, times, and locations were confirmed by the historical record and other independent sources. Zeitoun – called by his surname throughout the story – is a Muslim Syrian immigrant to the USA whose hard work and diligence when new to the country paid off, leading to him building a successful painting contractor business in New Orleans. He is the embodiment of the story that is represented in the CANE of the American Dream – that anyone, regardless of origin, race, class, or more, can achieve success in a society of equally accessible upward mobility for all, if one works hard and sacrifices enough. This CANE structures a collective American identity in which Zeitoun partakes. It is conveyed to readers within the book through an exemplary anecdote which itself contains within it an exemplary anecdote, the mise-en-abyme effect reinforcing the idea of the self-replicating truth of the CANE.

At the beginning of his time in New Orleans, Zeitoun eventually gets a job with Charlie Saucier: 'Charlie owned his own company, had built it from scratch. He'd become wealthy' (Eggers, 2010: 36). When travelling on his bike to one of Charlie's work sites, Zeitoun blows a tire. He can't leave the bike, which is his only form of transport to work, and is in danger of being 'late for work for the first time in his life' (37), so he begins the four mile run to work with the bike on his back, only to be passed by his boss who gives him a lift the rest of the way. Charlie is impressed by Zeitoun's commitment and work ethic: 'After that day, things moved quickly forward and upward for Zeitoun. Within a year, he had saved enough to buy his own truck. Two years later, he was working for himself and employing a dozen men' (38). This is the story of the American dream, one that is intended to cohere the collective national identity of all alike, transcending differences of background, in the land of opportunity.

However, in *Zeitoun*, this story is almost immediately ruptured by the discrimination with which the Zeitouns and their employees contend on a regular basis. Zeitoun, the reader is told,

> tried to be amused by the fickle nature of clients' tastes; it was part of the job, and if he got exasperated every time someone changed their mind, he'd never survive. The upshot was that it ensured no day was dull. The intensely personal nature of his business, the subjectivity of taste, the variables of light and curtains and carpets, guaranteed that minds would reevaluate and work would have to be redone.
>
> *(Eggers, 2010: 46)*

With the repetition of 'taste', this passage minimises the 'fickle nature' of some of the clients, lulling the reader into thinking it's discussing aesthetic preferences regarding the colour of interior design choices. The example that follows, however, is of 'a Southern belle in her sixties' whose 'fickle tastes' extend to the colour of her workmen's skin: 'I only want white people working on my house' (46). Zeitoun, the reader is told twice, is usually able to laugh these things off, but such incidents reveal his success might well be in spite of, not because of, other aspects of America's collective identity, including its sharply delineated racial divisions. The prejudices these give rise to, and the reactions in response to such prejudices, form collective identities at odds with any form of coherent shared national identity. This part of the collective identity system is primarily conveyed to the reader in the early stages of the book through Zeitoun's wife Kathy's experiences.

Times of crisis – be they linked to a global virus, or global climate change – can expose and heighten such tensions. Zeitoun's sense of his own belonging to a collective national identity is challenged by the events of Hurricane Katrina, during which his altruistic actions as a result of this sense of collective identity lead to his violation and mistreatment based on collective identities at national and institutional levels that are defined by shared stories of racial and religious prejudice and profiling. Zeitoun remains in New Orleans as the hurricane approaches, despite his wife and children leaving for safety. He does so due to the same work ethic that is rewarded in the American Dream CANE – a commitment to maintaining his business and protecting the properties it manages. When the extent of the damage the hurricane has caused becomes clear, he paddles his kayak around the neighbourhood, feeding abandoned dogs and rescuing trapped locals. In return, he is racially profiled by the police, falsely accused of being an 'al Qaeda' terrorist (Eggers, 2010: 222), and falsely imprisoned under inhumane conditions, a trauma that has lasting consequences for himself and his family.

Zeitoun weaves together a number of narrative strands: that of Zeitoun's upbringing in Syria; that of his life in the USA; that of his own experiences as a result of Hurricane Katrina; that of others affected by the hurricane, primarily his wife Kathy. In doing so, *Zeitoun* is able in narrative form to evidence the network of consequences of extreme weather events – not just their economic effects (in terms of damage to properties and livelihoods), not just the very different cost of lives lost (both of which categories can be rendered in numerical form) – but the way in which such events can exacerbate already existing tensions between different collective identities, magnify existing social differences, and have differential effects for different members of society. The storycontent of *Zeitoun* is just one example of stories that show how climate change is not just a socio-political issue, but an issue the socio-political effects of which are felt very differently by different groups of people.

In contrast to many climate stories which organise their narrative around the plight of one man – for instance, *Zeitoun*, Cormac McCarthy's *The Road* (2006), or Nathaniel Rich's *Odds Against Tomorrow* (2013; discussed further below) – Barbara Kingsolver's *Flight Behaviour*, while still focalised through a single individual (Dellarobia Turnbow), explores in detail her relationship to a number of different collective identities, of which she feels both more and less a part. *Flight Behaviour* explores these relationships in the context of climate change, as the novel revolves around the relocation of a population of monarch butterflies to Dellarobia's local mountain in the Appalachians, which should ordinarily have roosted in Mexico. The novel explores the collective identity of the family into which she has married, defined by its poverty, as is most of the local population. This is contrasted to the collective identity of the scientists, led by entomologist Ovid Byron, who come to study the butterflies. The novel explores the differences and tensions between these groups, brought together by the appearance of the butterflies. Dellarobia notes: 'There were two worlds here, behaving as if their own was all that mattered. With such reluctance to converse, one with the other. Practically without a common language' (Kingsolver, 2012: 209). These divisions extend nationally beyond her family and the scientists, and it is membership of a collective identity that influences people's beliefs and actions, not the unbiased processing of facts and figures:

> It was the same on all sides, the yuppies watched smart-mouthed comedians who mocked people living in double-wides who listened to country music. The very word *Tennessee* made those audiences burst into laughter, she'd heard it. They would never come to see what Tennessee was like, any more than she would get a degree in science and figure out the climate things Dr. Byron described. Nobody truly decided for themselves. There was too much information. What they actually did was scope around, decide who was looking out for their clan, and sign on for the memos on a wide array of topics.
>
> *(228)*

Dellarobia worries that her extended family's collective identity is inhibiting them from making the best decision they can about whether to log the hillside on which the butterflies have settled. Her husband Cub insists that they need the money, especially if they are to provide for their intelligent son:

> 'If you want them to have a computer and stuff, we need the logging money. Or' – he spread his hands – 'we can keep our trees. And be hicks.'
> 'Right. We cut down the trees and get ourselves buried in mud like a bunch of hillbillies, because we're afraid of raising our kids to be dumb hillbillies. Really you're saying we just do it because *that's who we are*,' she said, too loudly. 'Who *are* we?'
>
> *(240)*

The arrival of the butterflies challenges the coherence of established collective identities by bringing them into close relation with other groups – the scientists, the population of butterflies, and the media – about whom there is disagreement. It also demonstrates the way in which group identity influences the types of stories and information sought out and processed – stories that confirm, rather than challenge that identity. Ovid states that 'a journalist's job is to collect information'; Pete, another scientist, disagrees: 'Nope [...]. That's what we do. It's not what they do' (317). When challenged by Dellarobia, Pete insists that the media write in order 'to shore up the prevailing view of their audience and sponsors' (317); Dellarobia points out that people from all groups do this:

> 'You're saying people only tune in to news they know they're going to agree with?'
> 'Bingo,' said Pete.
> 'Well, see, I agree with you,' she said. 'I've thought that too. How often do you tune in to Johnny Midgeon?'

'You're right,' Pete said. 'I don't want to hear those guys.'

'So,' she said, 'you're the same as everybody.'

'Well, but it's because I already know what they're going to say.'

'That's what everybody thinks. Maybe you do, and maybe you don't.'

(317–318)

Evidence regarding echo chambers, filter bubbles, and confirmation bias is of course available from other disciplinary sources such as psychology and behavioural science.[12] Confirmatory narrative evidence from a story such as *Flight Behaviour* re-enforces understanding of this kind of phenomena, and stories can communicate and illustrate such information in ways that might inform different people more effectively than other forms of knowledge storage and transmission, such as scientific papers or policy reports.

Turning from our climate change to our nuclear case study, a final example of a story modelling a collective identity system is the HBO and Sky UK 2019 miniseries *Chernobyl*. This example is particularly instructive because it demonstrates the importance of understanding into which systems and collective identities a story is actually providing insight. Storylistening must not immediately dismiss a story that appears to be inaccurate, but must determine what exactly it is wrong about, but also whether it might be right about, and therefore provide useful narrative evidence about, something else. For example, through expert narrative analysis, including setting the series aside other forms of evidence, it is clear that *Chernobyl* contains infelicities about Russia in the 1980s; but it still contains useful narrative evidence with regard to contemporary UK and US politics.

The TV series tells the story of the people involved in the Chernobyl nuclear disaster in April 1986, focusing on the different individuals and groups involved, and their interactions. It portrays the three men convicted of being responsible for the disaster, showing their professional ambition getting in the way of following all the necessary rules and protocols, and it explores tensions between the scientists and the politicians that arise in particular from each group's different relationship to the truth. As a result, it might be easy to assume that the value of *Chernobyl* is its insight into the complicated identity system in the Soviet Union at the time of the disaster. However, the series has been criticised for misrepresentation in this regard. For instance, characters are presented as being afraid of being summarily executed, whereas Russian-American journalist Masha Gessen notes that that was a feature of life in the 1930s, not the late 1980s. Gessen (2019: n.p.) also criticises the classic Hollywood trope of the single heroic man standing up against the corrupt system, stating that the series' continued representation of the scientists standing up to the bureaucrats is 'repetitive and ridiculous': 'Resignation was the defining condition of Soviet life'.

Chernobyl is far more useful to storylistening in the West if understood as a representation of the identity systems – including, in particular, the relationship between the science and policy communities, and the dangers of misinformation, propaganda, and disregard for truth – that characterised the USA and the

UK at the time the series was made, rather than as a reliable or realistic model of such structures in the final years of the Soviet Union. In fact, writer Craig Mazin stated explicitly that he was motivated to create the series because of what he called 'the global war on the truth' playing out in the West at the time of the series' creation (Topel, 2019).

Relatedly, it has been asserted that the series – through its storycontent and storysharing – has cohered the younger generation in Belarus who have learnt more about the extent of the disaster through watching it, and who have received the series through a lens of stronger generational environmental consciousness. Belarusian Nobel laureate Svetlana Alexievich, whose book *Voices from Chernobyl* strongly informed the series, observes:

> It's no accident that a lot of young people have watched this film [*sic*]. They say that they watch it together in clubs and discuss it. They are different. For them, questions about the environment, especially in the West, it is through that lens that they understand life.
>
> *(quoted in Sous and Wesolowsky, 2019: n.p.)*

Narrative evidence derived from further empirical research to test Alexievich's assertion regarding the series' storysharing among young people in Belarus would usefully inform that nation's public reasoning regarding both nuclear and climate issues.

Indigenous stories

While *Zeitoun* and *Flight Behaviour* model collective identity systems in which race and class play a part in complicating the idea of a homogeneous national identity, Alexis Wright's *The Swan Book* (2013), set in a future Australia, explores the collective identity systems produced by settler colonialism and its effects on Indigenous life, culture, and identity. (Wright is a member of the Waanyi nation of the southern highlands of the Gulf of Carpentaria, Australia.) *The Swan Book* is a story about stories, about the ways in which they are produced, received, and circulated, about how they influence individual and collective identity, store and transmit social knowledge, and facilitate social interactions: 'We use stories all the time', says Wright in interview, 'Telling stories is a very big thing about who we are, and it is often the way that we do business with each other' (Wright and Zable, 2013: 28). As Álvaro Fernández-Llamazares and Mar Cabeza (2018) note in their exploration of the potential of Indigenous storytelling for conservation practice:

> Storytelling among IPs [Indigenous peoples] helps to forge a number of purposes, such as entertaining, passing down a repertoire of culturally built knowledge, maintaining a sense of community, and instilling moral values, all of which laid the groundwork for social collaboration (Nabokov 2006;

Lawrence & Paige 2016). A key feature of indigenous storytelling is the intergenerational transmission of experience, allowing for human adaptation to different environments (Brown 2013; Egeland et al. 2013). Indigenous stories are made up of extremely complex, finely coded information on human subsistence and infused with dramatic elements that ensure their transmission, engaging the heart with the mind (MacDonald, 1998; Archibald, 2008).

(Fernández-Llamazares and Cabeza, 2018: 2)

The Swan Book is set in a world in which climate change has mobilised a mass body of migrants, forced to take to the seas in search of survival: 'millions of white people were drifting among the other countless stateless millions of sea gypsies looking for somewhere to live' (Wright, 2013: 23). It tells the story of Oblivia, an aboriginal girl who is gang raped at a young age, and then found and taken in by Bella Donna (a white Western climate refugee). They live together in the hulk of a rusting ship in a swamp that was formerly Indigenous land but is now a fenced-off, Army-policed, detention camp for Aboriginal people, both those originally of that land, and those trucked in from elsewhere in Australia: 'the traditional owners of the land locked up forever: Key thrown away' (40).

The Swan Book traces the tensions within the collective identity system it models in both its content and its form. For example, in its content, Bella Donna insists on her membership of an Australian national identity because she lives on the old boat, not the camp land, and she is bemused as to why 'the swamp people' (Wright, 2013: 57) resist such assimilation:

The detention camp was now a settled population of traditional owners from kingdoms near and far, and swamped with a big philosophy about the meaning of home. Why do they do it? *They could also seek asylum and permanent Australian residency by living on navy junk*, the old woman claimed, referring to her hull as a solid piece of Australia that was immune to traditional land ownership laws. She liked being a part of mass Australia and owning her own home. It gave her a sense of authority when it suited her. *You think that they would want to grab the chance to become fully Australian. A chance to live like everyone else.*

(58)

But 'the swamp people were not interested in being conquered by other people's stories' (33) and fiercely reject Bella Donna's position: 'They yelled at her: *Yea! That's your story.* Patriotism! *Ha! We'll show you what bloody patriotism means.* A blaze of colour of Aboriginal flags unfurled in the wind' (6).

In its form, *The Swan Book* is syncretic, weaving together different modes of storytelling, burying a linear narrative within the structures and styles of Indigenous storytelling, flowing around and through repeated themes and motifs (swans, the viral power of stories, the characters themselves as motifs) which are nevertheless constrained and detached from their embodied, performative and interactive context by the shift from oral to written form, and into English.[13] In its storytelling, the novel foregrounds nature or Country and its vitality in Aboriginal culture – the collective identity systems constructed and sustained through these stories include the agential non-human (the animal and land), the ancestral, and the spiritual (see also the discussion of *Sila* and ethical relationality in Chapter 1). Such an understanding, manifest equally in laws, stories, and epistemologies, provides tools for conceiving of collective identity beyond the bounded categories typical of Western thought, which separates some humans from other humans, and from the animate and inanimate non-human. Storylistening sensitive to, and informed by, such thought requires an attention to location (Sundberg, 2014), and respect for and understanding of Indigenous Place-Thought (Watts, 2013), in order that Indigenous thought might carefully inform practical tools for reconceiving stories, for instance of climate change, beyond the Western impasse of atomised collective identities.[14]

Indigenous peoples have played and continue to play a crucial role in drawing attention to climate change at a global level (Todd, 2016), for instance through organisations such as the International Work Group for Indigenous Affairs (IWGIA), and the work of Indigenous advocates such as Rosemarie Kuptana and Sheila Watt-Cloutier (the latter of whom was reportedly nominated for the 2007 Nobel Peace Prize, although not awarded it – it went to Al Gore and the IPCC [Moore, 2007]). Storylistening to Indigenous stories about climate change would complement the intentions of such organisations, and activist interventions. This would include storylistening to apocalyptic textual stories such as *The Swan Book*, as well as to results of practical initiatives exploring how positive stories about desirable futures can inform community identity and actions towards sustainability (Fernández-Llamazares and Cabeza, 2018; Chabay et al., 2019).

Apocalyptic stories

Many of the example stories explored in this chapter tend towards the apocalyptic. Extreme stories can be hugely effective in mobilising collective identities and social action, but extreme stories can also create narrative lock-in, re-enforcing boundary construction between different collectives, inhibiting social action and interaction, and leading to narrative deficits (the failure to attend to, or the actual absence of, alternative stories).[15]

Nathaniel Rich's *Odds Against Tomorrow* (2013) provides one such example. *Odds Against Tomorrow* tells the story of Mitchell Zukor, a brilliant mathematician whose paranoia and apocalyptic fears make him expert at selling worst-case scenario stories to wealthy business people on behalf of his new employer, FutureWorld, 'a private consulting firm – in a manner of speaking – based in New York', which specialises in 'minimizing losses that may result from unforeseen or worst-case-imaginable scenarios' (Rich, 2013: 21). As with *Zeitoun*, the narrative of this primary character intersects with his love interest, Elsa Bruner, a fellow student who suffers from a life-threatening condition. While Mitchell profits from selling stories of impending disaster, Bruner sets up a utopian agricultural experiment in the countryside. This experiment is only possible, however, because a friend owns the land, and because of the availability of contemporary materials and technologies such as 'solar tubes, bidirectional net meters, and metal flashings' (63). In the same way, Mitchell's own retreat to a utopian independent existence after the floods that inundate New York subside is only possible because of the supplies his friend Jane regularly brings for him from the city. Nevertheless, Mitchell becomes a celebrated figure, his story providing a rallying point around which a generation of young people create a collective identity committed to starting afresh: 'There are others coming. Others like us. We want to start something here' (286).

The novel examines and exposes the fallacy of a CANE around the Anthropocene that idealises the rural and condemns the urban. Mitchell is well aware of this fallacy at the outset of the novel – his letters to Elsa 'made a point of listing the virtues of metropolitan life' (Rich, 2013: 64) – but at the end of the novel the story remains trapped in these only options, albeit the inhabitants of these positions have switched. Mitchell now represents the attempt to create a disconnected existence, even while recognising its futility:

> He was under no illusions. Out here in the neighbourhood formerly known as Flatlands – or was it Canarsie? – he wouldn't unearth Eden, or even some agrarian ideal. Most likely his work here wouldn't amount to very much at all. He knew nothing, after all, about farming, fertilization, engineering, construction. Problems would arise that he could not anticipate, and he'd be comically unprepared to fix them. The weather would only become increasingly erratic. The fields might go fallow or flood. Winter would be excruciating. And a single serious injury or illness would force him to give up.
>
> *(286)*

Jane takes his place within corporate America and business as usual within a recovering New York. What the novel cannot imagine is thinking beyond urban or rural as the only options – it doesn't consider a reimagined urbanity, for instance, one that might challenge its hierarchies of collective identities and the stories of wealth and power that cohere them (and which unite individuals like Mitchell's father and his clients who were both 'obsessed by financial gain [...] seeking profit at the expense of human dignity' [239]).

Mitchell berates himself when the floods come for having 'suffered a failure of the imagination' (Rich, 2013: 122) – he had concentrated only on drought scenarios, not those of a deluge. But the novel itself could also be said to suffer from a failure of the imagination, in not finding a way out of the binary between urban and rural even while recognising that the two are intimately and inextricably connected, and in potentially misrepresenting the advantages and disadvantages of both. That said, given climate affects everything, and overlaps with general environmental concerns (place, pollution, biodiversity, and more), a novel such as *Odds Against Tomorrow* can offer important insight into some of the risks and possible consequences of our current structures and dominant CANEs and collective identities. It also acknowledges – even if it cannot find a way out of – the problematic romanticism of a total rejection of contemporary life and the benefit of the urban centres around which it so often coheres and which support it. Narrative evidence from stories such as *Odds Against Tomorrow* might help decision-makers see the need for new stories that would transcend existing divisions, creating new kinds of collective identities around which sustainable futures could be built.

The increasing narrative lock-in and associated polarisation of collective identities in relation to climate change, again in the US context, can be seen in the 2017 film *First Reformed* (directed by Paul Schrader) which, even more than *Odds Against Tomorrow*, foregrounds divided collective identities, here of big business, climate activism, and institutional religion. Again, the film offers no vision for transcending these identities, no new story that might reform them, and thus no hope for a viable future. Like *Odds*, it ends with a focus on one individual white man and the possibilities for his own future identity, rather than exploring any new story about structures that might mobilise new collective identities.

The representation of the collective identity that is Christianity in relation to climate change in *First Reformed* renders US institutional religion as aligned with a CANE of evil corporate capitalism, and personal religious faith as a source of individual mystical salvation that does nothing to address wider social or systemic issues. A formal statement from the Alliance of Religions and Conservation, a secular body which 'helps the world's major faiths develop environmental programmes based on their own core teachings, beliefs and practices' (ARC, n.d.), acknowledges the need for more stories in relation to climate change, but focuses on the need to deploy the power of storytelling to mobilise action, rather than the need to find and listen to stories that better represent the complex system itself:

> Without [...] these areas [of narrative, myth and metaphor], policies will have very few roots [...] the climate change 'activist' world and indeed the environmental world has all too often sought refuge in random use of apocalyptic imagery without seeking to harness the power of narrative. Without narrative, few people are ever moved to change or adapt.
>
> *(ARC, 2007)*[16]

In *Apocalypse Never: Why Environmental Alarmism Hurts Us All* (2020), Michael Shellenberger proposes that apocalyptic environmental narratives have arisen to cohere a collective identity around a secular desire for transcendence, but hinder actual environmental progress. *Apocalypse Never*, and Shellenberger's earlier work, has been strongly criticised for factual errors, inaccurate science, and bad arguments (Pope, 2005; Gleick, 2020; Swain et al., 2020), but in his review of Shellenberger's essay 'The Death of Environmentalism', Carl Pope (2005), Executive Director of the Sierra Club, does concur with Shellenberger's claim that 'the environmental community [has] still not come up with an inspiring vision, much less a legislative proposal, that a majority of Americans could get excited about' (Shellenberger and Nordhaus, 2004: 16). Apocalyptic climate narratives are not functioning to cohere a non-partisan collective and mobilise multilateral positive action.

Apocalyptic narrative lock-in around climate change has distinct generational effects. Attending to novels for, or featuring, young adults, for instance, reveals the cohering of a teenage generational identity around the story of climate emergency as an apocalyptic threat to their futures. Storylistening to works such as Saci Lloyd's *The Carbon Diaries 2015* (2008) or John Lanchester's *The Wall* (2019) can complement attention to the global environmental youth movement and school strikes, most prominently represented by Greta Thunberg (Sweden), but with leading young activists across the world, including Isra Hirsi (USA), Autumn Peltier (Canada), Vanessa Nakate (Uganda), Wanjiru Wathuti (Kenya), and Adenike Oladosu (Nigeria). Attending to the dominance of apocalyptic and dystopian stories in cohering this collective identity can help to shed light on the high levels of climate anxiety in young people and its effects (Pihkala, 2019), and again emphasises the need for new stories to cohere collective identities across existing divisions and to offer realistic hope concomitant with positive action.

Researcher collectives

As a final example in our exploration of the relationship between stories, collective identity, and social knowledge and action, we examine collectives of specific relevance to science policy: researchers. Researchers constitute important collective identities for the purposes of our argument because in matters of policy, especially where science or wholly new expert knowledge is involved explicitly, they play significant roles. Shared stories contributing to shared identities are associated with research groups. While it is difficult to prove causality, careful storylistening to what stories are shared and between whom can provide insight into who is doing the research, what is – or is not – being researched, and why. For instance, evidence that science fiction plays a role in the formation of AI researcher communities, their constituents, and the type of research undertaken is anecdotal, historical, (auto)biographical, and, emergently, empirical. Science fiction can influence career choice, and the types of research undertaken and technologies designed and created.

By influencing individual career choice, stories can play a role in determining the type of people and thought styles that constitute a research collective. This is true of science and technology in general, and computer science and AI in particular. With regard to the former, for instance, David L. Ferro and Eric G. Swedin (2009: 86) note that 'a 2006 Discovery Channel television program entitled

"How William Shatner Changed the Universe" had the stories of a number of technologists and scientists crediting the 1960s television show *Star Trek* as influencing their career choices'. Joshua Cuneo (2011) also notes the influence of *Star Trek* on many researchers going into science fields. Kenneth R. Fleischmann and Thomas Clay Templeton's (2008: 5) interview study with scientists and engineers at the NASA Goddard Space Flight Centre provides examples that 'demonstrate the complex and multiple ways that science fiction influences the career decisions of scientists and engineers'. Ferro (2011: 1, 6), a computer scientist, ascribes his career choice to the 'defining moment' of receiving Isaac Asimov's *The Rest of the Robots* as a fifth grade Secret Santa-style Christmas present and states that 'science fiction [has] been an inspiration for those entering scientific and technical fields'.

Stories can also influence the research avenues explored and the types of technologies created. Examples of stories inspiring particular technological developments in computer science abound in academic (Abbate, 2011; Ceruzzi, 2011; Kirby, 2011; Bland and Westlake, 2013: 6–7) and popular discourse, for instance Brian Aldiss' short story 'Supertoys Last All Summer Long' influenced David Hanson's robot boy Zeno (Slagle, 2007). Contributors to James Frenkel's (2001) edited collection on Verne Vinge's short story 'True Names' write about the influence of the story on their development of imagined but yet to be realised computer technologies. Abbate (2011: 189) notes that 'Vinge's work, as well as other early cyberfiction, influenced actual thought and practice in computer science'. Isaac Asimov's stories are a particularly strong influence on Western roboticists, while the stories of *Tetsuwan Atomu* (Mighty Atom – known in the West as Astro Boy) influence many Japanese roboticists (Hornyak, 2006; Ndalianis, 2013).

Science fiction also serves as a form of communication within research collectives, the sharing and transmission of social and technological knowledge via stories contributing to their collective identity formation. Vinge's 'True Names' coalesced around it computer scientists such as Danny Hills, Timothy May, and Marvin Minsky, and was, anecdotally, required reading for graduate students in AI at Carnegie Mellon in the 1980s (Vinge, 2016). Murray Campbell, Daniel Dennett, Ray Kurzweil, Donald Norman, and David Stork have mediated discussion of advances in computer science through *HAL* from *2001: A Space Odyssey* (Stork, 1997). Science fiction stories provide a shared vocabulary for researchers (Abbate, 2011; Alvarado, 2011; Bardini, 2011). Powerfully charismatic individual stories have ensured the cohesion of a specific research community despite fragmentation and dispersal across other more established identity categories such as industry and academia. Allucquere Rosanne Stone (1991: 98–99) identifies William Gibson's *Neuromancer* (1984) as one such work:

> The critical importance of Gibson's book was partly due to the way that it triggered a conceptual revolution among the scattered workers who had been doing virtual reality research for years: As task groups coalesced and dissolved, as the fortunes of companies and projects and laboratories rose and fell, the existence of Gibson's novel and the technological and social

imaginary that it articulated enabled the researchers in virtual reality – or, under the new dispensation, cyberspace – to recognize and organize themselves as a community.

Stories, in particular but not exclusively science fiction ones, can also serve as an important site of, and provocation for, thinking about the social and ethical consequences of AI and other computing technologies (Joy, 2000; Dillon and Schaffer, [forthcoming]).

Preliminary and emerging empirical work is confirming the widespread and systemic influence of stories in AI research collectives. A small survey of the influence of science fiction on different disciplinary cohorts at a university in the USA and in Finland found computer science students to have higher consumption of science fiction stories across different media (games, TV, film, and literature) and the majority of such students thought science fiction had influenced their views (Ferro and Swedin, 2009: 89).[17] Sarah Dillon and Jennifer Schaffer's (forthcoming) qualitative study of the influence of storyimbibing (not restricted to science fiction) on 20 active artificial intelligence researchers based in the UK demonstrates that stories play a role in research focus, career choice, and community formation, as well as enabling social and ethical thinking, providing anticipatory narrative models, and both inhibiting and aiding science communication.

Science fiction in particular serves a community formation function for AI researchers, aiding communication of research ideas within research networks and with students. In consequence, if the dominant stories circulated are from within a specific branch of the science fiction tradition – for instance, primarily works produced by white Anglo-American men – this has the potential to act as a gatekeeper to the field, alienating researchers from diverse backgrounds and contributing to a homogeneous thought-collective (Dillon and Schaffer, [forthcoming]). Attending to such narrative evidence can aid public reasoning about the social and ethical implications of AI, and the need for and nature of public initiatives to diversify the types of researchers in the field.

Stories function in this way in relation to other communities of researchers, for instance those related to environmental and climate science. Stories inform the motivations and identities of researchers, the shared interests and assumptions within communities of researchers, the shape of research questions that are asked and funded (and those that are not), and the extent to which new evidence or ideas are picked up more widely. For example, the practices of research about endangered species may begin with studies of artefacts such as photographs and film, but they inform the creation of the Red Lists of endangered species and the laws that affect them. Similarly, stories of the Anthropocene – of loss and anticipation in connection to humans' relations with plants, animals, and other living and inanimate aspects of the Earth – influence today's academic and public directions (Heise, 2016). Shared stories about preserving or conserving the past drive directions of research, potentially closing off other stories that might conceivably help imagine the Anthropocene as a positive future. Ursula Heise identifies the links between stories of longing and stewardship, and a research orientation towards creating lists, databases, and policy that protects endangered species, potentially at the expense of observing how systems might 'naturally' evolve in the future. These stories can direct individual behaviour within collective settings.

The role of stories in conveying knowledge within or between social groups has come to inform recent research work in computer science which proposes that stories serve as a repository and conduit of socio-cultural knowledge – for example, shared values, beliefs, and social behaviours – which can be used as data for machine learning (Riedl and Harrison, 2015). Mark O. Riedl and Brent Harrison (2015) propose that learning from stories might offer one way of solving the value alignment problem in AI, by compelling an artificially intelligent entity to adhere to the values of a culture. One problem with such an approach, however, is evidenced in their recognition that *all* the stories of a given culture would be required in order to achieve this. They propose that this would ensure that stories that challenge socio-cultural norms would be outweighed by those that conform to them. However, many stories can serve both functions simultaneously, and this begs the question of which or whose socio-cultural norms are being replicated in AI systems, and whether all humans, as well as the animate and inanimate entities with which humans already share the planet (let alone artificial beings) benefit from conforming to them and/or their continuation. This question of power is left worryingly unanalysed in Riedl and Harrison's conclusion:

> In a future in which there are many encultured artificial intelligences, those that conform to sociocultural values would neutralize or marginalize the AIs that do not because maintaining social order is perceived as optimal – just as humans also do with each other.
>
> *(Riedl and Harrison, 2015: n.p.)*

What is also clear from the current research is that the 'stories' AI systems are trained on are not in fact stories at all since they are stripped of all the formal qualities that constitute them as such: 'we ask crowd workers to simplify their language to make learning easier, avoiding smilies, metaphorical language, complex grammar, and negations' (Riedl and Harrison, 2015: n.p.). They are in fact closer to what Roger Schank and Robert P. Abelson (1977) call 'scripts'. In stripping out the 'noise' to achieve an order of events that resembles an algorithm – for instance, instructions on how to order coffee at a coffee shop – such research fails to recognise that the 'noise' in stories is in fact essential to how they function so effectively in communicating social knowledge, and doing so in ways that continually provoke reflection on the very values they are encoding and transmitting.

Stories also play a role in the formal constitution of researchers in institutional structures. For example, the IPCC is constituted by, and reinforces, shared stories about the forms of knowledge that are or are not legitimate or relevant to the issue of climate change. The IPCC is an example of an institutional structure that created power for one type of story (about climate change), based on its storytellers (physical scientists and economists), while excluding other types of knowledge and collective narrative networks of researchers (humanities academics). Andreas Bjurström and Merritt Polk's (2011) research into the disciplinary constitution of the IPCC reveals a strong disciplinary bias towards the physical sciences and, where the social sciences are present, primarily economics.[18] Some scientific fields are also siloed. They argue that the lack of diverse disciplinary representation, and effective interdisciplinarity, 'distorts comprehensive understanding of climate change and [...] hinders climate change from being fully addressed as an integral environmental and social problem' (Bjurström and Polk, 2011: 1). Hulme and Mahony (2010) note that this bias towards the physical sciences is a matter of record (Shackley and Skodvin, 1995; Cohen et al., 1998; Malone and Rayner, 2001; Hiramatsu et al., 2008; Yearley, 2009; Victor, 2015; Corbera et al., 2016). Howard Newby (1993, quoted in Cohen et al., 1998: 341) calls it the 'IPCC fallacy'. This work exposing the fallacy focuses on the exclusion of the social sciences, however, with the value of the humanities in the context of climate change research rarely acknowledged or interrogated.

Mike Hulme and Martin Mahony (2010: 708) do attempt to bring humanities research into the conversation, stating that Hiramatsu, Mimura, and Sumi (2008) observe the areas of climate change research in which 'social sciences and humanities research had most to contribute', but humanities research is in fact not mentioned in that paper. More recently, anthropologists have begun to play a part in the IPCC as authors of reports, not just in ethnographic study of it (O'Reilly, 2015), although not extensively. Anthropologist Pamela D. McElwee (2020: n.p.), a lead author on the IPCC's Special Report on Climate Change and Land (2019), notes that 'there were more authors (3) specializing in the chemistry of atmospheric aerosols than those of us with expertise on the 7.5 billion people on the planet'. Echoing arguments we make in this book regarding storylistening, she adds that 'anthropologists' skill with using ethnography, local voices, and modes of storytelling, among other techniques, as a way to convey unique lived experiences can bring useful context into these reports'. Two moral philosophers were included as lead authors on the IPCC's Fifth Assessment Report (out of 800 lead authors) (Broome, 2014, 2020). Corbera et al. (2016: 94) note 'insignificant participation of scholars from the humanities' in the IPCC Working Group III report, noting that 'disciplinary biases [...] constrain how climate change is known and acted on, with only certain forms of knowledge and expertise authorized to construct a problem with global implications'.

According to our brief analysis conducted in late 2019, all four members of the IPCC Bureau (Chair and Co-Chairs) specialise in either the physical sciences or economics. Of the 46 members of the Executive Committee, only 5 members appeared to be either economists or to have clear interdisciplinary interests, the majority being scientists. Of the authors of the five chapters of the special report *Global warming of 1.5°C* (IPCC, 2018), 7% were social scientists, 0% were humanities academics.[19] This IPCC structure has helped give power to a particular type of story about climate change – that it is not a socio-political issue – to the exclusion in the public space of other types of story that would more fully address the complicated system of which the phenomena studied by the physical sciences constitute only a part. The thought-collective of the predominantly physical scientists who constitute the collective identity of the IPCC excludes the humanities as a set of academic disciplines, and renders irrelevant the knowledge they produce. It also makes it harder for academics in the humanities and sciences to engage with each other's emerging knowledge, engagement that might otherwise inform significant new directions of research. Bert Bolin (1994: 29), first Chairman of the IPCC (from 1988 to 1997), stated that 'only scientists can grasp the intricate interactions that take place in the complex system of the global environment'. As Naomi Oreskes and Erik M. Conway (2014: 2) speculate in *The Collapse of Western Civilization: A View From the Future*, such an exclusion in fact has the opposite effect: 'the archaic Western convention of studying the physical world in isolation from social systems' is a key factor in their imagining of Western civilisation's collapse. The history of epistemology is a history of shared dominant stories about which forms of inquiry and knowledge are legitimate and which are not, stories that constitute the collective identities of researchers and influence their research practices and findings.[20]

The stories cohering the collective identity of a global institution such as the IPCC, tasked with assessing how climate is changing and what appropriate responses might be, need to change. Mike Hulme's (2011: 177) work foregrounds the need for new types of stories, ones that attend to how 'nature and culture are deeply entangled' and that recognise that the knowledge produced by the humanities is essential to understanding that entanglement. The humanities are not of cognitive value merely as a means of science communication (Hulme, 2011: 178). A change in shared stories would lead to an expansion of the IPCC's collective identity to include more social scientists and humanities researchers. This identity expansion would be concomitant with the incorporation of forms of knowledge previously excluded, including local knowledges, Indigenous knowledges, and social knowledge stored and transmitted in stories (Ford et al., 2012, 2016; Hulme, 2011). In her reflections on working with the IPCC, McElwee (2020: n.p.) observes that the 'power of the knowledge itself is often less important than the power of the networks [associated with the production of reports] to promote new ideas'. New stories would necessarily mean more diverse networks with the power to promote consequently different new ideas.

The continued absence of explicit and thoughtful storylistening – whereby narrative evidence is considered by decision-makers alongside scientific and economic evidence – leaves public reasoning impoverished and liable to poorer or slower decision-making. Here we reiterate a point made throughout this book, one perhaps of particular relevance to climate change given the questions of truth and denial that so prominently revolve around it, at least in US discourse: to argue for the incorporation of narrative evidence into public reasoning is not to question the value of, or need for, scientific empiricism, nor is it to descend into post-truth. Rather, it is to recognise that there are forms of knowledge generated by a range of non-scientific disciplines (primarily located in the humanities) that are of value and relevance to decision-making. With its rigorous account of the functions of stories, storylistening, and narrative evidence, this book presents a framework for how such evidence can legitimately be taken into account without devaluing scientific evidence or sliding into the maelstrom of post-truth.

Consequences

The research explored and performative readings offered in this chapter make a case for the value to storylistening of attending to the role of stories in collective identity formation, and as transmitters of social knowledge. In this final section, we propose that storylistening can aid decision-makers by helping them to identify social groups in terms of narrative networks, leading to new understandings of motivations and actions and of the norms that inform them. We also consider the challenges – ethical and methodological – posed by the possibilities for new research in this area. We argue that for storylistening to be effective, decision-makers need to develop their own narrative literacy and understand the need for narrative expertise. We also make the case that public reasoning will be well served by the creation of greater narrative literacy within wider publics. Finally, we explain how storylistening can help decision-makers and academics become more aware of the operations of narrative lock-in, that is, how dominant narratives can cohere collective identities and limit the scope and quality of public reasoning.[21]

Narrative networks and identifying publics

Narrative networks are groups whose interactions and hence whose collective identities and behaviours are informed by storyimbibing, storytelling, storysharing, or storycreating. A narrative network may, therefore, be a public or may represent part of a policy system.[22] Through storysharing within narrative networks, stories function to create and cohere collective identities. Storylistening can inform public reasoning by providing new ways to delineate and gain insight into social groups by studying narrative networks. Evidence derived from exploration of narrative networks will sometimes enable wholly new categorisations of publics, rather than ones based on existing demarcations such as sex, age or wealth. Storylistening in this mode can also serve to illuminate publics who are otherwise under-represented in mainstream public reasoning because lack of numbers, or of power, disproportionately affects them. This is inverting the more common route of, for instance, seeking out the stories of previously identified minority or non-mainstream voices, and instead using storylistening to identify which voices might be relevant.

The implications of such storylistening for further practice and theory with respect to public reasoning need to be worked through in different disciplinary and practitioner contexts. For example, in the field of risk research (which in-cludes examination of perceptions of risk) publics' responses to particular types of, or presentations of, risks informs both the assessment of the risk and the policy responses likely to be considered, such as regulatory or institutional arrange-ments.[23] For those concerned with public policy studies, where terms such as networks, institutions, communities, actors, and systems are used in the context of multiple theorisations, the incorporation of storylistening will require adapta-tions specific to the frameworks being applied.[24]

As noted throughout this chapter, storylistening must be attentive to the dif-ferent benefits of attending to storycontent, and to story as social object, with a different emphasis required, and different research methods required and knowl-edge revealed, by each, in changing contexts. Storylistening should be informed by examination of the functioning, not just the form and content, of stories in order to determine which are (most) relevant and when. Storylistening to the sto-rycontent, the story as social object, and to the tellers and imbibers, can increase a decision-maker's insight into a system. This can help better to model it – as we explore further in the next chapter – since a model requires one to define the most important agents and relationships between them, an agent here being a centre of influence, through connectedness or power, which could be a group or an indi-vidual.[25] Storylistening to the shared stories of the group helps identify the players and their motivations, helps gain insight into their potential future behaviours, and hence informs (in anticipatory mode) the likely policy options.

Given the multiplicity of potentially relevant disciplinary approaches and terms, we here suggest a framework to use as a simplified starting point for future poten-tial applications of the concepts outlined in this chapter – see Figure 2.1. It is aimed primarily at policy practitioners and those experts working directly with them. The vertical axis distinguishes between highly networked groups and those that are com-posed of individuals who are storyimbibing more individually. The horizontal axis concerns the extent to which the storycontent in the network is related to the policy issue at hand and hence informs the potential behaviours of the network.[26]

		Content related to public reasoning?	
		No	Yes
Extent of network interactions	High	'Fans' (e.g. fan fiction networks involving co-creation of content)	'Actors and influencers' (e.g. scientists engaged in AI, or climate change campaigners)
	Low	'Audiences' (e.g. most readers of Jane Austen)	'Publics' (e.g. those opposed to nuclear power, when asked)

FIGURE 2.1 A starting point for creating evidence about narrative networks within a target system.

Our intent is that the terms 'Fans', 'Actors', 'Audiences', and 'Publics' might provide useful shorthands for initial assessments of the narrative evidence relating to identities and available in a particular context. For example, where a story was taken to matter, it might prompt questions about the extent to which the story's prevalence was likely significantly to inform relevant behaviours, or where a collective identity was taken to matter it might prompt questions about which stories were likely significantly to inform that identity, in turn directing further evidence-gathering.

Challenges and new research

The task of mapping stories to inform understanding of collective identities of relevance to public reasoning is ripe for new enquiry, combining both scholarly insights and framing, and the application of new and old technologies. New methods made available by developments in research technologies – in particular in relation to accessing and processing large datasets of stories – can enable identification of new narrative networks as well as enable mapping of existing networks for the first time, or in new ways.[27] Mapping narrative networks of course presents challenges, for instance, with regard to data access (much of the useful information is privately held), as well as with regard to the ethics of data gathering and the potential misuses of storytracking (for instance as a form of surveillance). If this kind of narrative evidence were to be produced from within academia, established ethical approval processes could act as a check and balance, and the digital humanities is already contending with the relationship between its methodologies and data access (Kaplan, 2015).

It is one of the aims of this book to provide a new shared framework for storylistening that would enable cross-fertilisation across disciplines and methodologies where that is useful, while recognising that disciplinary practices are deeply rooted and different, for fundamental and valuable reasons. Much literary criticism focuses on the relationship between the story and the individual reader. For the purposes of public reasoning, it is essential to bring these insights into conversation with the disciplinary fields that consider stories in a variety of different ways, such as anthropology, behavioural and political sciences, business, communication, and media studies, and a range of other social sciences. It is important for fields of research that engage with the cultures and communities of science and technology (including anthropology, ethnography, sociology, philosophy, history, geography, and STS) to take non-textual and textual stories seriously in a sustained and rigorous way. And it is crucial for literary studies to continue to expand its own methods to include sociological, empirical, and experimental research, and to attend to the relationship between stories and collectives. Echoing the Introduction, this is another both/and, rather than either/or point – these suggestions should be *in addition to*, not *as a replacement of*, existing disciplinary methodologies.

Another challenge is that of scale-up (note we discuss this same challenge but in a different context in Chapter 1). In other words, mapping a narrative network provides proof of concept, that is, that some people form a group whose collective identity is consistent with or informed by engagement with the story. But without greater insight into the transferable elements of the story and ways to identify them, it is hard to determine the numbers of people who are in the group who might have broadly similar identities but who do not have access to that particular telling of the story. We maintain that such difficulty should not deter further work given both emerging conceptual frameworks and the ability to observe storysharing in new ways.

Narrative literacy

Decision-makers as individuals are often already influenced by stories (knowingly or unknowingly), and as professionals or public figures often already take narrative evidence into account (effectively or ineffectively). Storylistening formalises and extends this practice, adding rigour to it, and aiming to improve the incorporation of narrative evidence into public reasoning by making it an explicit, effective, and informed activity. To do so, decision-makers need narrative literacy – an understanding of how stories function, and their effects at individual and collective levels. But they also need to recognise the importance of drawing on narrative expertise and to know when, how, and who to draw on. This will improve their own decision-making, and also enable them to recognise the limits of their competence. As with all evidence-informed public reasoning, the decision-maker must have a basic level of competence in the relevant area in order to know what evidence to seek out and to fully understand it when it is provided. A decision-maker typically knows they may need a lawyer or an accountant or a physicist, because they know they do not know what they need to know, but they know enough to know they probably need the expert or that they should consider designing an advisory system that incorporates the expertise. For storylistening to be effectively built into public reasoning, the same ought to be true in relation to stories, narrative evidence, and narrative experts.

Whereas formal systems can be important for defined policy questions, major developments in public reasoning also derive from the more distributed flow of ideas throughout a democracy. We have argued in this chapter that how individual storyimbibers engage with stories can determine, and be determined by, the collective identities of which they are a part, influencing their beliefs and their behaviours. Developing heightened and widespread narrative literacy among wider publics will enable individuals and collectives to be more in control of how they engage with stories, more aware of their effects, and less susceptible to some of stories' hazards, for instance those of misinformation and disinformation. The integration of storylistening into public reasoning ought therefore to be concomitant with the widespread development of narrative literacy among decision-makers and publics. Humanities academics, as well as humanities education across all educational levels, have a fundamental role to play here.

Narrative norms and narrative lock-in

In this chapter, we have pointed to the importance of storylistening as a way of identifying narrative networks and of gaining new forms of insight about publics, or about the systems in which particular publics have a significant stake. Storylistening can also aid in the identification of social norms, how they are, might be, or ought to be, changing, and how they are being challenged. Storylistening can aid decision-makers in determining when stories are, or are essential to, safeguarding knowledge – interestingly, Galafassi et al. (2018) indicate that one example of this is precisely in the area of science policy (see also Tengö et al., 2017) – and when stories (from a multitude of sources) might be essential to changing established social norms or generating the new knowledge required to meet societal challenges.

The normative role of stories can of course be exploited, for instance to persuade or manipulate, and stories remain deeply implicated in questions of social power and control. Societies are not homogeneous but heterogeneous. If stories transmit normative social information, they are in fact transmitting only the social norms of the storytellers who are in power. If storylistening is attending to such stories for social information, decision-makers must be aware of the stories they might not be hearing, which might represent very different social information. They must attend to stories that circulate in a range of collective identities – both the dominant and the marginalised – since these will reveal diverse, even conflicting, social values and norms, providing a more detailed picture of a society's coherence, or lack thereof. They must also be careful of assuming that the most dominant stories are the most accurate representations of societal knowledge. In particular with regard to mainstream cinema, for instance, its status as a high finance art means that risk is avoided by revisiting previously established storylines, meaning that the range of stories produced might be more a reflection of conservative business practices than of dominant societal or cultural norms (Polletta, 2006: 16; Dillon, [forthcoming b]). At the same time, a single story can contain knowledge that both reinforces dominant societal norms and challenges them. Storylistening must therefore take into account the multiple meanings of even dominant stories, in order to gain a full picture of societal positions on policy issues.

To meet these challenges, effective storylistening needs narrative experts who can identify and explain how dominant stories function, as well as identify and circumvent certain story gatekeeping structures, providing narrative evidence from stories that have been barred because of them.[28] Decision-makers involved must be cognisant of the role of different forms of power and influence in the context of who tells, shares, and listens to stories. Brian Wynne's (1996) work on the Cumbrian sheep farmers around the Sellafield nuclear site, for example, demonstrates how the social knowledge associated with a collective identity, in this case of a 'public' group of farmers, was considered inadmissible in the context of expert advice informing public decisions, leading to a poorer outcome.[29]

It is imperative for academics and decision-makers to be strongly self-aware of their own narrative lock-in, in terms of both the stories that define and delimit their own collective identities and the stories that they attend to or, in academia, teach and study. Such lock-in can restrict the value of humanities scholarship for public reasoning since it can lead to narrative evidence being distrusted as partial and/or such evidence simply failing to offer insight beyond stories and collectives of which decision-makers are already aware. Narrative lock-in needs to be challenged across academia to expand the members of the research collective in order to change the type and topics of research being conducted, and the forms of knowledge considered legitimate. Narrative experts need to be aware of their own narrative lock-ins and the boundaries created by the narrative networks in which they participate, so as to diversify the kind of research conducted and the stories attended to, and to avoid the narrative and cognitive deficits that result if this awareness is lacking. For policymakers, narrative lock-in raises similar challenges and opportunities to those created by consideration of framing. A frame is not the same as a story (as discussed in Chapter 1), but both have power at the individual and collective level to influence where the decision-maker directs their time, what evidence they seek, and who they seek it from.

Notes

1 In 1988, James M. McPherson (1988: 88-89) noted that 'this was comparable to at least three million today [...] the best seller of all time in proportion to population'.
2 A single text does, of course, operate powerfully in multiple ways and may have both negative and positive outcomes. *Uncle Tom's Cabin* has been strongly criticised for its misrepresentation of African Americans:

> Stowe's treatment of slavery hardly satisfied all in her own day, and "Uncle Tom" has since become a byword of racist complicity. Victorian abolitionists, white and black, sometimes hesitated to praise a book that urged a procolonization policy and apparently emphasized black docility [...]. In 1949 James Baldwin excoriated the novel as subversive of black dignity and worth.
>
> (Douglas, 1986: 11)

See Baldwin (1984: 13–23).
3 As is the case throughout this book, readers are encouraged to refer to the Glossary for clarification of terms, in this chapter for instance with regard to the differences between our usage of 'group', 'audience', and 'publics'.
4 We use these terms in alignment with Cassandra Phoenix and Andrew C. Sparkes (2009: 222) who define them thus: 'big story' refers to 'the grand narratives of ones life [sic]'; 'small stories [...] refer to stories told during interaction, generally within everyday settings, about very mundane things and everyday occurrences'.
5 Synthesising approaches to consideration of identity across a wide range of disciplines, the Foresight report on Future Identities discusses how a single individual has many identities including ethnic, religious, national, age, family, financial, social, and leisure ones:

> Understanding which of a person's identities are most relevant in a given situation depends on the context. Identities are, therefore, culturally contingent and highly contextual, but can also be strongly linked to behaviours, both positive (for example volunteering in a community) and negative (such as antisocial behaviour).
>
> (Government Office for Science, 2013: 3)

6 Polletta et al. (2011), Bamberg (2012), and Tilly (2002) place an emphasis only on the latter, but we maintain, and demonstrate in the performative readings in the next section, that storylistening to both story form and content *and* story as social object produces important narrative evidence.

7 For an introduction to the sociology of literature – which includes ethnographic approaches – see English (2010a), and the contents of the *New Literary History* special issue (English, 2010b) it introduces. A case for the incorporation of ethnographies of reading into anthropology is made by Rosen (2015).

8 Such questions are central to much thinking in sociology (including work previously cited in this section), which is often influenced by Michel Foucault's extended theories of power, knowledge, and discourse. See, for instance, Foucault (1970, 1972, 1979, 1980, 1984, 2000, 2007). Kenneth Plummer (2019) focuses on narrative and power in the context of '*tales of suffering in documented reality*' (xi) but excludes 'fiction' from his study of 'the sociological, ethical and political importance of storytelling and listening' (x).

9 We are not pursuing here the extent to which individual elite decision-makers or influencers are themselves influenced as individuals by the stories they have imbibed throughout their lives, or the extent to which they might choose to curate the public representation of their individual identity through the selection of stories. These are largely matters for biographers, modern historians, or political scientists.

10 Kasperson and Kasperson (1996: 96) discuss frameworks for considering the 'social amplification and attenuation' of perceptions of risk. Work on 'elite cueing' in the context of climate change proposes that elite individuals picking up a news story increases the extent to which the story may be promoted in the general media and hence imbibed by publics and so, it is inferred, influence behaviours (Carvalho and Burgess, 2005; Brulle et al., 2012).

11 See also the essays collected in Beckert and Bronk (2018: frontmatter) which show how 'in conditions of uncertainty, economic actors combine calculation with imaginaries and narratives to form fictional expectations that coordinate action and provide the confidence to act'; the essays demonstrate how narratives influence behaviour, and together they provide 'the rationale for a new form of narrative economics'.

12 To access a useful source of references to current material on these topics, see Geschke, Lorenz, and Holtz (2019).

13 Sarah Hunt (2014: 27) notes that to indicate the limits of Western theorisations of ontology and epistemology, 'a number of Indigenous scholars have pointed to stories, art, and metaphor as important transmitters of Indigenous knowledge. Stories and storytelling are widely acknowledged as culturally nuanced ways of knowing, produced within networks of relational meaning-making'. See, also, Tuhiwai-Smith (1999), Wilson (2008), Kovach (2009), Iseke (2013), and further references therein.

14 *The Swan Book* provides one such story – as a novel it is complicated and difficult, its form perhaps necessary in order for it to open up attention to Indigenous knowledge and the function of stories therein (in particular in relation to climate change), while at the same time not presuming to provide easy or direct access to such knowledge (Ravenscroft, 2012: 77).

15 See Mulgan (2020) for a discussion of contemporary narrative deficits in positive, or even utopian, Western social imaginings of the future.

16 We are grateful to Mike Hulme (2009: 356) for alerting us to this statement.

17 See also Geraci (2010: 54) for a summary of the result of informal, unpublished, survey work.

18 See Paul Roscoe (2016: 655) on the 'growing dissatisfaction with its [the IPCC's] heavily economic and econometric approach to analyzing the climate-relevant aspects of human thought and behavior' and an exploration of 'why the IPCC has been reluctant to model non-economic realms of culture'.

19 Out of 61 Drafting Authors for the 1.5 degree special report 'Summary for Poli-cymakers', there were 11 members who were not purely scientists, or who had in-terdisciplinary interests. Out of 269 authors over all five chapters of the 1.5 degree special report, there were 19 social scientists and no humanities academics. Note that attributions are inevitably subject to interpretation, and that the 269 authors include individuals who are counted more than once, because they appear as authors on more than one chapter. An in-depth analysis of authorship and author networks in relation to Working Group III's contribution to the IPCC Fifth Assessment Report does not include attention to the disciplines of the authors (Hughes and Paterson, 2017); nor does Venturini et al.'s (2020) network analysis of bridge individuals in the IPCC.

20 Smith and Stewart's (2017) work on social scientists' engagement with policy points to a further challenge, not specific to the social sciences, around the ways in which some of the current requirements for academic engagement with policy reinforce the notion of a small group of trusted or elite advisers and experts whose selection may not be wholly meritocratic but biased by the nature of the engagement required, which can require personal flexibility and career security.

21 Science policy experts may wish to note that we are not discussing the concept of the narrative policy framework (NPF) here. The NPF is one of several policy process frameworks discussed extensively in the science policy literature and to which Heik-kila and Cairney (2018) provide a recent overview. The implications of consideration of narrative networks operate across such frameworks.

22 As noted in the introduction to this chapter, definitions of our key terms can be found in the Glossary. Within more detailed consideration of policy systems there are a variety of terms such as actors, institutions, sub-systems, and agents. These are not included in the Glossary as they are not used explicitly in our arguments, but de-scribe a variety of groups, including those with expertise, influence, or power, which are defined and selected for the particular area of policy or public reasoning under consideration.

23 For very different approaches to this question, see, for example, Nick Pidgeon's (2020) personal account of the development of public engagement thinking within risk communication research and Science and Technology Studies (STS) over the last 25 years, and Heise (2008).

24 For an introductory discussion of descriptions of the policymaking environment, see, for example, Cairney (2020: 101-109). Alongside actors, institutions, and networks, Cairney here (and in Cairney and Weible, 2015) also discusses the definitions and roles of 'ideas' and of paradigms – yet another area to which storylistening might be relevant.

25 Note that Oliver and Faul's (2018) review of networks and network analysis points up the gaps in current theorising with respect to networks in evidence, policy, and practice.

26 The names are intended to make it easy to identify and to refer to quadrants. In prac-tice, for any given story or issue, there will be overlap. For example, whereas most readers (by number) of a Jane Austen novel are members of an audience, a smaller number would classify as fans.

27 Such mapping is of course highly relevant to the sharing of textual and non-textual stories on social media and other digital platforms (see, e.g., Alleyne, 2015).

28 See, for instance, Saha and van Lente (2020), the first detailed academic study of the effects of the UK publishing industry's structures and operations on writers of colour and their work.

29 For wider discussion, see Jasanoff (2006).

3
MODELLING

Introduction

In 1946, Jorge Luis Borges published a very short story which has become a not uncommon reference point in discussions of modelling and representation.[1] The story – entitled in English 'On Exactitude in Science' – is presented as an extract from a fictional travelogue by the equally fictitious Suárez Miranda, in which he recounts the development and deployment of map-making in one of the regions he visits:

> …In that Empire, the Art of Cartography attained such Perfection that the map of a single Province occupied the entirety of a City, and the map of the Empire, the entirety of a Province. In time, those Unconscionable Maps no longer satisfied, and the Cartographers Guilds struck a Map of the Empire whose size was that of the Empire, and which coincided point for point with it. The following Generations, who were not so fond of the Study of Cartography as their Forebears had been, saw that that vast Map was Useless, and not without some Pitilessness was it, that they delivered it up to the Inclemencies of Sun and Winters.
>
> *(Borges, 1999: 325)*

This satirical story is useful when discussing models because it exposes the mirror fallacy, that is, the mistaken idea that models are exact copies – mirror images – of that which they represent. Models are not direct representations of their target systems. If they were, as the citizens of Borges' imagined land discover, they would be of no use whatsoever. Models need to be close enough to that which they are representing to be of relevance to it, but different enough that they are more manageable and manipulable to investigation.[2] Our definition of a model,

DOI: 10.4324/9780367808426-5

which we will unpack and explain during the course of the chapter, is an idealised description or conception of a target system, which can help perform some cognitive function with respect to that system, yielding knowledge through surrogative reasoning.

The Government Office for Science report (2018) on 'Computational Modelling: Technological Futures' addresses both the *functions* of models and how models are *used*, understanding them as tools that are to some extent determined by their intended purpose: 'how one builds, checks and interprets a model depends on its purpose' (Government Office for Science, 2018: 17).[3] In addition, the results of a model need to be communicated, a stage which is 'the final and potentially most important part of the modelling process' (Government Office for Science, 2018: 33). The Government Office for Science report identifies many types of scientific models within the category of computational models alone: there are Excel spreadsheets, statistical models (also called probabilistic or stochastic), differential equations, formal logical statements, automata and algebraic models, system dynamics, agent-based models, and game theoretic models; there are ensembles of models, deterministic and non-deterministic models, dynamic and static models, discrete and continuous models, Markovian models, models of individuals, and models of populations.[4]

Similarly, philosophical discussions recognise the importance of models in a range of scientific domains, such as 'inflationary models in cosmology, general-circulation models of the global climate, the double-helix model of DNA, evolutionary models in biology, agent-based models in the social sciences, and general-equilibrium models of markets' (Frigg and Hartmann, 2020: n.p.). A whole range of model types have been categorised in the philosophical literature, including

> probing models, phenomenological models, computational models, developmental models, explanatory models, impoverished models, testing models, idealized models, theoretical models, scale models, heuristic models, caricature models, exploratory models, didactic models, fantasy models, minimal models, toy models, imaginary models, mathematical models, mechanistic models, substitute models, iconic models, formal models, analogue models, and instrumental models.
>
> *(Frigg and Hartmann, 2020: n.p.)*

Roman Frigg and Stephan Hartmann (2020) identify that models raise a whole host of questions that cut across philosophical sub-fields, including how models represent (semantics), what kind of thing they actually are (ontology), and how they enable learning and explanation (epistemology). While there is a wealth of work in these areas, there remains little philosophical consensus. Axel Gelfert (2016: vi) identifies the 'lively philosophical debate [...] which focuses on general questions concerning the nature of models and the possibility of model-based representation', but recognises the challenges of developing a unified philosophical theory when confronted with the diversity of actual models: 'How, one might wonder, can a philosophical account of scientific models aspire to any degree of unity or generality in the light of such variety?' (Gelfert, 2016: 3). Regarding the extensive literature on scientific representation, Roman Frigg and James Nguyen (2020a: v) observe that 'there is no stable terminology, no shared understanding of what the central problems are, and no agreement on what might count as an acceptable solution'.[5] As well as this divergence within the philosophical arguments, there also remains a gulf between abstract philosophical investigations of scientific models, the understanding and practice of the scientists building and using them, and those who use them to assist in decision-making.[6]

While in no way attempting to comprehensively bridge these gulfs, in this chapter we bring philosophical discussion of models and scientific representation into dialogue with our investigation of the functions of stories and their role in public reasoning, in particular with regard to our case studies. We do so in order to establish a rigorous philosophical basis for understanding stories as narrative models. This provides another way of understanding the cognitive value of stories, and therefore the role they can play in providing narrative evidence for public reasoning.

In the first section of the chapter, we explore how models can be understood as functional tools, and address the role of stories in model usage. We then present one account of scientific representation – the DEKI account – which we extend to an account of narrative representation in order to ground our proposal that stories can function as, or can contain, narrative models. We close the first section by addressing the cognitive value of models, and by explaining how stories can function as mimetic narrative models (already explored in the previous chapter in the context of narrative models of collective identity systems) and anticipatory narrative models (to which we attend at greater length in the following chapter as part of a wider analysis of the role of stories in anticipation), depending on the target system.

In the second part of this chapter, we explore this modelling function more broadly in relation to our case studies. We do so through the frame of considering what storylistening needs to do or know in order to be effectively informed by evidence from narrative models. It is necessary to identify the relevant story, identify its target system, and determine mimetic legitimacy. And we demonstrate why it is necessary to identify whether the story is functioning as a mimetic or an anticipatory narrative model. Finally, we consider how stories navigate between the global and the local, the general and the particular, another reason why they are important as complements to, not replacements of, scientific models. In the final section, as we have done in the previous chapters, we draw out the implications for both decision-makers and humanities academics of understanding stories as narrative models, including identifying the need for a pluralistic evidence base, synthesis, interdisciplinarity, and long-term relationships.

Function description and evidence

Models are structures created to indirectly represent parts of the world in which the model creator or user is interested. These parts of the world are called the model's target system. The model is a simpler, hypothetical, system that resembles in useful ways the more real-world system. Models are therefore easier to study and derive results from than the target system. Reasoning about the model and its results then enables inferences of cognitive value with regard to the target system. Chris Swoyer (1991) calls this 'surrogative reasoning'. That models have cognitive value in relation to the target system is a point at least on which most philosophical theories of scientific representation agree. But, as we have noted, there remains widespread philosophical disagreement regarding a range of other questions: what is the nature of a model? What is the relationship between a model and a target system? How does this enable surrogative reasoning? What cognitive functions do models serve? In this section, rather than provide a survey of the philosophical literature on scientific modelling, we foreground salient theories that are robust, persuasive, travel across the disciplinary and sectoral divides to which we are attending, and in relation to which discussion of stories already features. First, we address a functionalist approach to models that aligns itself most fully with their practical use and in which stories play a significant role. However, we note that even a functionalist approach still begs the question of how models represent. We therefore introduce Frigg and Nguyen's (2020a) DEKI account of scientific representation to answer that question. We explore how that account extends to artistic representation, and therefore provides a philosophical basis for understanding stories as narrative models. Finally, we address the cognitive value of models, which serves to usefully bring together the philosophical, scientific, and public reasoning perspectives.

Models as functional tools

As noted above, Gelfert (2016: 3) questions whether, in the face of the diversity of types of scientific models, it is reasonable to aspire to 'a unitary philosophical account of models'. Instead of attempting such a theory of what models *are*, one strategy instead is to propose that what all models have in common is their function, not their nature (Ducheyne, 2008; Contessa, 2010; Mahr, 2012).[7] Gelfert (2016: 4) breaks down this functional approach to models into the instantial view and the representational view. Here we will remain with the representational view, which can itself be divided into the informational and the pragmatic. The informational approach holds that a scientific representation contains information about the thing it represents, independent of the model user and the model's techniques. The pragmatic representational approach holds that a scientific representation provides information about the thing it represents as a result of the cognitive uses to which it is put by the model user. In emphasising the cognitive activities that the model facilitates (equivalent to what the Government Office for Science [2018] report describes as modelling functions), and the necessary role of the user, the pragmatic representational view aligns most closely with the understanding of models found in the scientific and policy contexts.

In the pragmatic representational view, a model is a 'tool of inquiry *for a model user*' (Gelfert, 2016: 20) and the proper subject of philosophical enquiry becomes the range of functions and uses to which a model can be put. This does then yield, in fact, a definition of what a model is, such as Uskali Mäki's (2009: 32) proposal that the necessary and sufficient conditions for an object M to count as a model are that an '[a]gent A uses object M as a representative of some target system R for purpose P, addressing audience E, prompting genuine issues of resemblance to arise; and applies commentary C to identify and align these components'. Understanding how models have cognitive value requires understanding how this configuration of user, model, and target system works, and this is where stories come in. Mäki proposes that 'commentary' is necessary; Gelfert (2016: 121) proposes that models require 'hermeneutical' work, analogous to that of reading a text, but Mary S. Morgan's remains the fullest account of the role of stories in model usage.

Morgan (2001: 361) proposes that 'stories form an integral part of models'.[8] Aligned with the functionalist view, Morgan (2001: 361) states that a full understanding of a model requires an understanding not just of its structure, but of 'how it works and what it can do', and she places an account of the relationship between stories and models as central to this understanding. Stories are necessary to set a model off – in the form of a narrative device such as a question – and to explain the model's results, thereby enabling those results to be applied to the target system. Models generate stories about the world producing narrative explanations in response to the narrative devices which prompt the modelling (usually phrased as 'what happens if…?' questions). One model can produce a suite of stories depending on the questions asked and the parameter values in the model. Narrative explanation (Morgan, 2001: 376) is therefore a cognitive function whereby stories do not just communicate the results of a model but serve as prompt and explanation of a model run, thereby functioning as part of the model system. Stories therefore play a fundamental role in model usage: 'our ability to relate our models to the world and use models to understand the world depends upon narrative devices' (Morgan 2001: 365). In Morgan's account, although she does not make the connection to Swoyer, surrogative reasoning from model to world takes place through stories and is therefore a form of narrative reasoning (see also Morgan, 2012). Stories are therefore essential to the cognitive value of scientific models.

The DEKI account of scientific representation

A pragmatic representational functionalist view of models still has to account in some way for how models usefully represent their target system: 'If we want to understand how models allow us to learn about the world, we have to come to understand how they represent' (Frigg and Nguyen, 2020a: x). A philosophical account of scientific representation therefore forms an essential but not comprehensive part of the wider understanding of how models function in science and in informing decision-making outlined here.[9]

Frigg and Nguyen (2020a) provide an assessment of existing views of scientific representation, including the similarity view, the structuralist view, the inferential view, the fiction view of models, and representation-as. On the basis of an assessment of the strengths and weaknesses of each view, Frigg and Nguyen (2020a; see also Frigg and Nguyen, 2016) present the DEKI account as providing the most rigorous theory for understanding how models represent. It is so called because of its key elements: denotation, exemplification, keying up, and imputation. A model *denotes* a target system. The model *exemplifies* certain properties of that system – this is a selective act determined by context. These properties are *imputed* to the target system by the model designer or the model user – that is, s/he stipulates that the properties exemplified in the model hold in the target system. But an exact correspondence is rarely proposed. A precise articulation of the relationship between the properties of the model and their imputed correlates in the target system is needed. In scientific representation, this precise articulation is a *key*, which explains exactly how the properties of the model relate to the target system.

The DEKI account of scientific representation provides what Gelfert (2016: 114) states is, at the very least, needed philosophically: 'an account of how it is that we can so easily move between the concrete world of representational media and the (real or fictitious) target systems that are being modeled'. But as such, DEKI can also offer an account of narrative representation, providing an explanation for how a story represents, and therefore providing grounds for our proposal that a story can be understood as, or as containing, a *narrative model*. We define a narrative model as an idealised description or conception of a target system, through narrative means, which can help perform some cognitive function with respect to that system, yielding knowledge through surrogative reasoning.

Stories as narrative models

There already exists a tradition within the history of philosophy, literature, and literary criticism that essentially understands stories as models. It is contained in the history of the idea of mimesis. In the Western tradition from Plato to the present, there is a tension between a 'world-reflecting' understanding of mimesis, and a 'world-creating' understanding of mimesis (Halliwell, 2002: 15). In the former the work of art reflects the real world; in the latter it creates a separate or alternative world (a heterocosm). As a result, the relationship between the story-world and the real-world is more complicated than one of direct reflection. In his history of mimesis, Stephen Halliwell (2002: 15, 23) proposes that the relationship is one of 'correspondence or equivalence' or of 'coherence or congruity'.

We have already swiftly dispelled the 'world-reflecting' understanding of models at the opening of this chapter, and we propose here to also reject it as a useful way of understanding stories as models. Shakespeare's Hamlet might be blamed for its persistence, with the claim that 'the purpose of playing' is 'to hold, as 'twere, the mirror up to nature, to show virtue her own feature, scorn her own image, and the very age and body of the time his form and pressure' (3.2.21–22). Hamlet's mirror metaphor obscures the precise nature of the relationship between story (model) and world (target system).[10] Adopting instead Aristotle's definition of mimesis, which Halliwell (2002) has shown is best translated not as 'representation', but as 'world-making' or 'modelling', the same question can be posed for stories as for scientific models – how does a narrative model represent the world?

Since the relationship is not one of direct reflection, Halliwell's proposed formulations for the nature of the relationship between story and world in the 'world-creating' understanding of mimesis are too loose. Deploying DEKI as an account not just of scientific but also of narrative representation offers a tighter formulation of the nature of the relationship between story and world or, as it can now be termed, between narrative model and target system. Frigg and Nguyen suggest as much in the final chapter of *Modelling Nature*, where they propose that DEKI could be extended to explain the workings of symbolic art, film, and literature. (They give example readings of Frans Pourbus the Younger's painting of Anne of Austria, the 1987 film *The Way Things Go* [dir. Fischli and Weiss], George Orwell's *Animal Farm*, and Voltaire's *Candide: or, Optimism*.) Frigg and Nguyen (2020a: 210) suggest that extending DEKI to art, film, and literature could provide a new account of 'the epistemic value of art'. It also places artistic and narrative representation as similar in kind, but not degree, to scientific representation, the primary differences being the greater license for reader identification of the target system in the former, and the greater flexibility of interpretation in relation to artistic or narrative representation.

Here we provide another worked example of how a story can be understood to represent, according to the DEKI account. Our example for this purpose is Jane Austen's novels. Austen's novels *denote* late eighteenth-century English society. They *exemplify* the landed gentry, marriage, and the economic and social prospects for women within that class at that time. The author and/or reader *imputes* that the nature of marriage in late eighteenth-century England possesses the properties explored in Austen's novels. The *key* to the relationship between the properties of the narrative model and their correlates in the target system is provided by expert narrative engagement, including textual attention to the story form (the materiality of its representation) as well as historical and biographical knowledge. Erich Auerbach's *Mimesis: The Representation of Reality in Western Literature* (1953) might be understood as just such a key. DEKI provides one account of how stories can be understood to represent – through denotation, exemplification, keying up, and imputation – and therefore provides grounds for understanding them as models in the wider context in which we outline the functioning of models in this chapter. Stories are narrative models that represent (parts of) a target system and which, through surrogative reasoning, enable inferences of cognitive value with regard to that system.

The cognitive value of models

Scientific and narrative models are epistemic tools (Boon and Knuuttila, 2008; Gelfert, 2016: 113–117; Currie and Sterelny, 2017: 20).[11] The philosophical literature is in agreement that models – and here we would include narrative models – can facilitate a wide variety of cognitive activities. Gelfert (2016: 4) gives examples including 'drawing of inferences about a target system, the derivation of predictions, or perhaps a deepening of the scientific understanding'. Frigg and Hartmann (2020) identify learning (about the model, and about the target system), explaining, and understanding. They also point to other cognitive functions proposed in the literature, including concept formation (Nersessian 1999, 2010), theory construction (Leplin, 1980; Hartmann, 1995), and the construction of other models and generation of new target systems (Peschard, 2011). The Government Office for Science (2018) report also focuses on the cognitive activities that models enable. Here then there is agreement between philosophical theories of modelling and models as understood in a practical and policy context.

The same caveats around the use of scientific models to inform public reasoning identified in the Government Office for Science (2018) report apply to narrative models: certain models are only useful in certain contexts; the same model is not (necessarily) useful in different contexts; the knowledge produced needs to be used carefully. Both narrative models and scientific models need to be deployed judiciously and in appropriate contexts but, in both cases, the existence of the models helps structure evidence and collective reasoning. The Government Office for Science (2018: 8) report notes that 'models can be powerful assistants in decision-making, they can also be dangerous and misleading if misused and misapplied' – this is equally true of scientific and narrative models. Both scientific and narrative models must be regularly reviewed in relation to changing real-world conditions. Just as decision-makers must ask questions of scientific models, such as 'what data are available and how robust are they? What assumptions are being made?' (Government Office for Science, 2018: 9), they must ask questions of narrative models regarding their robustness and relevance to decision-making. They must also be aware that both scientific and narrative models may provide insight into, but not the resolution of, uncertainty: 'Decision-makers should understand that models may not resolve uncertainty in difficult decisions but may illustrate how large it might be and how it might come about' (Government Office for Science, 2018: 9).

In the following section, in the context of our case studies, we explore what some of the questions asked of narrative models might be, including: which stories are relevant to the issue at hand? What target system does the story enable surrogative reasoning about? Is the narrative model functioning in mimetic or anticipatory mode? And, if the former, is the story mimetically legitimate? Asking, and answering such questions (with the help of narrative experts), can enable narrative models to be effectively and explicitly incorporated into a pluralistic evidence base to inform decision-making. Storylistening provides a framework and a language with which to do so in a rigorous way.[12] Narrative models are not a replacement for scientific models, but can complement those methods (Currie and Sterelny, 2017). Although they lack scientific precision, they are particularly useful in representing complexity and in modelling that which cannot (yet) be modelled scientifically.

Performative readings

Identifying the relevant story

Whether stories are mimetic or not, and the extent to which they enable surrogative reasoning, does not align with the traditional distinctions in literary studies between realist and non-realist textual stories. This distinction is heavily value-laden, with 'serious fiction' (regularly aligned with realism) often defined through an exclusion of popular or genre fiction (regularly aligned with non-realism). In the Introduction, we make clear that storylistening is ineffective if it only takes stories seriously that have previously been designated as such according to a priori criteria such as those of literary canon formation. Such criteria are not an effective way of identifying the stories of most relevance to decision-making issues. In the previous chapters, we have seen how this is the case, for instance, with regard to the need to incorporate stories from marginalised communities and perspectives into storylistening. Here, we explore how this is the case in relation to genre.

Take, for example, climate change stories. In 2005, Robert Macfarlane (n.p.) asked, 'where is the creative response to what Sir David King, the government's chief scientific adviser, has famously described as "the most severe problem faced by the world"?' While Macfarlane (2005: n.p.) notes the extensive documented literature around the nuclear issue, he bemoans the lack of a comparable 'intensity of literary engagement with climate change'. Macfarlane's lamentation is echoed just over a decade later in Amitav Ghosh's *The Great Derangement* (2016), although with a significant difference. While Macfarlane laments a universal artistic absence, Ghosh recognises that climate change has been engaged with in genre fiction, in particular science fiction. However, his focus remains on its absence from what he predominantly calls 'serious fiction'. He examines why so-called 'serious fiction' – by which he in fact means the realist novel – has been unable to engage with climate change, but does not make a case to take stories seriously that fall outside of that category. Although Ghosh (2016: 7, 24, 66) repeatedly acknowledges a problem with 'serious fiction''s exclusion of genre fiction, it is unfortunately an exclusion he maintains rather than undoes. It is therefore possible to revise more accurately two much quoted lines from the book (Ghosh, 2016: 135): when future generations look back upon the Great Derangement, they will certainly blame the leaders and politicians of this time for their failure to address the climate crisis. But they may well hold artists, writers, and critics of so-called 'serious fiction' equally culpable – for failing to take seriously the imagining of possibilities to be found in stories excluded from that definition, and for failing to draw attention to such stories. Listening to those stories should, indeed, have been part of the job of politicians and bureaucrats (irrespective of the state or capacity of the realist novel).

The major academic critical surveys of literature and climate change have appeared since Macfarlane and Ghosh's lamentations (Trexler, 2016; Goodbody and Johns-Putra, 2018; Johns-Putra, 2019a, 2019b). In such work, there has been a focus on establishing a new genre – cli-fi – which consists primarily of mainstream stories concerned with climate change. However, this new category still maintains a problematic distance from science fiction and has begun to be challenged or expanded (Milner and Burgmann, 2020; Sperling, 2020a).[13] Within the history of Western anglophone SF as a genre, changes in climate have been a long-standing concern, although it is not until the 1970s that human culpability was consistently considered as a cause. Late twentieth-century storylistening might usefully have attended to early anthropogenic climate change stories published as public consciousness of climate science and its findings began to rise, such as Frederik Pohl's 'The Snowmen' (1959), James Blish's 'We All Die Naked' (1969), Ursula Le Guin's *The Lathe of Heaven* (1971), and Arthur Herzog's *Heat* (1977).[14]

The importance of not disqualifying the relevance of narrative models to storylistening on the basis of non-relevant criteria is also evident in relation to economics, in particular as it intersects with climate change. Some of the most productive narrative models of ecology and consumption in a Japanese context, for instance, can be found in the films of director Hayao Miyazaki. His animated fantasy films such as *Princess Mononoke* (1997) and *Spirited Away* (2011) prompt helpful surrogative reasoning about the fast-growth period in the Japanese economy from the 1960s onwards, and related issues of consumption, waste, and the environment (Mayumi et al., 2005; Russell, 2017). The fantastic as a mode is also crucial to Lucy Prebble's play *Enron* (2009), written and performed in response to the Enron scandal and the 2008 financial crash. *Enron* deploys fantastic theatrical elements, such as the use of reptilian predatory figures to represent Enron's phantom companies, in order to model the almost unbelievable fictionality of Enron's operations and its creation of a 'virtual economy'. Prebble has explained in an interview that her intention 'was to show the theatricality of business and the illusions on which it thrives' (quoted in Billington, 2009: n.p.).[15]

Productively mimetic narrative models can therefore be found across media, across genres, and across the supposedly high/low culture divide. Storylistening must not determine in advance what stories are worth listening to, based on non-relevant criteria. Narrative experts with extensive knowledge of stories relevant to policy issues are of crucial importance here in aiding the identification of relevant stories. Experts – both scientific and narrative – are also essential to identifying or explaining the target system that such stories are modelling, and whether they are doing so legitimately or not.

Identifying the target system

The mimetic status of a story, in particular in terms of the legitimacy of its representation of the science in relation to contentious issues, can be the subject of severe public disagreement. For example, the film *The China Syndrome* (1979) depicts a near-accident at a nuclear power plant, the attempt to expose it by a whistle-blower and a journalist, and the machinations to cover it up to protect corporate interests.[16] Uncannily, it premiered 12 days before the Three Mile Island accident – the partial meltdown of reactor number 2 of Three Mile Island Nuclear Generating Station in Pennsylvania on 28 March 1979. The film enables surrogative reasoning about control of nuclear technology, its potential possibilities as an alternative source of energy (as well as its dangers), the trustworthiness of those in power (be that corporate or governmental), and the reasons for and nature of anti-nuclear sentiment. But response to the film was divided regarding the plausibility of its representation of the near-accident and the reaction to it: one expert interviewed by *The New York Times* for a piece on expert responses to the film noted that 'the nuclear critic would point to the film as a documentary on reactor safety while the industry would say it was totally unrealistic' (Burnham, 1979: D1). This was indeed the case, as the *Times* piece reports:

> John Taylor, an executive of Westinghouse, which makes reactors, calls the film 'an overall character assassination of an entire industry.' On the other hand, Daniel Ford a leading critic of nuclear power, says, 'The film highlights the central problem with the nuclear program — safety precautions are being compromised by an industry whose major concerns are power generation and money making.'
>
> *(Burnham, 1979: D1)*

In the context of climate change, Michael Crichton's *State of Fear* (2004) provoked a similar response. Following its publication, controversy raged over to what extent, and about what, it was mimetic. Scientists exposed its misrepresentation of climate science and its data. At the same time, experts from the social sciences and humanities have identified that the novel remains useful, and must be taken seriously, as a narrative model that enables surrogative reasoning about the politics of knowledge, facts, and truth (Trexler, 2016: 35–46; Radin, 2019).

In an example of partisan selective deployment of narrative evidence, Republican Senator James M. Inhofe (who had described global warming as 'the greatest hoax ever perpetrated on the American people' [quoted in Kluger, 2015: n.p.]) made *State of Fear* required reading for the members of the Senate Committee on Environment and Public Works, at a hearing of which Inhofe called Crichton to testify. But attention to the story by decision-makers was not informed by expert advice regarding the novel's mimetic illegitimacy with regard to the science; nor with regard to the surrogative reasoning it enables about its actual target system – namely the politics of truth that it in fact highly effectively models; nor was the novel attended to as part of a synthesis of narrative evidence on climate change. This is an example of the kind of mislistening that discourages public reasoning from taking stories seriously. But in fact it demonstrates the need to use narrative evidence properly within the framework of storylistening. The partisan selective deployment of scientific evidence is also a danger, but the solution there is not to dispense with scientific evidence altogether. Rather, it is to ensure that there are systems in place that ensure (as far as is possible) the robustness of both the evidence and its use in decision-making. The same applies to narrative evidence – storylistening provides the necessary framework to ensure that robustness. The incorporation of storylistening into public reasoning would therefore help to prevent or debunk the political deployment of partial, selective, or misinterpreted narrative evidence.

Returning to *The China Syndrome*, that story is also mimetically valuable in that it does not focus on a nuclear meltdown but uses a *near*-accident to model contemporary challenges and concerns. Twice – at the opening and the close of the film – it builds its tension through the immanent possibility of such an incident in the plot, but each moment resolves before disaster strikes. For this reason, *The China Syndrome* is different to other nuclear stories which model the actual (for example, John Hersey's *Hiroshima* [1946]), or potential (for example, *The War Game* [1962], discussed in more detail in Chapter 1) effects of nuclear disaster in the form of nuclear war. The dominance in the imagination of stories of experienced nuclear disasters and of imagined bigger disasters affects regulation and has meant that there is a very tight set of constraints, a 'zero tolerance' attitude towards risk, when it comes to nuclear policy (Weart, 2012). Gillian Tett (2010) and others have argued there should be a similar approach to the regulation and behaviours associated with major financial institutions. In principle, this would mean less 'growth', but might mean more stability.

With regard to storylistening, the effect of dominant stories demonstrates the power they have to influence public reasoning and decision-making, evidencing precisely why and how, according to Ursula K. Heise (2008: 137; emphasis added), '*it stands to reason* that such conceptualisations, which tend to be more available to the general public than scientific information, play an important role in the selection and evaluation of risks'.[17] The same case can be made with regard to AI, where dominant stories of intelligent machines, often mistakenly received as mimetically modelling the capabilities of the technologies themselves rather than their sociotechnical context, form the backdrop against which AI systems are developed, received, and regulated (Royal Society, 2018; Select Committee, 2018; Cave et al., 2020). In relation to AI stories, as with climate stories, it is important for storylistening to understand exactly what target system stories are modelling. That is, stories might be mimetic, but not about the thing one might actually think they are representing. Take, for example, *The Terminator* (1984) and the dominant image of the red-eyed killer robot that circulates as representative of it (already discussed briefly in the Prologue). Exposed here is the difference between an image from a story being taken out of the context of that story in order to metonymically represent a speculative fear – that of the rise of the machines, killer robots, and the extermination of humankind – versus proper attention to the mimetic qualities of the original story in order to understand the thought and reasoning it in fact enables.[18]

The original film can be understood as a mimetic narrative model of contemporary fears regarding the wider systems within which new technologies are developed and deployed. In that context, the relevance of the story is not to do with the embodied robot in any technological sense; instead, the story models the sociotechnical system in which current (much less sophisticated) technology is embedded. *The Terminator* models concerns in the target system about the power of those developing or controlling the technology. Those forces and that power are not represented in fact in the figure of the humanoid robot at all, but in Skynet – the conscious, artificial neural network-based group mind AGI system that is the real antagonist in the film, and which controls the Terminator machines. Skynet is not visually depicted in any of the original three films of the Terminator franchise. (The attempt to portray it on screen begins only with the critically panned *Terminator Salvation* [2009] and *Terminator Genisys* [2015].) In its lack of physical instantiation, Skynet represents fears of the unnamed and distributed structures of human corporate and other power, reflecting a contemporary sense that various publics do not have control over, or influence on, technology's use or consequences, and that the values and intents of those that do are not benign. Skynet is also productively mimetic not of the threat of AGI, but of the fact that disembodied AI systems – in the form, for instance, of automated decision-making or facial recognition technologies – pose much more of a threat to human life at present, than do humanoid robots of any description.[19] Storylistening would be usefully informed by paying attention to the productive interpretation of other dominant AI stories as mimetic of contemporary concerns, rather than as actual imaginings of future technologies.

To provide another AI-related example, storylistening to Isaac Asimov's work does seem to be taking place, for instance within current public reasoning around robotics and ethics, with recent resolutions, principles, and discussions referencing Asimov's laws of robotics (BBC, 2007; McCauley, 2007; Sawyer, 2007; European Parliament, 2017; Murgia, 2017; Marnell, 2018; UKRI, [n.d.]). But such attention might be made more sophisticated by storylistening which takes into account a fuller understanding of Asimov's stories. That is, not to reject them because they are fictional, nor to adopt them as blueprints, but to realise that the stories are helpful to robot ethics in that they demonstrate the way in which programming is not determinant of outcome, that laws produce unexpected consequences. Asimov's stories are all about how the laws go wrong, where their limits are, how they are circumvented, and how they lead to unanticipated outcomes. The stories demonstrate this in a range of entertaining but informative scenarios which might inform contemporary reasoning about the relationship between the rules contained in coding and algorithms, and questions of control, prediction, and value alignment. What Asimov exploited for literary plot purposes is what is now being contended with in reality – the unpredictability of programming in particular with regard to its real-world effects.

Public reasoning therefore needs to attend to stories in a carefully nuanced way (informed by narrative experts), and also attend to the most informative stories for the issue at hand. For instance, in addition to understanding Asimov's robot stories more fully, attention might helpfully be paid to Asimov's Foundation trilogy, in which he interrogates the limits and effects of using big data, and predictions based on it, in systems of governance. While for some contemporary thinkers Asimov's fictional science of social prediction – psychohistory – is a goal to be actualised (Ingham, 2018; Leetaru, 2011; Bodas-Sagi and Labeaga, 2016; Qiao et al., 2017; The GDELT Project, 2020), considering the limitations Asimov builds into his imagination of the concept – for instance, that it is effective only for large populations, only over extended periods of time, and that it requires secrecy, lack of transparency, and the restriction of freedoms – would be highly instructive to contemporary public reasoning regarding the benefits and risks of big data-based decision-making (Naqvi, 2018).

Identifying the modelling mode – mimesis or anticipation

One of the challenges when storylistening is to understand in what mode a narrative model is functioning, whether mimetic or anticipatory. The same story may be functioning in one or both modes, depending on what its target system is taken to be, and whether that target system is actual or hypothetical. Identifying the modelling mode informs what context of public reasoning the model would be best used in, for instance mimetic models might aid surrogative reasoning about nearer term or narrower areas of public reasoning in which more elements of the target system are fixed, while anticipatory models might be used in longer-term areas where more elements of the target system might vary, and over greater ranges.

Consider, for example, Kim Stanley Robinson's novel *Aurora* (2015). The novel follows the story of a group of human beings who inhabit a large, life-sustaining ship which, generations earlier, left Earth in search of a new planet to inhabit. The ship is operated and overseen by an artificial intelligence, and its inhabitants are required to manage its every resource in such a closed system with meticulous care. The novel's imagining of a sophisticated artificial general intelligence that has achieved consciousness and makes independent judgements regarding its role in governing the human population of the ship is hypothetical, and thus in this respect the novel would be functioning as an anticipatory narrative model. But if *Aurora*'s target system is taken to be planet Earth and its human inhabitants, the novel serves as a useful mimetic narrative model in relation to climate change, in particular possible adaptations strategies. If we mobilise here the DEKI account of representation presented in the first section of this chapter, we can see that *Aurora*'s target system of planet Earth and its human inhabitants is a large target system, but an important one given that climate change is a global issue, even as it has radically different local effects. *Aurora* exemplifies certain properties of that system. That is, the novel represents many properties of our present-day situation. These include unstable environmental effects with consequences for the planet's ability to sustain human (and other) life, the possibility that one mode of adaptation is the colonisation of other human habitable planets, and the challenge of governing resources and people in a closed system. The novel is affective and effective because the reader imputes that these properties exemplified in the model hold in the target system; that is, the novel has relevance to its readers – it enables them to engage in surrogative reasoning about contemporary circumstances – because the reader is convinced that its themes and concerns correlate with their reality. For the story to enable such reasoning, an articulation of the precise nature of that correlation is needed. This precise articulation, the key, is provided through the act of careful reading and interpretation which unlocks the knowledge relevant to the target system contained in the narrative model.

To offer some of that interpretation here, the novel prompts its readers to consider possible policy responses to climate change. One is the relocation option; the other is the resource management and collective governance option. The relocation option is imagined in detail, drawing attention to: the levels of scientific achievement that would be required to relocate a proportion of the human population to a potentially inhabitable planet – assuming humankind could be sure enough in advance that it really would be; the amount of time it would take to do so; and the potential consequences on arrival. When the ship and its inhabitants do arrive at Aurora, their joy at reaching land is short-lived when their immune systems are unable to cope with an Auroran virus. Many die of the virus; the others who have been down to the planet are murdered in an act of civil disobedience when their re-entry to the ship is opposed. Discovering that Aurora is uninhabitable, the population of the ship is divided over what action to take next. Roughly half want to stay and attempt to inhabit a neighbouring planet, the other half want to return to Earth. The population divides, and the story follows the group that return to Earth. The implication – although the reader never does find out for certain – is that those who stay will not survive. *Aurora* therefore provides a narrative model of the relocation option that enables reasoning about its viability as an option in the target system, contemporary Earth.

Aurora also prompts consideration of the other option – resource management and collective governance. It does so because the relocation ship serves in fact as a model of Earth – it has different zones, inhabited by different peoples, different traditions and practices, different flora and fauna, and local leadership structures. It is also an entirely closed system – all its energy, minerals, metals, food, waste, is contained within it. Meticulous management of its resources and communities is necessary in order for the ship to continue to sustain life. Both scientific and humanistic expertise is needed here, as well as collective governance which ensures all the ship's inhabitants are cognisant of the need to maintain their environment through their individual and collective actions. Such governance is not idealised – while its aim is to be as democratic as possible, the novel does not shy away from modelling the way in which the sustainability of their environment is also dependent on the restriction of some individual freedoms, for instance, the right to reproduce, or to travel in certain areas of the ship. In recreating the closed system of Earth on an imagined interplanetary relocation ship, *Aurora* models the resource and governance challenges and options that Earth currently faces, but which both individuals and collectives have been slow or resistant to confront, countenance, and address.[20]

Whether a story is functioning as a mimetic or as an anticipatory narrative model is also dependent on changing historical circumstances. Stories with target systems that were once considered merely speculative or hypothetical are turned to for their mimetic modelling when they are perceived to enable understanding of, or reasoning about, new contemporary events. Their mode and function therefore changes, in line with the fact that the same model may serve many purposes (Government Office for Science, 2018). While not one of our case studies, it is impossible to make this argument at the current time of writing without pointing to an example of this phenomenon in response to the COVID-19 pandemic. Sales of Albert Camus' *The Plague* ([1947] 2002) and Dean Koontz's *The Eyes of Darkness* (1981) rocketed in the first few months of 2020 (Flood, 2020), and the 2011 film *Contagion* had shot up to number 2 on the iTunes movie rental chart by 13 March 2020 (N. Sperling, 2020). While one reaction to this phenomenon is concern that the stories might be misleading or unhelpful, a more careful approach would be to note the fact that people turn to stories in order to understand contemporary events, and then to examine those stories, and the patterns and nature of their consumption, in order to understand how they might be informing – perhaps helping or hindering – people's behaviour, reasoning, and emotional states.[21]

Returning to an example from one of our case studies, Lonna M. Malmsheimer's (1986: 36) cultural study of how the public responded to the Three Mile Island accident focuses on 'how people in mass society create meanings essential to projection and, thus, to rational decision making'. Malmsheimer notes that people sought analogies in order to help them understand their current situation, and in doing so, they did not distinguish between stories and historical events:

> In imagination, people turned to analogs like *On the Beach, Fail Safe, Dr. Strangelove, Hiroshima Mon Amour,* and *Canticle for Liebowitz.* They thought of the Nevada tests, the Cuban Missile Crisis, and the Cold War (bomb shelters, air raid drills and the like). Most important of all, informants drew upon their understanding of the World War II bombings of Hiroshima and Nagasaki.
>
> *(38)*

Malmsheimer (1986: 38) is uncertain how to handle this lack of distinction between stories and historical events, repeatedly using inverted commas to describe the '"loose" thinking' and '"irrational" thinking' she associates with the turn to stories to inform individual decision-making, in particular at times of unprece-dented crisis. But storylistening provides a framework for taking such individual thinking seriously and, at a collective level, for understanding both the benefits and risks of stories functioning as mimetic narrative models.

The global and the local

Public reasoning is not just shaped by textual stories, but also by non-textual stories about experienced realities. Here, a fundamental challenge is that for most people their lived experience bears no relation to the stories told by the scientists. Taking the climate change case study as an illustration (Corner and Groves, 2014; Rapley and De Meyer, 2014; Corner and Clarke, 2017), the reasons for this gap include differences in temporality and differences in physical scale. In the first instance, the scientific stories of use to public rea-soning are invariably about the future, whereas people's lived experience is primarily about the present (and the recent past). In the second instance, the scientific stories are about the general, whereas lived experience is about the particular. For example, in terms of physical scale, scientists cannot yet tell easily defensible stories about the implications of climate change by specific household or by agricultural field, by minute, day, or month (see Shaw et al., 2009 as an illustration of the challenges). This challenge has long been exacer-bated by a strong scientific distinction between weather and climate, whereas in common public usage the terms weather and climate are much less clearly distinguished. This easily leads to a public presumption that a changing cli-mate should be simply linked to changes in weather. In scientific practice, the robustness of the attribution of specific weather events, such as floods or droughts, to climate change is improving but intrinsically very difficult. A changing climate does not necessarily 'cause' any specific weather event, and any single change in weather does not 'prove' the climate is changing.[22]

As we explore in the next section, the relationship between the general and the particular is an important space into which stories as narrative models step. Here, closer examination through the lens of extreme weather events further il-lustrates significant questions about the relationships between different scientific approaches, the scientific questions being asked, and their roles in public reason-ing. Climate change is global and differing degrees of probability are typically assigned to its trajectories, most of which have not happened and, in the case of the future, never will.[23] As might be expected with matters of such public signif-icance, the focus is on risk assessments and aimed at avoiding a 'Type 1 Error' – that is, the error of saying something is true when it isn't. But a complementary way of considering the factors determining a specific extreme weather event is the 'storyline' approach, 'which examines the role of the various factors con-tributing to the event as it unfolded, including the anomalous aspects of natural variability, and answers the question deterministically' (Shepherd, 2016: 28; see also, Trenberth et al., 2015; Lloyd and Shepherd, 2020). In discussion of the two approaches Elisabeth A. Lloyd and Naomi Oreskes (2018: 311) describe the storyline as being 'like an autopsy: it gives an account of the causes of the extreme event – the flood or storm – and can indicate whether climate change was one of these causes'. For the risk-based approach, the underlying question is: what is the probability of a certain class of weather events, given global climate change, relative to a world without? The latter may underestimate the risks, while the storyline approach carries the risk of 'Type II Errors' or false alarms, and of overstating the role of climate change. As we discuss later in this chapter, public reasoning requires a pluralistic evidence base and, as the example of extreme weather events begins to show, the plurality is not just of discipline but also of scientific approach and of the scientific questions being asked which, in turn, inform and are sometimes informed by, the public framing of the issue.

Shepherd et al.'s (2018) 'storyline' approach is a further example of the role of stories in scientific model usage (discussed in the first part of this chapter). Turning back again to stories as models, extreme events such as storms, floods, and droughts are a form of fast violence that, compared to more gradual change, is noticed, more likely to be remembered, and more likely – in real-world terms – to cause measurable damage or disruption with personal and shared consequences.[24] Fast violence is also more storyable. But, while there are many textual stories focusing on eco-apocalypse or extreme weather events (consider, for example, *The Day After Tomorrow* [2004]), different stories are now emerging that have mimetic value for their engagement with climate change outside of the lens of fast violence. The *Sunday Times* top ten bestseller *The Lost Man* (2018) by Jane Harper provides one such example, which links global climate system changes with a very local experience.[25] Such stories do not have to defend precisely why they concentrate on the areas they do, nor the point in time. They can also incorporate knowledge from different types of models – climate, ecological, socio-economic, familial – in one story that plausibly portrays the interaction between them and draws attention to their connections. Importantly, in *The Lost Man*, the climate is not the explicit focus of the story, but it is both the backdrop against which the action takes place and a key actor in the murder mystery plot.

The Lost Man is set in rural Australia in a region where the temperature is such that human beings cannot survive exposed in open spaces for any significant length of time.[26] All motor vehicles used to navigate the landscape are equipped with the supplies necessary for survival, and the vehicles themselves are crucial to sustaining life – their air conditioning systems are essential to creating temperature-regulated micro-environments. The plot of the novel revolves around the mysterious death of one man, spotted at the opening by a helicopter pilot, lying near an isolated headstone:

> From above, from a distance, the marks in the dust formed a tight circle. The circle was far from perfect, with a distorted edge that grew thick, then thin and broke completely in places. It also wasn't empty.

In the centre was a headstone, blasted smooth by a hundred-year assault from sand, wind and sun. The head-stone stood a meter tall and was still perfectly straight. [...]

The temperature the past few days had hit forty-five degrees at the afternoon peak. The exposed skin was sun-cracked. [...]

The headstone threw a small shadow. It was the only shade in sight and its blackness was slippery, swelling and shrinking as it ticked around like a sundial. The man had crawled, then dragged himself as it moved. He had squeezed into that shade, contorting his body into desperate shapes, kicking and scuffing the ground as fear and thirst took hold.

He had a brief respite as night fell, before the sun rose and the terrible rotation started again. It didn't last as long on the second day, as the sun moved higher in the sky. The man had tried though. He had chased the shade until he couldn't anymore.

(Harper, 2018: 1–4)

The man dies of exposure after a desperate struggle to take advantage of the small shade the headstone affords. In the mystery plot, the climate is not to blame explicitly for his death – he was in fact technically murdered by a member of his family who, wishing to bring his abusive behaviour to an end, drove his car away from his location so he had no escape or refuge from the sun. But the murder could not have happened without those climate conditions. The story does not model a major apocalyptic event, but models what 'normal' life is required to constitute to survive in such conditions. In doing so, its engagement with climate change might be less explicit than that of other stories, but in representing sustained high temperatures as a fact of life, it is more interesting mimetically as a model that enables surrogative reasoning about the societal effects of temperature rises. At the same time, by making the temperature a key actor in the murder mystery plot, the novel is also able still to create a suspenseful and entertaining story, without resorting to extremes of dystopia or apocalypse.

Generality, particularity, complementarity

Staying with the idea of the general and the particular, but turning to our economics case study, Morgan (2001) makes a strong case for the importance of stories in mediating between the generality of economic models and the specificity of cases in the target system that those models might be used to understand:

To the extent that we make use of general theoretical claims we have embodied in the structure of the model, then we make use of theoretical (scientific) explanation, but when we use the model to discuss specific cases, we also rely on the complementary explanatory power of narrative.

(Morgan, 2001: 378)

She gives numerous examples, including a simple one such as the theoretical explanation of the law of demand: when price is high, demand is low. She calls this 'a powerful, but thin, explanation, because it uses the power of the law, but explains nothing of the detail' (378). Narrative explanation can complement this theoretical explanation, for instance, by telling stories 'to explain the specifics of why coffee prices are high in 1976' (378). In Morgan's account, economic models are 'mixed instruments' (378) in which, as we have seen above, stories play an integral role in model usage, both in prompting specific runs of the model and in relating the results to the target system.

Stories therefore function as part of economic model usage, which combines theoretical and narrative modes of explanation. Morgan does not consider that stories might function as economic narrative models in their own right, independent of, but as a complement to, scientific models. Such an argument is proposed here. It is indicated (although not made in these terms) in Bruna Ingrao's (2001) exploration of what economists might learn from literature, in which she echoes both Morgan's insistence on the cognitive value of stories and Martha Nussbaum's criticism of the limited mode of rationality deployed in economic modelling which determines the type of data it incorporates.[27] It is found in Deirdre McCloskey's (2021: 3) *Bettering Humanomics*, in which she argues for 'an economic science that accepts (with commonsense repairs) the models and mathematics and statistics and experiments and the like of the orthodoxy circa 2021 but then adds the immense amount we can learn about human action in the economy from the myriad forms of human speech if we will but listen, really listen'.

An example of treating a textual story as a narrative economic model is found in Nussbaum's extended analysis of Charles Dickens' *Hard Times* (1854) in *Poetic Justice* (1995), in which she engages with the story as a mimetic narrative model that enables surrogative reasoning about the nature and effects of political economy. Her analysis is founded upon her proposal 'that economic science should be built on human data of the sort novels such as Dickens' reveal to the imagination, that economic science should seek a more complicated and philosophically adequate set of foundations' (Nussbaum, 1995: 11). She argues that

> there is every reason to think that an approach that includes the sort of insight [found] in literature permits a kind of modelling and measurement more predictively fruitful, and more capable of giving good guidance to policy, than the types otherwise available in economic science.
>
> *(11–12)*[28]

Nussbaum is not alone in being deeply critical of dominant modes of economics and the decision-making it informs. In her words,

> If economic policy-making does not acknowledge the complexities of the inner moral life of each human being, its strivings and perplexities, its

complicated emotions, its efforts at understanding and its terror, if it does not distinguish in its descriptions between a human life and a machine, then we should regard with suspicion its claim to govern a nation of human beings; and we should ask ourselves whether, having seen us as little different from inanimate objects, it might not be capable of treating us with a certain obtuseness.

(Nussbaum, 1995: 24)

At the same time, Nussbaum emphasises throughout *Poetic Justice* that stories are not a replacement for scientific techniques and models, but that they can complement these methods, and that to maintain this is not to undermine the importance or relevance of the former.

With regard to the relationships between narratives of science (including economics) and real-world target systems, economics has both parallels with and differences from climate science, in particular in relation to questions of generality, specificity, and complementarity. For the former, generalised statements about economic wealth are experienced as individual wealth only for some. Stories can engage with parts of the target system that scientific economic modelling cannot reach, such as the disparity between global and local accounts or experiences of wealth.[29] *Hard Times* remains a key mimetic story for its modelling in this respect, and with regard to the local effects of large-scale industrialisation, and the problematic effects of the dominance in governance of economic models of scientific rationality, to the exclusion of other forms of knowledge and reasoning. A classic example of the global-local discrepancy is found in young Sissy's account to Louisa of her 'lack of understanding' of political economy in her school lesson:

'And he said, Now, this schoolroom is a Nation. And in this nation, there are fifty millions of money. Isn't this a prosperous nation? Girl number twenty, isn't this a prosperous nation, and an't you in a thriving state?

'What did you say?' asked Louisa.

'Miss Louisa, I said I didn't know. I thought I couldn't know whether it was a prosperous nation or not, and whether I was in a thriving state or not, unless I knew who had got the money, and whether any of it was mine. But that had nothing to do with it. It was not in the figures at all,' said Sissy, wiping her eyes.

(Dickens, 2003: 60)

The parallels and differences between economics and climate change continue when considering complexity. In both, there is scope for modelling that represents formal complexity deriving from the model's mathematical expressions, and for informal complexity as an attribute of modelling systems in which direct causality is difficult to establish and which may exhibit emergent behaviours.[30] But there seems to be some difference in forms of engagement between stories and what cannot be known in the context of target systems considered to be created by humans, such as markets, than in the context of target systems that are, at least initially, based on observation of the natural world, such as the climate or weather. It is rare to hear climate modelling spoken of as 'a recurring task of twentieth-century aesthetic experimentation', as Nicky Marsh (2016: 16) speaks of representation of finance, or the weather spoken of as 'a form of fiction, a myth that was widely believed', as Katy Shaw (2015: x) speaks of the banking system before 2007. We note here, however, that the broadening of consideration of climate change better to incorporate economic and social effects means there may be value in considering the emerging similarities in the functioning of stories as narrative models, as the abstractions of economic change begin also to be embedded in them. Saci Lloyd's use of carbon as a currency in *The Carbon Diaries 2015* (2008), which foregrounds otherwise abstract notions of the carbon consequences of a transaction or action, may be performing a similar function to the use of time credits by Andrew Niccol in *In Time* (2011), to concretise the role of labour in wider economic systems. Of course, carbon is, in fact, a physical quantity, but its place in public reasoning is sometimes no less abstract than that of labour.

We reiterate that both scientific and narrative models are necessary, that the availability of a narrative model should not deter the development of a scientific one, and, likewise, that the availability of a scientific model should not deter the development of a narrative one. To borrow a term from climate science, public reasoning can be informed by evidence from *ensembles of models* of different types, including narrative models.

Consequences

We have explored in this chapter how stories can function as narrative models that enable surrogative reasoning about target systems, thereby producing narrative evidence that can valuably inform public reasoning. In the previous section, we focused on the considerations needed for storylistening to take narrative models into account and effectively incorporate narrative evidence from them into public reasoning. As a result, some of the arguments that in other chapters might have come in this final section have already been made: for instance, that, for storylistening to be effectively informed by narrative models, expert advice is needed in order to identify the relevant stories to the policy issue in question, identify the target systems that they are modelling, analyse their mimetic legitimacy, and perform the surrogative reasoning. These processes must happen while taking into account other issues of relevance to storylistening and public reasoning already outlined in previous chapters, including those of scale-up, narrative deficits, and expert knowledge (discussed in Chapter 1), and narrative literacy, narrative norms, and narrative lock-in (discussed in Chapter 2).

We have also emphasised the need to avoid deeming stories irrelevant to public reasoning based on non-relevant criteria. In this respect, an area of further research and of experimental practice might be to examine how to change the ways in which individuals or networks decide which stories are taken seriously by schools, by subsidised media, and by civic societies. This also means expanding practices in academia, in particular story selection for research and teaching, since these of course influence the world outside of academia.

In addition to the implications for storylistening of understanding stories as narrative models already considered above, in the remainder of this final section we discuss further aspects of the task of incorporating evidence from narrative models into public reasoning alongside other forms of evidence, particularly that from the scientific models which often play a very visible part in public reasoning. We therefore consider the need for a pluralistic evidence base, for synthesis, and for interdisciplinarity. We outline how the knowledge generated by using narrative models can reach and inform public reasoning, and delineate what more is needed − in the structures of public reasoning, and of academia − for storylistening to be embedded effectively and productively.

Pluralistic evidence base

An essential starting point is the recognition of the value to public reasoning of all rigorous forms of modelling as indirect representations of the target system, even while models display their entirely fictitious natures and their inevitably selective choices about which aspects of the target system matter most and which to ignore.[31] This is as true of a scientific model as it is of a critically examined story. To caricature, it is as easy to criticise some sciences for being unable to adequately take into account the complexities of human social behaviours, as it is to criticise some humanities for being deeply specific and unable to generalise beyond a particular, non-repeatable, circumstance. What is needed is a pluralistic evidence base that combines the strengths of different forms of modelling and knowledge-generation. As discussed above, all types of modelling can be more or less well done, and can be used or misused in the public sphere.

Juxtaposing narrative models next to scientific ones might also cause valuable debate about the evolution of the latter by raising questions about the relationships between the large-scale or abstract, and the more local or context-specific framings, as in the case of studies of extreme weather, for example (Lloyd and Oreskes, 2018; Shepherd and Sobel, 2020). This is not, here, about linking evidence-based modelling or systems-thinking to the individual's lived experience in order to draw attention to it, important as that may be of itself. Rather, it is about finding rigorous ways to create ensembles of models that can better inform public reasoning across all areas where climate change is relevant.[32] We argue here that some of the most long-standing and difficult issues, such as how to move to a circular economy, or how to shift buying and sourcing patterns to more sustainable bases, might effectively be explored through storylistening, to improve the selection of models deployed. We also note that the extremes and disruptions that scientific models sometimes struggle to model effectively often also provide narrative opportunities for suspense and surprise.

Across all areas of public reasoning, stories have hitherto played a significant but largely unacknowledged role when it comes to their influence on decision-making, rather than their part in communicating decisions (the latter has been rigorously attended to). The purpose of this book is to enable an open, transparent, and informed assessment of the benefits, and limitations, of incorporating narrative evidence into decision-making. Considering stories as narrative models of parts of the real world that matter for public reasoning about a policy issue has the effect of placing them at the heart of judgements about ways to use different forms of evidence. Formal advisory systems are frequently informed by scientific, often computational, models (economic, climatic, epidemiological, for example). In the earlier sections of this chapter, we have examined ways in which narrative models functioning in mimetic mode might extend this range of models available, enabling social, cultural, and political models to be brought into play in addition to whatever models the relevant fields would usually deploy.[33] Stories can function as part of a scientific model system and, when functioning as a narrative model themselves, can enable surrogative reasoning about things about which there is no scientific evidence, or provide an alternative approach to, and perspective on, things also known through scientific means.

Synthesis

Lessons learnt from areas where the interplay between research and public reasoning has been made explicit and studied, such as climate change or public health, show repeatedly that a key requirement for that evidence to have the greatest possible effect is a shift away from reporting individual studies, towards forms of synthesis (Whitty, 2015; Donnelly et al., 2018; Royal Society and the Academy of Medical Sciences, 2018; Stirling and Mitchell, 2018; Economic and Social Research Council, [n.d.]). Given the inevitable limits on their time and cognitive bandwidth, any decision-maker engaging with a complicated matter in a well-founded way needs to be able to draw on some overview of the best thinking in the relevant disciplines. The alternative, while desirable in terms of the visibility of an individual scientist's published paper, or an individual humanities academic's book, means that the public reasoning is more febrile: dependent on what publics or decision-makers have most recently seen or remember, and drawing insights only from the single discipline or perspective the publication in question represents.

Practices towards synthesis vary greatly across disciplines, and much of that difference reflects very different forms of enquiry and knowledge creation. However, overall, there is relatively little, and where it does happen in any sustained and visible way, as with the IPCC, or in the fields of medicine (Cochrane) and international development (Campbell), it requires considerable investment.[34] Researchers are inevitably drawn to, and rewarded for, creating new knowledge, and the generative effects of synthesis tend not to be included within that categorisation. The task of bringing together existing knowledge within a discipline, or knowledge across disciplines but relevant to a policy question, is neither fully recognised within most research structures, nor comprehensively within policy structures (where, to caricature, the political focus is often on immediate decision-making and delivery).

However, as the Royal Society and the Academy of Medical Sciences (2018) argue, it is both important and possible to synthesise evidence, and the practice should be more often rewarded. It may be different from original research, but it requires its own forms of rigour, creativity, and judgement. In some fields this is not only for the benefit of public reasoning but because, increasingly, synthesis within fields which used to be done by individuals at the start of their academic career takes so long that it significantly reduces the time available for fresh research.[35] The academies' report outlines four principles for good evidence synthesis, which can be applied to rapid work (such as the UK's Scientific Advisory Group in Emergencies [SAGE] mechanism) or to long-term work (such as through the IPCC). They are inclusivity – in the sense of bringing in to the process both the best experts and those for whom the evidence is intended; rigour – engaging the best experts from the most relevant fields, and ensuring scrutiny by their peers; transparency – describing the academic processes that create the knowledge, acknowledging uncertainty and controversy within fields, and declaring personal, political, and other interests; and accessibility – making sure that the language of the final product is aimed at the target audience and, wherever possible, made publicly available, even if it is aimed at a particular audience such as government or business. Storylistening would benefit from drawing on syntheses of narrative evidence, both within and across the humanities, undertaken according to these principles. At the same time, the incorporation of narrative evidence into the wider mechanisms of synthesis across all disciplines would strengthen those syntheses and the public reasoning they inform. This would mean storylistening becomes part of the work of national academies, of disciplinary societies, of policy institutes and think tanks, of business analysts, and of civil society groups.

Interdisciplinarity

Because any significant policy issue requires multiple forms of evidence, the challenges of creating structures that allow evidence, synthetic or other, to inform public reasoning are also challenges of working across academic disciplines.[36] There are deep structural reasons as to why this is difficult and, indeed, dangerous, for academics (British Academy, 2016). Despite the existence of research funding programmes and institutional initiatives to support interdisciplinary and multidisciplinary research, peer review, promotion, and status are all based primarily around disciplines whose shapes evolve very slowly compared to variations in the scope and nature of many areas of public reasoning, or to variations in public structures.

The challenges of working across disciplines are, in many ways, the same as those of working in public engagement. They require an academic to communicate and engage with language that is less accurate and nuanced than that they would use for the same purposes within their discipline. (It is worth noting that the only language two disciplines have in common is that of the public so, helpfully, the practice of working across disciplines and of public engagement reinforce each other.) But adopting a language that works outside their discipline can make the academic vulnerable to criticism from those at the core of the discipline. It requires a kind of bilingualism that not all are capable of, nor comfortable with. The argument here is not that everyone in a discipline should practice in this way, but that public reasoning would benefit from more academics being able to engage across disciplines, across sectors, and across other divides (for instance expert and public). The choice to do so should be valued and rewarded as an essential addition to traditional scholarly and disciplinary practices, not an undermining of them. Such engagement is essential as a performative proof of, rather than merely rhetorical defence of, the value of humanities disciplines, their methodologies, and the forms of knowledge they produce (Dillon 2018; Dillon, [forthcoming a]; see also 'Evolving the Humanities' in Chapter 4).

Long-term relationships

While synthesis can in principle be carried out very rapidly, the best synthesis and the best conditions for expert knowledge to inform public reasoning are also associated with strong relationships between academics and decision-makers and, for major policy areas, between academics in different disciplines too. To illustrate, Susan Owens' (2015) study of the work of the Royal Commission on Environmental Pollution (a study conducted over two decades) shows how a group of people from very different disciplinary backgrounds and sectors were able to develop sufficient common language and understanding over time to enable scientists both to provide work immediately relevant to policy and to anticipate future needs. Jonas Meckling and Bentley B. Allan's (2020) study of policy from 1990 to 2017 suggests that it took decades for the fields of climate science and economics to ask new questions, create new evidence, share, debate, and evolve mental models, and to bring many forms of evidence into conversation with each other, supporting the emerging presumption that actions to mitigate climate change might also be economically beneficial.

Embedding expertise in relationships has many benefits: it makes it more likely that the decision-maker will listen to the expert even if what the expert says is counter to the decision-maker's values and beliefs, or if it is likely to be unpopular with significant publics; it enables the development of new terms and shared understanding of common terms; and experts and decision-makers understand each other's rhythms and timescales better, and are able more effectively to act as allies across sectors. Alongside the benefits derived from long-term relationships, there are also potential risks and losses. The existence of such relationships risks blurring the roles of the expert and decision-maker, or creating the conditions in which they are publicly perceived as blurred (Cairney and Oliver, 2020). Experts, even when acting with integrity in the sense of providing only evidence that is fully consistent with the rigour of their discipline or practice, may be seen as less trustworthy because of their relationships with decision-makers. This can in fact risk making their evidence less influential in the wider context of public debate and scrutiny. In addition, in creating or gathering evidence that is relevant to the immediate interests of decision-makers – valuable in itself – academics may be doing so at the expense of following lines of enquiry that could be wholly disruptive but beneficial, or that might in the future meet needs as yet unanticipated by anyone. The arrangements for public reasoning therefore also need to include capacity for the creation and promotion of evidence that is, and is seen to be, separate from the structures of decision-making.

Notes

1 See, for example, Jeevanjee et al. (2017) and Frigg and Nguyen (2020b).
2 Models provide 'simplified versions of systems of interest which are easier to study and generate hypotheses about' (Jeevanjee et al., 2017: 1763); 'No model is complete: every model presents a view, usually termed an abstraction, of a more complex system' (Government Office for Science, 2018: 38).
3 Calder et al. (2018) provide a useful summary of the Government Office for Science (2018) report.
4 There may also be machine learning (ML) models, although there is disagreement about whether machine learning techniques constitute models since 'the algorithms offer no indication of causality, or the underlying mechanisms of the system, and so may not provide explanations' (Government Office for Science, 2018: 43). ML could be thought of as 'a form of "hypothesis-free modelling"', which differs from traditional computational and mathematical models which combine data with 'prior knowledge or hypotheses about the system being modelled' (Government Office for Science, 2018: 43). Where ML modelling is of particular use is where 'we have no prior knowledge or intuition about how a system works' (Government Office for Science, 2018: 43), for instance identifying a handwritten number.
5 Gelfert (2016) and Frigg and Nguyen (2020a) provide comprehensive literature reviews and critical assessments of the respective philosophical arguments, their strengths and weaknesses, which should be referred to for detailed disciplinary insight.
6 With a different focus, Gelfert (2016: vi) notes that the 'in-depth study of specific cases of scientific models and the abstract concern for model-based representation – have stood side by side with one another, without entering into a true dialogue' (Gelfert, 2016: vi). The division he addresses is between history of science case studies and philosophy of science investigation into modelling – a different division to the one we identify here.
7 Gelfert (2016: 25) notes that an alternative strategy is 'quietism', but that this is 'usually a position of last resort in philosophy'.
8 For earlier accounts of the relationship between stories and models in relation to which Morgan situates her work, but which her arguments supersede, see Gibbard and Varian (1978) and McCloskey (1990a, 1990b, 1994). See Morgan (2012: 217–255) for a reiteration of her arguments regarding stories and economic models.
9 For example, as Hilborn and Mangel (1997: xii) observe, once models have been constructed they need to be confronted with data and tested against the world:

> there can never be a "correct" model. There may be a "best" model, which is more consistent with the data than any of its competitors, or several models may be contenders because each is consistent in some way with the data and none clearly dominates the others.

10 Even if a model were a direct copy, mirrors reflect by reversing, so even a mirror image is not a direct representation, rendering the mirror metaphor doubly unhelpful. See Felski (2008: 77–79) for a brief engagement with the mirror metaphor in discussions of literature's cognitive value, as well as cartographic, window, and lamp metaphors.

11 One alternative categorisation is that between models that are deterministic and specific, and those that are probabilistic and general, and in which either category can be quantified in some way, or not. However, this alternative does not capture the purpose of the distinction between scientific and narrative model, which is intended to enable discussion of the differences between public reasoning based on evidence where the structure of the modelling, and of the analysis, is inherently plural and sparse in word-based detail, and that where the investment in the presentation is more specifically determined and typically richer in word-based detail.

12 The language and framework of storylistening would, for instance, help decision-makers, scientists, the media, and other publics understand how Health Secretary Matt Hancock's imbibing of the film *Contagion* (2011, dir. Steven Soderbergh) usefully influenced the UK's COVID-19 vaccine strategy (Bland, 2021; Grafton-Green, 2021; Manthorpe, 2021). Of course, not all stories about pandemics would be useful in this context, and of course decision-making ought not to be made on the basis of narrative evidence alone, but it appears that, as a mimetically legitimate narrative model, *Contagion* did contribute usefully to public reasoning in this context.

13 Note *The Encyclopedia of Science Fiction*'s (2018: n.p.) entry on cli-fi:

> coined by obvious analogy to Sci Fi and denoting speculative fiction about Climate Change [...]. The term appeared and became fashionable outside sf circles in the early twenty-first century; journalist Dan Bloom claims that he coined it in 2007, and Margaret Atwood was an early adopter. As with the use of Counterfactual in place of Alternate History, there tends to be an associated distancing from the perceived downmarket nature or Pulp roots of Genre SF, bringing this area of speculation within the comfort zone of Mainstream Writers of SF. Hence the symptomatic newspaper headline "Don't call it 'science fiction'. Cli-fi is literary fiction." (26 April 2013 Christian Science Monitor)

14 For an introduction to climate fictions and the literature on them, and for further critical reading suggestions, see Sperling (2020b).

15 Interestingly, stories had a role to play in the activities of Enron itself – Prebble notes that

> Andy Fastow, [...] chief finance officer, was a fan of fantasy films and sci-fi, and gave Enron's shadow companies names like Raptor and Talon – an idea I seized on, so that on-stage raptors become a scary, sinister way of showing how Fastow's ideas spun out of control.
>
> (quoted in Billington, 2009: n.p.)

16 For an extended reading of *The China Syndrome*, see Halden (2017).

17 As example, Heise points to Turney (1998) for an account of how Mary Shelley's *Frankenstein; or, The Modern Prometheus* (1818) affects current discourses on genetic engineering.

18 Heise (2008: 137) notes the important need to attend to such images: 'a culturally inflected study of risk perceptions stands to gain from closer attention to the way certain visual images come to function as shorthands for particular dangers and crises', such as, for instance, 'images of so-called charismatic megafauna – panda bears, mountain gorillas, or whales, for example – that synecdochically evoke the beauty and value of entire ecosystems [...] at risk'. Heise (2008: 137) also identifies an absence of storylistening and narrative scholarship from the humanities in the study of risk:

> while the work of Sheila Jasanoff, Brian Wynne, and other scholars has successfully established bridges between social studies of science and risk theory, the

interface between risk analysis and literary and cultural studies has so far been less frequently addressed. Risk theorists have paid relatively little attention to the role that particular metaphors, narrative patterns, or visual representations might play in the formation of risk judgments.

For a rare example of an attempt to use narrative to categorise different types of systemic risks associated with new technologies, with reference to characters from Greek mythology, see Klinke and Renn's (2001) account of work by the German Scientific Advisory Council for Global Environmental Change, in turn picked up in the UK Government Office for Science's *Blackett Review of High Impact Low Probability Risks* (2012).

19 Again, as with the argument made about confirmation bias and filter bubbles in the reading of Barbara Kingsolver's *Flight Behaviour* in Chapter 2, such criticism of contemporary AI technologies has been made elsewhere (O'Neil, 2017; Noble, 2018; R. Benjamin, 2019; Eubanks, 2019); narrative evidence complements this work, adding another form of knowledge and communication of such ideas to decision-makers.

20 Storylistening to *Aurora* might usefully be placed alongside planetary boundary arguments from other fields, for example Rockström et al. (2009) and Steffen et al. (2015).

21 See Dibdin (2020) on the mimetic legitimacy of *Contagion* (both scientific and social), of relevance to our brief discussion of its influence on Hancock above. In order to promote the film at the time of its cinema release in 2011, there was a special screening for people involved in science advice in epidemiology. At one point in the film, the audience broke into spontaneous applause in shared delight at seeing a clear and accurate representation of the R number included in a popular film.

22 There are many studies on the relationships between specific major weather events and global climate change. For an authoritative overview, see National Academy of Sciences (2016).

23 As Shepherd and Sobel note (2020: 8):

> Yet if the earth's climate history is just one of many equally possible histories, it is a deeply privileged one, scientifically and otherwise, in that it really did occur. No future climate trajectory is similarly privileged. Thus there is a fundamental disconnect in time between our knowledge of the climate's history, with all its specificity, richness of detail, and undeniable reality, and our knowledge of its future, about which even a perfect prediction can only be probabilistic even in principle. In some respects, this disconnect mirrors that between the global scale—at which we truly understand the human influence on climate—and the local scale, at which its impacts are felt.

See also Shepherd et al. (2018) and Lloyd and Shepherd (2020).

24 See Amos Tversky and Daniel Kahneman (1974: 1127) on the effect of availability bias on judgements about uncertainty: 'recent occurrences are likely to be relatively more available than earlier occurrences. It is a common experience that the subjective probability of traffic accidents rises temporarily when one sees a car overturned by the side of the road'. See also Government Office for Science (2014), Hulme (2009), and Harcourt et al. (2020).

25 Recent novels by Sarah Moss – for example *Ghost Wall* (2018) and *Summerwater* (2020) – provide further examples of stories in which climate change is not the explicit focus but in which, as Toby Lichtig (see 'Front Row', 2021) describes it, there's a 'hum of anxiety' about it in the background.

26 That time is of course now. Another factor determining whether a story is received as mimetic or anticipatory is the geographic (not temporal) location of the reader, and the extent of their knowledge of the target system, for instance here knowledge of the climate state of different regions on Earth.

27 Ingrao (2001: 12) details examples of occasions on which 'economists have literally built scientific explanation on parables, recounting short stories centred on fictional characters with the purpose of conveying meaning and insight'.

28 See also Gary Saul Morson and Morton Schapiro (2018: ix), who argue that 'infusing humanistic approaches and sensibilities into economics would make its models more realistic, its predictions more accurate, and its policies more effective and just'.

29 Katy Shaw (2015: 6) notes that 'fictional works may tell truths about economic realities, while apparently factual works on economic realities may be infiltrated by fiction, so that they offer covert myths or fantasies, or disguised dramas with heroes and villains'.

30 Complexity as a term is also sometimes (mis)used simply to indicate that it is very difficult to study the target system and, occasionally, as a reason not to try to model it at all.

31 All models, scientific and narrative, can be understood to be fictions. Peter Godfrey-Smith (2006: 734–735, 736) in fact develops his account of scientific models as 'imagined concrete things' out of an extended analogy between them and literary fiction, or what he calls 'ordinary fictions', although he does not draw the logical conclusion that if scientific models are like stories, stories might be usefully understood as narrative models.

32 For discussion of the relationship between types of model, the questions they are intended to answer, and their relationships with policy framings in the context of climate science, see Lloyd and Oreskes (2018).

33 In their review of guidance to social scientists, Marshall et al. (2017: 2) say that 'despite decades of evidence on the importance of incorporating knowledge of people and their lives into the policy design and implementation process, policy-makers generally find it difficult to do so'.

34 Cochrane is an international network providing information and evidence for healthcare workers, funders, and researchers to enhance decision-making (https:// www.cochrane.org/). Campbell's International Development Coordinating Group (IDCG) 'is a multidisciplinary network of researchers, policymakers and practitioners' that 'prepares, edits, updates and disseminates systematic reviews of high policy relevance with a dedicated focus on social and economic development interventions in low- and middle-income countries' (https://www.campbellcollaboration.org/contact/coordinating-groups/international-development.html).

35 Jones (2009) discusses what he calls 'the knowledge burden mechanism' in relation to innovation, and academic research.

36 Heather Douglas (2012: 156) notes that 'the more complex an explanatory account is, the greater the range of evidence that supports it needs to be for the account to appear simple or unifying, and thus to gain the requisite assurance'; see also SAPEA (2019). More broadly, Douglas (2012) assesses existing approaches to weighing complex sets of evidence (e.g. from multiple disciplines) and the criteria for doing so. See OECD (2020a) for further investigation of the challenges and benefits to public reasoning of interdisciplinary (or in the OECD's language, transdisciplinary) research.

4

ANTICIPATION

Introduction

In 1931, 11-year-old Frederick Pohl (2012) discovered the future, or at least what was to be his future. His eye was caught by the cover of an unusual magazine abandoned by visitors to his home, which seemed at first sight to feature a giant green gorilla tearing apart a city. On closer inspection, he discovered that the gorilla was in fact an alien, and that the magazine was full of stories of entertaining, if seemingly far-fetched, adventures – he had discovered science fiction. Pohl would go on to have a career of more than 75 years in science fiction writing, editing, and fandom, winning many of SF's most important prizes (the Hugo, Locus, and Nebula Awards as well as the John W. Campbell Memorial Award), receiving the Damon Knight Memorial Grand Master Award in 1993, and being inducted into the Science Fiction and Fantasy Hall of Fame in 1998.

Pohl was already an established science fiction writer and editor, with a sideline in lectures about the future at management meetings, when he encountered *The Futurist* magazine (the publication of the World Future Society (WFS) established in 1966) on its first publication in 1967. 'It was not SF', says Pohl (2012: n.p.). In contradistinction to the 'SF as trash' conviction of his parents and peers when he discovered science fiction, *The Futurist* was respectable, covering the serious efforts of research establishments to predict the future, and explaining the techniques developed in order to do so. At the time, Pohl recalls, these included scenario writing (developed by Herman Kahn) and the Delphi technique (developed at the RAND corporation). Pohl was immediately intrigued and flew to Los Angeles to meet people who had worked on Delphi. Captivated by the technique, Pohl (2012: n.p.) added it to his lecture presentations and 'became a sort of honorary futurologist'. While SF and futurology were held distinct by their reputations and the seriousness with which they were imbued, Pohl (2012: n.p.)

DOI: 10.4324/9780367808426-6

notes that 'even the most respectable of them [futurologists] had to admit that science fiction writers were a kind of cousin to themselves'. In fact, SF writers were welcomed into the WFS: the final session of the WFS's first annual conference was devoted to Arthur C. Clarke and Pohl himself; both writers frequently took part in WFS studies.[1] More widely, from 1970 to 1990 the journal *Futures* had a regular feature in which Dennis Livingston reviewed new science fiction releases for both their literary and futurological merits (until 1979 under the title 'Science Fiction Survey', then under the title 'Science Fiction') and, dating earlier than Pohl's participation, Michael Burnam-Fink (2015: 51) notes that 'some of the earliest scenario exercises in the 1960s brought science fiction authors into dialog with defense planners, businessmen, and sociologists to seriously attempt to predict the future'. 'This friendly symbiosis went on for years', reflects Pohl (2012: n.p.) regarding his own involvement: 'For ten of them, in fact – but by Year Ten, troubles began to arise'.

The symbiosis between SF and futurology started to fissure at this ten year mark in part because by then the 'future' of some of the earlier predictions had arrived, and they could be tested against reality.[2] The results were mixed. Pohl explains,

> As futurology study groups pondered over these hits and misses, they noticed a clean split. Predictions about space missions, weapons, aircraft and giant engineering projects were pretty often reliable. About cures for cancer, sociological stresses and other matters biological or psychological, the predictions were all over the place, and very rarely exact. In other words, the futurologists were great at predicting devices and events for which the plans had already been laid, funds had been budgeted, and construction had sometimes already begun. At other things, not so much.
>
> *(Pohl, 2012: n.p.)*

This did not of course mark the end of futurology (Pohl points to French Futures Studies' theoretical development of the idea of *futuribles* [possible futures]), nor of course of science fiction.[3] Pohl continued to maintain his SF practices, and his belief in the value of the vast databank of SF stories:

> And well, as a matter of fact, I developed a kind of little idea of my own. It spins off the RAND Delphi – a sort of Delphi in reverse – and I call it Phi-Delphi. The Parisians put a lot of effort into generating floatable ideas – "futuribles". My plan saves a lot of that work by tapping a vast natural resource of ready-made futuribles: I'm talking about science fiction stories.
>
> *(Pohl, 2012: n.p.)*

As Pohl's decade was playing itself out, modern Futures Studies (FS) was developing, and its understanding of itself, and of the future, was changing. The significance of FS was not to predict the future – 'There is no knowledge of the future' (Bell, 1996: 14; see Riner, 1987) – but to anticipate possible, probable, and preferable futures in order to make better decisions in the present.[4] In the foreword to one of the foundational works of the field – Fred Polak's *The Image of the Future* (1973) – Kenneth Boulding (1973: v) identifies this essential relationship between the future and decision-making: 'The human condition can almost be summed up in the observation that, whereas all experiences are of the past, all decisions are about the future. The image of the future, therefore, is the key to all choice-oriented behavior'.[5] In his history of the field, Wendell Bell (1993) notes that one of the contributions to the development of FS was parallel progress in the policy sciences, with leading American political scientist and communications theorist Harold D. Lasswell being one of the first academics to recognise that policymaking and decision-making depend upon anticipations of the future.[6]

The 1970s also saw the publication of a foundational theoretical work in science fiction studies: Darko Suvin's *Metamorphoses of Science Fiction: On the Poetics and History of a Literary Genre* (1979). Paralleling the move away from prediction in modern FS, for Suvin the value of SF lies not in its predictive value but in its socio-political function: SF is 'a diagnosis, a warning, a call to understanding and action, and – most important – a mapping of possible alternatives' (Suvin 1979: 12).[7] For Suvin, SF imagines futures that prompt its readers into better decisions and actions in the present.

Neither FS nor SF is about predicting the future, but about anticipating a range of futures which can enable better decision-making. In Chapter 3, in order to understand the function of stories as narrative models, it was necessary to dispense with too simplistic an idea of stories as a 'reflection' of reality. In order to understand the function of stories in relation to anticipation, it is necessary to dispense with this too simplistic idea of stories as 'predicting' the future. For the most informed storylistening, it is also necessary to be open to listening to all relevant stories, moving beyond existing definitions of value or worth based on non-relevant criteria, and sometimes simply on genre prejudice, for instance against science fiction. (We reiterate here a point made both in the Introduction and in Chapter 3.)

We will return to the nature of the relationship between FS and SF below, as part of the first section's wider mapping of the intersections between stories and anticipation.[8] In that section, we will consider the methods and techniques developed in FS as a response to the need to anticipate the future, and the place and role of stories within and across them. We also make the case for the value to storylistening of narrative futures methods, including attention to anticipatory narrative models. Informed by narrative evidence drawn from stories' role across futures techniques, as well as from stories themselves as anticipatory narrative models, storylistening can contribute to the work of anticipating the future, in order to enhance the quality of current decisions by bridging from scenarios to action. In the second section of the chapter, we explore the relationship between stories, anticipation, and decision-making in relation to our case studies. We consider how stories can offer mimetic narrative models of FS, and suggest the need to move from thinking about individual stories as predictive to considering the usefulness of collective narrative anticipation. We propose that stories function as data, and highlight the need to decolonise the future in FS. Finally, we note the need for both stories about end-states (that prompt immediate action), and stories about pathways, risk, and adaptation (that prompt long-term planning). In the final section, we address how the structures and definition of public reasoning and the humanities can evolve to enable and incorporate storylistening, and we introduce the concept of narrative responsibility.

Function description and evidence

Stories and scenarios

Using Bishop et al.'s (2007) map of current futures techniques, we can demonstrate how and where stories feature on this map, and what stories-futures intersecting terrain the map does not cover.[9] In the first instance, stories feature in relation to scenarios. Scenarios are the paradigmatic output of FS. They describe a possible future state and/or the pathway to that state (Bishop et al., 2007: 8).[10] Scenarios are either stories themselves or require a story to frame and use them, for instance, where the scenario takes a quantitative form (such as a trend database or a strategic plan) or is an expansive account of a wide range of elements. In the first category, scenarios are 'stories or future histories' (Bell, 1996: 18) which present what could happen or might happen given a certain set of circumstances. They are the product of both qualitative and quantitative futures methods: 'Scenarios contain the stories of these multiple futures, from the expected to the wildcard, in forms that are analytically coherent and imaginatively engaging' (Bishop et al., 2007: 5). Stories (in the form of the produced scenario) are therefore an integral component of futures practice. Insights from narratology (Miller, 2007; Raven and Elahi, 2015; Liveley, 2017), and from the study of SF storytelling practices (Burnam-Fink, 2015), can enhance the creation of narrative scenarios. Narrative literacy and storylistening can enhance an understanding of how to bridge from the scenario to decision-making. Narrative literacy and storylistening are therefore an essential component of what Riel Miller calls futures literacy:

> a Futures Literate policymaker is able to identify and distinguish different forms of the "potential of the present" to use the future in the same way that an accomplished reader can distinguish and invent (co-create) many meanings from a given text.
>
> *(Miller, 2011: 27)*

Bishop et al. (2007: 6) note that a narrow definition of scenario would more properly restrict it to defining alternative histories in story form, but that a wider understanding of scenario – as denoting alternative futures no matter in what form – prevails in practice. Stories play a role in this wider definition, framing quantitative scenarios and facilitating their usage. Marta Pérez-Soba and Rob Maas (2015: 59) point to the importance of stories in the fourth phase of the policy formulation process – scenario description: 'here, each scenario comes to life, that is, it is described in a credible and salient way, for example, using figures, images, narratives and metaphors'. In this context, Miller (2006: 7) maintains that all futures activity is a form of storytelling since,

> any statement about the future necessarily assumes a context, a set of as-sumptions, that even if not explicit nevertheless exist and provide the setting within which the observation, including a snapshot image of the future from a Delphi or whatever forecasting/foresight tool, is made mean-ingful/intelligible as "a story about x".

This claim is not dissimilar to the role of stories in model usage as defined by Morgan (see Chapter 3). Stories are therefore essential to FS with regard to the products of futures techniques: they function as narrative scenarios, as the 'what if' prompt for quantitative methods, and as the framing and use-facilitation of non-narrative scenarios.

Stories as Futures Studies techniques

Stories also function as futures techniques in their own right. Bishop et al. (2007: 7) define a technique or method (again, they note that strictly these terms name different things, but that in practice they are used synonymously) as 'the sys-tematic means that a professional uses to generate a product'. They provide an extensive overview of different futures techniques and their attributes, including comparison of their starting points, processes, and products, as well as advantages and disadvantages of each. Storytelling, storyimbibing, and/or story analysis al-ready define the processes of some known techniques. For example, in incasting, the story functions as a prompt for speculation on impacts of alternative futures:

> incasting is a simple matter of having participants divide into small groups and read a paragraph that describes a rather extreme version of an alternative future. [...] They are then asked to describe the impacts on a series of do-mains, such as law, politics, family life, entertainment, education, work, etc.
> *(Bishop et al., 2007: 12)*

Comparably, in backcasting, a future state is envisioned and then a story is cre-ated about the events that would lead from the present to that future state – this is in fact a technique used in creative writing pedagogy. Future mapping also uses predefined narrative end-state scenarios, but also includes ideas for events leading up to those states. Participant teams then select and arrange the events, in essence creating a 'full story' but with the assistance of having the story pathway parts provided, although with their ordering and connection to be determined: 'the technique offers participants a deeper understanding of how events can interact to create different futures, and how different end-states can occur from the same set of events' (Bishop et al., 2007: 14).

We propose that these known techniques should be classified as *narrative futures methods*, a category which should also include Science Fiction Prototyping (SFP), collaborative storytelling games, and surrogative reasoning from existing stories (primarily, but not exclusively, SF stories) functioning as anticipatory narrative models. Narrative futures methods can be used to anticipate under conditions of uncertainty and contingency, can help avoid, or raise critical self-consciousness about, colonial attitudes towards the future, and can extend futures practice beyond experts, leading to enhanced civic engagement and deliberative democracy.

Science fiction prototyping (SFP) is an 'emerging foresight technique' (Graham et al., 2014: 2) inspired by 'hard' science fiction. SF prototypes are defined by Brian David Johnson (2011: v) as 'short stories, movies and comics that are created based on real science and technology'.[11] They have a twofold function: one, commercial and instrumentalist, to help develop new products and technologies; the other, social and ethical, using science fiction to explore the use and implications of those future technologies. SFP develops out of a keen respect for science fiction as a genre, but also distances itself from it on the grounds of intention, context, and purposiveness (Graham et al., 2014: 2; Schwarz et al., 2014: 6): 'what makes SF prototypes different is that they use these fictional creations explicitly as a step or input in the development process' (Johnson, 2011: v). Unlike most genre science fiction, the creative process in SFP is often collaborative, rendering it a useful futures method for engaging a wide variety of participants – for instance business professionals, engineers, scientists, and wider civic engagement, including, for example, children and young adults (Graham and Mehmood, 2014: 91). As such, SFP can play a role in widening civic participation with regard to the development of, and reflection on the societal implications of, new technologies or scientific developments. Extending SFP, Merrie et al. (2018) use SFP to explore radical ocean futures-scenarios. They identify the limits of scientific scenarios in dealing with complex socio-ecological futures due to the difficulty such scenarios have in accounting for non-linear change and 'the co-evolutionary dynamics of socio-ecological systems' (Merrie et al., 2018: 22). They deploy SFP in order to circumvent these limitations and develop radical ocean futures that extrapolate not just from existing science and technology but also from existing economic, social, and environmental trends (Merrie et al., 2018: 22).

Storylistening can be informed by narrative evidence drawn from SFP exercises, widening the sources of evidence included in decision-making (both the form of evidence and the source of people generating it), contributing to a more deliberative democracy. Collaborative storytelling games can function similarly, with the same benefits, in particular offering an important avenue to further include non-experts in futures work (Avin, 2019). Collaborative storytelling games allow for structured participation that both renders the process of futures-making more accessible for less futures literate audiences, and encourages participants to think 'divergently' about possible implications of future technology (Candy, 2018). For example, the structure of Stuart Candy and Jeff Watson's game 'The Thing from the Future' (Candy, 2018) ensures that desired and undesired futures (preferable and non-preferable) do not merely manifest as dystopian and utopian extremes, but emerge through detailed micro-narrative imaginings of possible futures via the description of hypothetical future objects. Olivia Belton and Sarah Dillon (2021) developed and trialled a collaborative storytelling futures game inspired by the tabletop role-playing game *Microscope* (Robbins, 2020) in order to assess non-expert anticipatory assumptions (AA) with regard to autonomous flight.[12] While Belton and Dillon's initial research stops at what Miller (2007) defines as 'awareness' (level 1 of futures literacy (FL) – the revelation of existing AA), there is potential to develop the method in order to move participants on to further FL levels and more rigorous imaginings. The fact that games are already used as futures tools in public reasoning offers the opportunity to incorporate more storytelling games into such practices.[13]

Science fiction and Futures Studies

While SFP and collaborative storytelling games are therefore emerging as futures methods, the continued exclusion of engagement with extant science fiction stories demands to be revisited.[14] Many works of SF are written with similar intent and purpose to SFPs and collaborative storytelling games, and have a wide effect on public views, actions, and decision-making. Given they are produced by creative professionals, they are also usually significantly more sophisticated and rewarding in their rigorous imagining than lay products. While not (necessarily) collaborative in creation, critical engagement with such stories can indeed be collaborative, and can take place within a futures context.[15] Moreover, literary theory has long dispensed with authorial intention as an arbiter of the meaning and effects of a story, so critical engagement with SF stories irrespective of author intention can yield rich insights into possible and preferable futures.

A reconsideration of the relationship of FS and SF is beginning to happen.[16] Jan Oliver Schwarz et al. (2014) engage with an SF prototype found within the pages of a novel and encourage this practice alongside (but not as a replacement for) other futures practices, although they do not treat the novel as a whole as potentially useful within a futures context. Schwarz (2015: 511) does make this move, arguing that 'the vast body of cultural products, and not only the science fiction genre, represents a large, interesting and mostly untapped source for developing foresight'.[17] Gary Graham and Rashid Mehmood (2014: 91) end their reflections on an SF prototype with the question: 'Does one need to make science fiction prototypes to find them useful, or is consumption of the right kind of science-fiction adequate for foresight?'. Michael Burnam-Fink (2015: 50) suggests that SF should be considered in its own right 'as a mode of thought about the future'. However, he does not demonstrate how futures practitioners and decision-makers might engage with existing SF works, instead pursuing the 'science fiction as informing other methods' approach. Ashley Winstead (2017: 229) puts Margaret Atwood's *Oryx and Crake* (2003) into dialogue with nonliterary forecasting methods, in order to demonstrate 'the indispensability of fiction – specifically speculative fiction – to the production of knowledge about the future across economic, political, and artistic fields in the twenty-first century'.

Clark A. Miller and Ira Bennett (2008) propose both SF storytelling and SF storylistening (although they do not use the term) as viable futures methods in particular in the context of widening participation in imagining technological futures. They identify that 'the challenge […] is to find ways to bring the construction and deliberation of science fiction narrative productively into engagement with technological assessment and decision-making' (Miller and Bennett, 2008: 604). They offer some practical suggestions, such as the integration of science fiction storytelling and critical storyimbibing into science education and outreach programmes, and the development of SF writing courses to include development of 'skills necessary to take maximal advantage of science fiction as a public good' (604).[18] They identify that 'the most important project may be to try to identify mechanisms through which science fiction could be meaningfully integrated into society's practices and institutions for public engagement and technology assessment' (604) – storylistening is one such mechanism.

Such recent work is revisiting and revitalising arguments made in the 1970s (Livingston, 1971; Elkins, 1979) that science fiction should be taken seriously within FS. This means not just using science fiction techniques in existing and new FS methods, but engaging seriously with the extant body of SF work. Most recently, Alessandro Fergnani and Zhaoli Song assert:

> we need to stretch the boundaries of the foresight imagination, to revive the field with an injection of transformational thinking, to think the unthinkable more systematically and plan for it. That is why much attention in our field has recently turned to science fiction.
>
> *(Fergnani and Song, 2020: 1)*

They note, however, that the community 'has been slow to translate insights from science fiction into [their] foresight methods in a systematic manner' (Fergnani and Song, 2020: 1–2).[19] Again, the theory and practice of storylistening, in the context of anticipation, offers ways forward for achieving this.

Anticipatory narrative models

SF stories are anticipatory narrative models that enable surrogative reasoning about future states, and the pathways to those states, reasoning which – through storylistening – can inform present decision-making.[20] In public reasoning, such models may also allow participants to side-step competition between narratives about the present, as they offer the possibility of considering alternative futures that can be perceived as equally valid (and equally speculative). The first section of Chapter 3 has presented the theoretical basis for understanding stories as narrative models – this applies equally to narrative models functioning in the mimetic or anticipatory mode. The difference is one of target system, not of structure or consequence. While mimetic narrative models represent a present-day target system, anticipatory narrative models represent imagined future states. Both of course contribute towards shaping the future through storylistening-informed decision-making. The surrogative reasoning process, as outlined in Chapter 3, draws on all the existing skills and tools of narrative criticism – from engagement with the details of plot, character, structure, and style, to situating stories within their authorial, historical, generic, and other contexts. Storylistening can gather narrative evidence from narrative experts deploying such tools in relation to anticipatory narrative models, and through storylistening to critical engagement with SF texts by lay publics, whether in the wild or in futures-specific environments. Like the other narrative futures methods explored here, engaging with anticipatory narrative models offers the opportunity for gathering evidence from a wider range of publics, as well as offering the opportunity for greater civic participation, engagement, and deliberation beyond that of experts (Miller and Bennett, 2008; Milojević and Izgarjan, 2014; Paschen and Ison, 2014; Miller et al., 2015: 66–67; Reason and Heinemeyer, 2016; Merrie et al., 2018): 'tools built on science fiction might serve as means for building a reflexive capacity into the governance of technology: for helping individuals and communities to meaningfully deliberate technologies and to democratically construct technological futures' (Miller and Bennett, 2008: 598).

Performative readings

Following the pattern of Chapters 1–3, this section illustrates and further explores the functioning of stories in the context of anticipation in relation to our four case studies. Performative readings demonstrate the role of stories as mimetic narrative models of the theory and practice of FS itself, enabling surrogative reasoning about its aims and effectiveness that might inform how and in what ways it is incorporated into public reasoning. We propose that thinking about collective narrative anticipation (of particular use for detecting weak signals) is more important for storylistening than looking to individual stories for predictions, and we introduce the idea of treating stories as data. We then move on to exploring how stories can expand FS's predominantly linear conception of time, and how their narrative structures and techniques can facilitate understanding of the expansive space-time sweep of latent futures.[21] Stories can make explicit the structures of power implicit in FS's commitment to 'our' ability to shape the future when it is left uninterrogated who is included in and excluded from that empowered collective, and we offer examples of initiatives deploying narrative methods to encourage civic engagement and expand whose stories of the future influence public reasoning. We then explore how stories function in the context of a move in futures practice from focusing on end-states to thinking about pathways, risk, and adaptation.

Modelling Futures Studies

Cixin Liu's *The Three-Body Problem* (2008), the first book in the Remembrance of Earth's Past trilogy, is set in mid-twenty-first century China. There, nano-materials researcher Wang Miao plays a virtual reality game called 'The Three Body Problem'. The game is set in a fictional world modelled on an intelligent alien civilisation's planet called Trisolaris. Trisolaris, as its name implies, is distinguished by possessing three suns that orbit each other in random and unpredictable ways. This leads in turn to random and unpredictable climate conditions on Trisolaris which resides primarily in Chaotic Eras (where there is no predicting the length of days or nights, or the temperatures), to less frequent Stable Eras during which Trisolaran civilisation moves swiftly to advance. The Trisolarans have evolved to possess a unique biological mechanism to survive such climatic chaos – they can entirely dehydrate their bodies so that populations can be stored in high volumes as dry husks, to be rehydrated by those monitoring the planet when a Stable Era is deemed to have arrived. The challenge is predicting when that is the case, as collective rehydration can lead to mass population death if it is mistakenly ordered during what in fact remains a Chaotic Era (for instance through the effects of extreme heat or cold).

Through Wang's playing of the game, the novel models the relationship between futures and governance, and the importance, despite its difficulties, of prediction. While it is a premise of modern FS that the future cannot be known, the game demonstrates that at least attempting to do so is essential to the good governance of Trisolaris, so its leaders can make decisions about when to rehydrate the planet's inhabitants. Wang witnesses a range of methods of attempting such predictions from early divination to modern mathematical solutions to eventually learning that there is no general solution to the three-body problem and that, therefore, no long-term prediction is possible. What the Trisolarans *are* able to predict, however, is that at some point their planet will be consumed by one of the suns. This is an important plot point, since it leads to their decision to find an alternative planet, and hence to the communication with Earth that is crucial to the story's events. But the challenge of governing Trisolaris under unpredictable chaotic conditions which allow for no general mathematical solutions – but within which scientific prediction is possible in some areas – enables surrogative reasoning about the relationship between governance, science, prediction, and decision-making in the real world, and cautions against rejecting the need for, or effectiveness of, scientific prediction, while also recognising its limitations and its specific use cases.

In Chapter 3, we discussed the need to identify in which mode a narrative model might be functioning. In this reading, *The Three Body Problem* is functioning as a mimetic narrative model, not an anticipatory one. Although it is possible that the novel might be read as an anticipatory narrative model of first contact, as a mimetic narrative model it explores the relationship between prediction, anticipation, and governance. In a similar way, Harlan Ellison's short story 'Soldier' (1957) (to which the original *Terminator* film may or may not be explicitly indebted) could be read as an anticipatory narrative model of high-tech war, but it can also be read as a mimetic narrative model regarding the role of stories in FS and public reasoning.[22]

'Soldier' is a self-reflexive SF story about what it means to imagine the future and how that imagining might affect current decision-making. It is a story about the theories and practices of FS. Within the story, the future scenario is 'real' due to the trope of time travel. 'Soldier' opens in the far future with a harrowing description of the nature and effects of high-tech-enabled killing in the Great War VII. Due to an accident of timing, a soldier named Qarlo is warped off the battlefield and materialises in a subway station in the present day. Lyle Sims, a special adviser within what might now be described as the X-Files branch of Internal Security, has to decide what to do with him when they realise he is from the future. One option is to deploy Quarlo as a soldier or military tactician in the present-day war, based on the reasoning that 'if he knows no other life than that of a soldier... why, make him a soldier' (Ellison, 2014: 133). This might be described as path-dependent reasoning, where history (in this instance Quarlo's history as a soldier) matters, and determines the future (Quarlo will be deployed in a military capacity again). However, Quarlo proves useless in this capacity because his understanding of tactics works only with the military capabilities of the future. Nevertheless, he makes an impression on those in the Department for Defense, as General Mainwaring reports:

> [...] the stories he tells of brain-burning and spore-death would make you sick. It isn't pretty the way they fight.
>
> I thank God I'm not going to be around to see it; I thought *our* wars were filthy and unpleasant. They've got us licked all down the line for brutality and mass death. [...] For a while there – felt foolish as hell – but for a while there, when he was explaining it, I almost wanted to chuck my career, go out and start beating the drum for disarmament.
>
> *(134)*

Mainwaring's comments give Sims 'the answer to the problem [of what to do with Quarlo], inadvertently' (134). Sims deploys him as a storyteller. His graphic stories of the horrors of future wars leave his audiences seeking for a solution to the experience he has given them. The solution offered is to sign a petition to prevent that future war, in fact all war, taking place.

Quarlo's futures storytelling leads to legislation both in the USA and globally: 'No more war... under any conditions' (138). Quarlo's storytelling makes people consider what their preferred future might be, and storylistening to his tales changes policy to ensure as far as possible that the world's possible and probable futures do not include Quarlo's:

> Quarlo has been more valuable just telling about his Wars, about how men died in that day in the future, than he could ever have been as a strategist.
>   It took a real soldier, who hated war, to talk of it, to show people that it was ugly, and unglamorous. And there was a certain sense of foul defeat, of hopelessness, in knowing the future was the way Quarlo described it. It made you want to stop the flow of Time, say, 'No. The future will *not* be like this! We will abolish war!'
>
> *(138)*

Despite this positive outcome, Sims worries that the future might still not yet be changed by such storytelling, storylistening, and global policymaking. He wonders, 'foolishly if he wasn't too much the idealist' (134–135). Here Sims is no doubt functioning as a mouthpiece for 'Soldier''s anti-war author Ellison's fears regarding the power of his own stories to effect change in public reasoning and decision-making. But Lawrence Freedman's (2017: xix) account of the role of stories – both textual and non-textual – in relation to nuclear war aligns with 'Soldier''s position and confirms how the stories told about the future affect present decisions and how the future plays out: 'how people imagined the wars of the future affected the conduct and course of those wars when they finally arrived'. Observing that 'there is no longer a dominant model for future war, but instead a blurred concept and a range of speculative possibilities' (xxi), Freedman urges that all stories about future war should be treated seriously:

> As in the past there will be a stream of speculative scenarios and anxious warnings, along with sudden demands for new thinking in the face of an unexpected development. *Whether couched in the language of earnest academic papers, military appreciations or fictional thrillers, these will all be works of imagination.* They cannot be anything else because the future is not preordained. [...] These works of imagination will often have value in helping to clarify the choices that need to be faced and at times will even turn out to have been prescient. For that reason many will deserve to be taken seriously.
>
> *(287; emphasis added)*

'They should all, however', he concludes, 'be treated sceptically' (287).[23] Freedman's 'scepticism' might be best understood as mandating the need for storylistening. Such storylistening needs to be informed by reliable methods of assessing the value of collective anticipations of the future.

Prediction and anticipation

Claims for the predictive power of individual stories are now widely discredited: the law of averages accounts for the fact that at least some things or events imagined in previous stories come true; most do not. Stories therefore ought not to be thought of as predicting the future when that predictive power is assigned retrospectively to one specific story which suddenly, due to contemporary events, has an uncanny similarity to those events. But stories could be understood as to some extent predictive when there is a collective weight of anticipation that current circumstances will lead to certain futures. In this sense, stories might be an important way of identifying weak signals, undetected by other means (Bina et al., 2017). Such a claim has been made, for instance, with regard to the 2008 global financial crisis. In a letter to the Queen addressing the question of why no one saw it coming, Tim Besley and Peter Hennessy (2009: 10) concluded that

> the failure to foresee the timing, extent and severity of the crisis and to head it off, while it had many causes, was principally a failure of the collective imagination of many bright people, both in this country and internationally, to understand the risks to the system as a whole.

While there may have been a failure of collective imagination in economic or other scientific circles, in *Crunch Lit* Katy Shaw (2015: 16) argues that stories could have been used as narrative evidence of a looming financial disaster:

> financial fictions set in the two decades preceding the 2007–8 financial crisis challenge dominant post-crunch narratives that the crisis was impossible to predict. These fictions suggest that the seeds of the millennial credit crunch can be found in the new systems and behaviours of finance in the years leading up to 2007–8.

Similarly, Aifric Campbell (2016: n.p.), a former managing director at Morgan Stanley, notes that 'novelists were picking up on troubling long-term trends in the financial sector long before the strategists'. She points to Don DeLillo's *Players* (1977), Martin Amis' *Money* (1984), Tom Wolfe's *The Bonfire of the Vanities* (1987), Brett Easton Ellis' *American Psycho* (1991), Don DeLillo's *Cosmopolis* (2003), Stephen Amidon's *Human Capital* (2004), and Anne Haverty's *The Free and the Easy* (2007) as narrative evidence of collective anticipation of the fragility of the financial sector and the likelihood of a crash. Note that it is the cumulative evidence of these stories that defines their anticipatory value, which is also a product of the storyteller's attention to the details of the present and perception of weak signals:

> if you tracked this long-term trend on a graph you'd see fiction was sounding the alarm. Writers could detect a wolf tone beneath the 'irrational exuberance', since the job entails listening in close, scanning frequencies for the drum beat of change.
>
> *(Campbell, 2016: n.p.)*

Such economic novels, published prior to the crash, could have been taken seriously within public reasoning as a site of collective imagining; doing so would have informed decision-making in ways that might have led to different possible futures. The challenge of course lies in identifying those relevant stories in the present, not retrospectively. This challenge can be met in multiple ways. First, by consulting narrative experts. As discussed in Chapter 1, this places an onus on humanities academics to ensure they engage with stories in their topic area across the political spectrum, or decision-makers must gather a range of narrative experts if their knowledge is restricted due to avowed personal politics. Second, by drawing on the continued expansion of narrative experts' digitally aided methods to enable the processing of large narrative datasets (so that patterns across, and of, stories can be more easily identified). These processes would enable robust analysis of anticipatory trends in contemporary stories, which could then, as part of a pluralistic evidence base, inform public reasoning.

Valuable storylistening is informed by multiple stories, so the pertinent question becomes not only 'what does this story say about future war/climate/economics etc.', but 'what do the stories in circulation today as a whole say about future war/climate/economics etc.'. Such a process is important because of course not all collective narrative anticipations turn out to be predictively correct, but many will carry information of value nevertheless. Consider, for example, mid-twentieth-century American nuclear stories. Until 1945, nuclear power and nuclear weapons existed only in the science fictional, and scientific, imagination.[24] With the bombing of Hiroshima, that fiction became reality, with significant consequences for the status, visibility, and wealth of SF writers, as Albert Berger (1976: 143) recounts:

> The writers of pulp-magazine science fiction found themselves in an ambivalent position after the explosion over Hiroshima of the first atomic bomb. On the one hand, they were acknowledged as prophets proven right by the course of events. Some of them began new careers as writers of popular science and participants in government and university sponsored seminars on social and technological change. Even those who remained close to their roots in magazine fiction found themselves newly prosperous as a result of the increased attention the bomb had brought to 'that Buck Rogers stuff'.

The prophetic nature of the pre-1945 nuclear stories was celebrated by fans and editors alike as proof of science fiction's predictive powers.[25] It was particularly gratifying for John W. Campbell, trained as a physicist at MIT and Duke University, who became editor of *Astounding Science Fiction* in 1931 (and remained so until his death in 1971). Campbell was committed to improving the realisticness and seriousness of the genre, encouraging and publishing stories that extrapolated based on current science. Berger (1979: 125) observes that 'with Hiroshima seemingly providing such powerful validation for both science fiction's anticipation of nuclear energy and for the metaphorical use to which the genre put the technology, there was a certain sense of pride in many of the letters flowing over Campbell's desk'.

Of particular note for its apparently predictive power was Cleve Cartmill's pulp story 'Deadline', published in *Astounding*'s March 1944 issue, about one man's heroic feat to stop the deployment of a nuclear weapon in a war on an alien planet. It is not a good story – judged on pretty much any criteria – but it is a hugely significant one, for it contains the following description:

> I'm stating fact, not theory. U-235 has been separated in quantity easily sufficient for preliminary atomic-power research, and the like. They got it out of uranium ores by new atomic isotope separation methods; they now have quantities measured in pounds. [...] But they have *not* brought the whole amount together, or any major portion of it. Because they are not at all sure that, once started, it would stop before all of it had been consumed.
>
> *(Cartmill, 1944: 164)*

While the bomb as described in 'Deadline' would not have worked, the story anticipated the creation of nuclear weapons and the defining effect the creation of them would have on modern warfare: 'They could end the war overnight with controlled U-235 bombs' (165). It also identified the most challenging engineering problem being faced by scientists at the Manhattan Project at that time – the separation of uranium into fissionable and non-fissionable isotopes. In his memoir 'Old Legends' (1995), physicist and SF author Gregory Benford, who worked with Edward Teller, remembers the latter's account of the impact of Cartmill's story on the Manhattan Project scientists, and the wartime intelligence officer observing them:

> 'Deadline' provoked astonishment in the lunch table discussions at Los Alamos. It really did describe isotope separation and the bomb itself in detail, and raised as its principal plot pivot the issue the physicists were then debating among themselves: should the Allies use it? [...] Talk attracts attention. Teller recalled a security officer who took a decided interest, making notes, saying little.
>
> *(Benford, 1995: 282)*

The security officer's notes on a lunchtime discussion of a group of scientists who were also science fiction fans led to a full-scale military intelligence investigation of Cartmill and Campbell (who it turns out provided the scientific content for the story), taking in other prominent SF writers of the time, to determine if there had been a breach of security regarding the research being undertaken at the Manhattan Project.[26]

The events surrounding 'Deadline' exemplify the seriousness with which the content and influence of SF stories was taken in the USA during WWII.[27] They were taken seriously by the government (evidenced in its policy of voluntary censorship of material relating to the development of atomic weapons, a policy Campbell knowingly breached with 'Deadline') and by scientists, who were readers of SF and looked to SF stories to raise and explore the social and ethical implications of their research: 'Time and again at Livermore I heard physicists quote sf works as arguments for or against the utility of hypothetical weapons' (Benford, 1995: 274).[28] Robert A. Heinlein's 'Solution Unsatisfactory' (1941) (first published under his pseudonym, Anson MacDonald), which anticipates the strategic situation of the Cold War, was another story that Benford recalls Teller saying influenced the scientists, for both its scientific and its social insight:

> Someone had thought that Heinlein's ideas were uncannily accurate [...]. In Heinlein's description of the strategic situation, Teller said, the physicists found a sober warning. Ultimate weapons led to strategic standoff with no way back – a solution unsatisfactory. How to avoid this, and the whole general problem of nuclear weapons in the hands of brutal states, preoccupied the physicists laboring to make them. Nowhere in literature had anyone else confronted such a Faustian dilemma as directly, concretely.
>
> *(Benford, 1995: 281)*

Not all stories were as helpful or predictively correct as Heinlein's, of course. Pre-Hiroshima stories of nuclear power were often set in a far enough future that the social and ethical implications of such scientific developments could be too easily side-stepped (consider, for example, nuclear energy in Isaac Asimov's Foundation series); others failed to account for government and university scientists' involvement in research, locating technological development only within market and business structures (Berger, 1979); others imagined miraculous usages, from energy too cheap to metre to flying cars (Strauss, 1954). Post-war stories of nuclear war invariably assumed that such conflict was inevitable, lacking faith in political structures to prevent it once the technology was available (Berger, 1976),[29] and indulged in unrealistic survivalism (Franklin, 2008: 174), or American exceptionalism, the latter of which is eloquently presented by a character in Philip Wylie's novel *Triumph* (1963) (Brians, 1984):

> There were also lots of prophetic books and movies about total war in the atomic age, and all of them were practically as mistaken as plain people and politicians and the Pentagon planners. In all of them that I recall, except for one, we Americans took dreadful punishment and then rose from the ground like those Greek-legend – Jason's men – and defeated the Soviets and set the world free.
>
> *(Wylie, 2007: 96)*

There were of course exceptions, such as British author Nevil Shute's *On the Beach* (1957) – to which Wylie's character is most likely referring – which anticipated the global impact of nuclear war.

Storylistening at that time, not just retrospectively, could have identified which stories had anticipatory value (in relation to possible, probable, or preferable futures, and the pathways to them) and which stories had mimetic value (for instance with regard to contemporary concerns, anticipatory assumptions, and insight into collective identities). This could have been done using the narrative methods suggested above, as well as by collating narrative evidence with evidence from other sources. Herman Kahn's modelling and his book *On Thermonuclear War* (1960), for instance, would have enabled an understanding of stories of American exceptionalism as a reflection not of a plausible future but of current American national ideology. Instead, public reasoning might have been informed by Theodore Sturgeon's 'Thunder and Roses' (1947) which 'foresees how the American quest for "security" would lead to creating the means to annihilate America and perhaps all humanity' (Franklin, 2008: 170). Chandler Davis argued that 'a whole generation of "strategy theorists" would be making an advance in their theory if they would throw out their treatises on mutual deterrence and read THUNDER AND ROSES' (Davis quoted in Berger, 1981: 290). Such storylistening might have productively informed contemporary futures thinking and related public reasoning and decision-making with regard to nuclear technology.

Stories as data

Stories do not just function as anticipatory narrative models. They can also function as data, evidence of the present and the past that can inform anticipatory systems. In *The History Manifesto*, Jo Guldi and David Armitage (2014: 57) refer to fairytales and books as data informing an understanding of the past: 'in their intense reckoning with archives, historians had to grapple with many kinds of data – the fairytale, the archival artefact, the book itself in its binding and illustrations'. Similarly, stories provide data informing anticipations of the future.

In *Narrative Economics*, Robert J. Shiller argues that stories change human behaviours which change market behaviours, so his economic model includes stories as functional elements, not just descriptions of what is happening. Stories change the target system because they are an influential (functional) part of the target system. Shiller argues that data-based modelling of economic systems should be complemented by study of (non-textual) narratives. The narratives affect the outcomes, and hence should act as data to those trying to model for anticipation. Stories function as data in a different way in relation to natural rather than market systems. Stories told about whether a volcano will erupt do not change whether it will erupt, but they do change the effects that eruption will have, for example, by determining whether people live on the slopes, or what their preparedness is, or how they respond during and after the eruption. Stories therefore serve as data for the modelling of the impacts of such natural events, not for the modelling of the likelihood of such events. Climate change offers an example that straddles these two instances of stories functioning as data. The climate changes for reasons unconnected to human activity but it also changes due to human activity – stories influence humans' contribution to the overall changes in conceptually similar ways to the ways they affect economic markets. Not least because, by changing markets and policy, they change the amounts of carbon emitted. They might therefore indeed serve as data for modelling future natural, as well as societal, phenomena.[30] Shiller's work demonstrates that economic stories affect actions and hence markets. In other areas of public reasoning, it would be reasonable to assume the same is true. For example, if telling stories about robots out of control makes people more fearful of them, then that will affect public reasoning, which in turn will affect outcomes.

Stories might also indicate a lack of data. For instance, every story that assumes climate change does not happen in the future reinforces its absence as the default and solidifies public understandings that exclude further change. The May 2019 *albert* report 'Subtitles to Save the World' analysed one year (September 2017 to September 2018) of subtitling data from the BBC, ITV, Channel 4, and Sky for the frequency and attitude of words associated with sustainability and human impact on the environment: food, travel, energy, climate knowledge. The analysis found that 'the climate related words that were mentioned most frequently are not those that contribute most significantly to an individual's carbon footprint' (albert, 2019: 3), and that coverage focuses more on problems than solutions. The analysis also compared the prevalence of sustainability words to other words – 'climate change (3,125) to Brexit (68,816), chocolate (32,919), cake (46,043), Shakespeare (5,444) as well as the BBC (87,875) and ITV (7,108) themselves' – starkly revealing that on British television climate change 'currently carries similar representation to urine (2,000) and zombies (2,488)' (3). The report concludes that 'climate and the environment are not integrated into programming in any meaningful way' (8), and encourages climate change discussion to be integrated naturally into the discussion of everyday topics, just as the discussion of money is, rather than being a focus of discussion or storylines in its own right. It is therefore possible to integrate climate change across story genres, which is one way of telling stories about it that do not tend to dystopic or apocalyptic extremes, because other factors are driving the plot (see discussion of *The Lost Man* in Chapter 3). In her closing thoughts, BAFTA Chair, Pippa Harris, notes the role that storytellers have to play in changing anticipatory assumptions, and therefore in creating different futures: 'Though it may seem that our future has been taken from us, history is still being created. It is time to write a different script and share it with the world' (8). The improved recognition and incorporation of climate change into mimetic stories would ensure that such stories include climate change-related information that might then inform anticipatory modelling. Mimetic stories can therefore contain, or fail to contain, important information to inform anticipatory narrative models.

A similar digital humanities method of analysing subtitles to produce data from stories can be found in relation to AI. Gabriel Recchia's (2020) computationally assisted analysis of the English-language portion of the Open Subtitles Corpus (a dataset of over 100,000 film subtitles ranging from the silent film era to the present) found a prevalence of the term 'control' in conjunction with artificially intelligent agents, with qualitative investigation revealing that many of these uses were linked to fear of loss of control. These findings are echoed in the Royal Society's (2017) Machine Learning report on its public dialogue, which shows that 'control' is a matter of concern and interest in multiple publics' anticipation of AI's futures. 'Control' is also an aspect of regulation, and is at the heart of both current policy related to data (who controls the personal information that is the data from which AI 'learns'?), and future regulatory environments (What degree of 'control' should there be over semi-autonomous vehicles? Who controls the car? Who controls the wider social setting in which the car operates?). In this instance, storylistening combined with public dialogue (as discussed later in this chapter) reveals important information for decision-makers and for public reasoning, in terms of directing both future debates and also policy evolution.

Decolonising futures

The idea of the future as empty possibility dominates the FS field, which predominantly conceives of the future as open and therefore subject to human control and mastery: 'if [...] the future is seen as ours for the making and taking then imagination may be employed for conjecture, creation, colonization and control' (Adam and Groves, 2007: 18).[31] FS therefore focuses not on past-based prediction but on mapping possible, probable, and also preferred futures, and their potential consequences, to aid collective decisions and actions now that will influence the future.[32] But the future is not virgin territory ripe for all to colonise, since it is both already constrained physically, and only some people have the power to decide and act in ways that will significantly influence it further – some will benefit, and some will suffer, from that colonisation, both in the present and in the future. Such an idea of the future also depends on a primary Western understanding of time as linear.

In an editorial introducing a special issue of *World Futures Review* on time and the future in a range of national cultures and regions, Jim Dator (2017: 6) identifies the Western and colonial philosophical underpinnings of FS:

> Modern futures studies emerged soon after the Second World War during the time the west seemed dominant everywhere in the world – or thought it was. With some exceptions, early futurists apparently unconsciously adopted the Abrahamic/western/Enlightenment view of the future that understood time to be both linear and ultimately (potentially) progressive. Most futurists, then and now, have simply assumed without question that Time's Arrow is real, headed toward 'the future,' and cannot be reversed or stopped, though it can be directed to a significant extent by human intentions and activities.

Keri Facer (2019) points to the need to incorporate more decolonial theory, for instance Boaventura de Sousa Santos' (2014) theory of 'epistemologies of the

South', into FS in order to expose the social, political, and epistemic consequences of this understanding of temporality.[33] These include the exclusion of
other understandings of time, the dependence of the story of progress on exploitation and violence, and the restrictions it places on the imagining of possible futures. Pupul Bisht, a multi-disciplinary futurist, is leading contemporary
futures practice on decolonising the future.[34] She established the Decolonizing
Futures Initiative in 2018, 'a global project that aims to engage marginalized
communities in imagining their preferred futures in order to inform and inspire
inclusive policy-making and innovation' (Bisht, 2021: n.p.), and stories are fundamental to her practice.[35] Her narrative futures method, inspired by the Kaavad
folk-storytelling tradition of Rajasthan, India, is one of the first to be derived
from a non-Western tradition (Bisht, 2017, 2020).

Attending to existing stories can also play an important role in the necessary process of decolonising FS (Feenberg, 1977). Stories can offer a different
perspective on time, modelling long temporal ranges, and offering alternatives
to the linear, teleological tendency of much futures thinking. This function is
particularly important in challenging the idea that the future is an empty space to
be colonised, exposing that not everyone has the power to do so, and that some
futures are latent and already in the making. Stories can contribute to what Johan
Galtung and Sohail Inayatullah (1997) define as macrohistory, that is 'the study
of social systems, along separate trajectories, through space, time, and episteme,
in search of soft laws of social change' (Inayatullah 2017: 26). They argue that
attention to grand patterns can contribute to futures thinking that is effective
in part because of its distance from the immediate present. Macrohistory brings
both long-term history and a far-future perspective to futures thinking. It can
take place as historical research, and the case for it to inform anticipation is also
made in Guldi and Armitage's *The History Manifesto* (2014). But it can also take
place in stories, which are able to model large sweeps of time from the distant
historical past to the far future in a compressed, comprehensible form.

With regard to climate change, one story functioning in such a way is N. K.
Jemisin's Broken Earth trilogy, comprising *The Fifth Season* (2015), *The Obelisk
Gate* (2016), and *The Stone Sky* (2017). Jemisin plays with temporality, and
achieves an astonishing historical range, through the literary technique of split
narrative. In the first book of the trilogy, there are three narrative strands, each
told by what the reader assumes is a different narrator. However, the novel reveals
that the three narrators are in fact the same woman, but at different periods in
her life – a child, a student in training, and a middle-aged mother (named Essun).
The split narrative here is able to present a lifetime, and explore the effects of
past and present actions on the future, but in a non-linear way. This technique
is replicated on a larger scale in the third novel, rendering the trilogy a powerful
story in modelling the slow violence, latent futures in the making, and extended
geological time of climate change.

In *The Stone Sky*, the narration is split between an unnamed omniscient narrator (who the reader discovers is one of the trilogy's main characters, Hoa), Essun,

and her daughter Nassun. These narratives take place in two different times. Hoa tells the story of a technologically advanced city called Syl Anagist, in the far, far past. That civilisation's hunger for more and more power, and its exploitation of certain of its peoples to gain it, led to its destruction. It also led to the destruction of the earth system in its then form. The story's present, where Essun and Nassun's stories continue, contends without realising it with the geological after-effects, centuries later, of Syl Anagist's actions. Their norm is a ravaged earth riven with earthquakes and other geological unsettlements (in a land ironically called the Stillness). This long view of the effects of humankind's actions on the Earth is possible through this split narrative and temporal structure, and through having an immortal narrator (Hoa) who brings knowledge of far past events and their consequences into the present. Through these techniques, the distinction between past, present, and future created by understanding time as linear is replaced with an understanding of time as palimpsestuous, that is, as layered and interwoven both in any individual's memory and experience, and on a planetary scale. Jemisin's story models the imbrication of the past, present, and future, which results in multiple directions of causation, including the influence of past actions on present and future circumstances, as well as the effects of imaginings of the future on present actions.[36]

Such an understanding of time mirrors that found in Indigenous epistemologies, in particular as they are mobilised in activist resistance to climate change-inducing activities. Shelley Streeby (2018: 51) discusses how the New York City Stands with Standing Rock Collective insists on 'the significance of long histories and connections among different flashpoints in time'. This understanding of temporality is also modelled in Native slipstream science fiction, which Grace L. Dillon (2012: 3) identifies as viewing time 'as pasts, presents, and futures that flow together like currents in a navigable stream', thereby 'replicating nonlinear thinking about space-time' (see also Dillon, 2016). Storylistening to such work – for example Gerald Vizenor's novel *Bearheart: The Heirship Chronicles* ([1978] 1990), Leslie Marmon Silko's *Almanac of the Dead* (1991), or the Māori science fiction web series *Anamata Future News* (2015) – would mean taking them seriously as anticipatory narrative models that could inform decision-making. Both dominant Western linear progressive narratives and linear apocalyptic narratives (Whyte, 2018) are decentred by including Indigenous perspectives.[37]

Bisht argues that 'we need to give prominence to stories as a legitimate way of knowledge production and communication, which then in itself can become an act of decolonisation'; included in this activity is a recognition that 'futures for all cannot be imagined by a few', and that this is 'not just about inclusion; it is about recognising where power is held' (quoted in Larsen, 2020). Storylistening to works such as Jemisin's trilogy can contribute to this work, prompting reasoning (often absent from futures thinking) about the unjustness of existing structures, and about who can actually influence and control the future and how. In Jemisin's trilogy, a race of humans called orogenes, who have the capacity to control tectonic activity, are repressed, enslaved, and persecuted by humans without that capacity (called 'stills'). They have no social or political power, no involvement in the governance of the Stillness, and no control over the future. The trilogy's story is put in motion when one extraordinarily powerful orogene revolts against these conditions, and perpetuates an act of colossal violence on the land and its peoples, overturning the established order. Here, the only way in which a member of a disempowered community can affect future change is through violent revolt.

This differentiated nature of access to power and capacity to influence the future often correlates with whose stories get told or heard in public reasoning and whose do not. Expanding the idea of the South into a metaphorical rather than a geographical concept, de Sousa Santos (2014: 19) includes within it certain groups within the geographic North that are also 'excluded, silenced and marginalised populations'. Nesta's Common Futures series (begun in 2018) on the future of work is a futures exercise that is attempting to listen to, and foreground, the stories of one such group. The series is gathering the stories of low-paid and precarious workers in Britain who will be directly impacted by technological change, for instance automation. Nesta offers their stories as a counterpoint to the more loudly heard stories from those developing and deploying the technologies:

> Entrepreneurs are expert storytellers. Their visions of colonies on Mars, AI powered everything and armies of workers with no obligation to provide them basic rights like holidays or the minimum wage are shaping the laws that politicians pass, the funding they make available and the rules they design to govern emerging technologies. We think that it's time for those who are never given the chance to tell their stories to talk to policymakers about how they see the future.
>
> *(Saunders, 2018: n.p.)*

These stories reveal that the obsession with killer robots, for instance, of many dominant textual stories about AI, or the 'replacement by a robot' narrative focus of policymakers, are not reflected in the stories of workers. Their anticipatory assumptions about an AI future reflect present and historical concerns, for instance regarding labour rights, social mobility, universal education, and retirement age and security. Storylistening to these stories could reorient public discussion and decision-making.

Narrative futures methods have a key role to play in expanding futures thinking and practice to include the stories of those traditionally disempowered and unheard, or habitually excluded from decision-making. For instance, Miller et al. (2015) deploy collective storytelling in order to widen societal engagement in reasoning about energy futures. They identify that other futures methods are produced and designed for expert engagement and do not engage a wider range of participations either in their production and use:

> the energy sector has a long track record of technocratic decision-making, with limited opportunities for broader public engagement, often portraying

energy choices to the public as relatively simple choices amongst fuels and technologies, rather than comprehensive choices among competing socio-technological arrangements.

(Miller et al., 2015: 66)

In contrast, their narrative method aims to widen engagement and deliberation. Involving more diverse participants in futures thinking, in terms of both background and knowledge, ensures that not just the technological and economic, but the environmental and social implications of energy policy are taken into account. It also ensures that those who will be affected by such policies have access to decision-making in modes other than that of protest. They propose that storytelling – and, we would add, storylistening – offers one of the new approaches needed to facilitate more productive dialogue between experts, decision-makers, and publics.

Turning to economics, in William Davies' collection, *Economic Science Fictions*, Laura Horn (2018) notes that some science fiction suffers from a lack of future imaginings of different forms of corporation, and is trapped in modelling future corporate dystopias that can only be resisted by a subversive individual. As examples, she points to novels from the 1950s, including Mack Reynold's *Mercenary from Tomorrow* (1968) and Frederik Pohl and Cyril Kornbluth's *The Space Merchants* (1953), and to recent televisual corporate dystopia stories such as *Mr. Robot* (2015–2019), *Continuum* (2012–2015), and *Incorporated* (2016–2017). But Horn also highlights textual stories that imagine alternatives to capitalism, including Ursula Le Guin's *The Dispossessed* (1974) and Kim Stanley Robinson's Mars trilogy, situating the latter in relation to non-textual stories of cooperative organisation of production. Combining our economic and AI case studies, another example would be Iain M. Banks' Culture series which offers a detailed future imagining of a post-scarcity socialist society in which sentient AGI and humans peacefully coexist. Stories must not just describe the need for alternative models of the future, but provide them. Such stories might also be the product of collective imagining, rather than of individual imagining. One insight of the Royal Society (2018: 22) report on *Portrayals and Perceptions of AI and Why They Matter* is that what matters is the space for creating collective stories, as well as what the stories are:

> an alternative approach to reshaping the narratives surrounding AI lies in changing the ways in which people create narratives, rather than focusing on the content of the narratives themselves. Spaces can be created that allow new stories to emerge through new approaches to dialogue and engagement.

If such stories are not created, or not listened to, public reasoning lacks or misses out on anticipatory narrative models that might help lead to a wider range of possible futures.

Pathways, risk, adaptation

Our exploration of the shift from prediction to anticipation has shown how stories can reveal and reframe assumptions about decision-making (decide x to achieve outcome y), and convey a more realistic sense of continuity along pathways. In some areas of public reasoning this would in turn encourage a shift or reframing away from debate about a desired end-state, and towards a debate about possible multiple pathways and timeline (rather than multiple possible steady states), and about the systems or capabilities necessary to manage prolonged uncertainty. For example, the question might not just be 'how do we deal with this flood?', but also 'how do we live with changing levels of flooding over time?'[38] Or, with regard to AI, the question of whether taxi drivers are replaced by AI is important, but how (with what consequences) and when (how evolving over time) also matters. Some futures thinking is therefore moving from developing future scenarios that are static to thinking of pathways (see Fazey et al., 2016, 2018), which involves considering how to live with emergencies or recurrent risks. With regard to climate change, for example, the risk of a climate catastrophe is one thing, imagining living in a future with multiple catastrophes over time is another. Narrative futures methods can help here.

Stories about extreme or apocalyptic events might be less useful in their anticipatory modelling of climate change, and therefore risk judgements in private and public reasoning, than stories functioning as anticipatory narrative models of living with recurrent risk. Jemisin's trilogy serves again here as a useful example of a recurrent risk narrative model. The trilogy models, and enables public reasoning about, the types of societal structures and organisation that might be needed in order to live with recurrent risk.[39] The social structures of the inhabitants of the Stillness (a single supercontinent) are organised around and in response to the recurrence, every couple of centuries, of what is known as the 'Fifth Season', a period of catastrophic climate change.[40] Such structures include identifying people not based on race or gender but based on their skill set and its specific contribution to society, and dividing society up into small local communities known as 'comms' which are responsible for their own leadership and management of resources, and on the support of which their members rely in particular at times of crisis. Resilience is dependent on local governance and resource structures, community, trust, allegiance, and a societal model that places value on the individual's role in the collective, not their own advancement, success, or power.

Which scientific or narrative models are included in an ensemble of models has significant implications for public reasoning and decision-making. Storylistening to extreme narrative models informs public reasoning differently, and produces different decision-making, than storylistening to recurrent risk narrative models. Both are needed. The extreme narrative models confront the fact that because carbon dioxide emissions accumulate, until net zero is reached, things will keep getting worse. They are intended to motivate mitigating action and short-term rapid response (although, as we have discussed in Chapter 2, they also risk provoking denial or paralysis). Recurrent-risk narrative models can motivate adaptation action and long-term anticipatory planning.[41] The 'wicked problems' analysis of complex systems that emerged from social planning is in the same direction. It asserts that wicked problems cannot be solved, but only continually tackled (Rittel and Webber, 1973; Rayner, 2017). Jem Bendell (2018) proposes a shift to a deep adaptation post-sustainability framework which focuses on resilience, relinquishment, and restoration. Climate policy now needs both to make decisions that reduce risk (attempting to control the future) and that adapt to risk (due to latent futures in progress). Stories can help with exploring these different ways of thinking about and modelling futures.

Consequences

In this final section, we pull out some of the key consequences for public reasoning and the humanities of this chapter's exploration of stories and anticipation. We consider how the structures and practices of public reasoning and the humanities can evolve to enable the incorporation of storylistening into the former, and to foreground the public value of the humanities more broadly. We close this chapter by introducing the idea of individual and collective narrative responsibility.

Evolving structures of public reasoning

Storylistening becomes even more important in public reasoning that is explicitly about the future, because of the greater ranges of uncertainty about the future compared to the past. Just as models act as convening spaces (Government Office for Science, 2018) and stories act as a safe space for public reasoning to explore matters that are hard to discuss directly, so too is the future sometimes a safe space to reason about the present.[42] For example, the Foresight Future Flooding Project (2004) created quantified scenarios for flood risk in the UK out to 2080. One of their functions was to tell a story about the inevitability of loss of land from coastal erosion, but to do so from a sufficiently futuristic perspective that people could discuss today's concerns at a distance. This parallels the cognitive estrangement from the time and space of the present that defines SF.

However, public reasoning that is explicitly about the future requires a wholly new level of collective comfort with, and confidence in the practice of, surrogative reasoning as creating one form of 'evidence about the future'. The question of what evidence is allowed to be suitable for public reasoning is potentially even more contested for evidence about the future than for that evidence acknowledged to be about the past.[43] There may be a particular form of value for those whose primary concern is the role of science here, in that the humanities can bring with them a degree of comfort with multiple potential futures that will help avoid the trap for scientists of having to 'prove' things about the future that are unprovable.[44] Incorporating evidence from narrative futures methods into public reasoning may mean that scientific evidence about the future will be listened to in more sophisticated and robust ways too.

In a world of complexity and uncertainty, attending to available scientific anticipations, and to narrative anticipations that can better take into account the specific, uncertain, and emergent, is of huge value. But to do so brings challenges for systems of public reasoning. Systems that bring together narrative evidence with scientific or technological anticipations will have to contend with much higher degrees of uncertainty: when applied carefully, they make uncertainties about the future more visible and enable those uncertainties to be engaged with more effectively. Selecting, bounding, and positioning possible futures becomes a greater challenge. Our suggestion here is that there might be scope for further enquiry bringing together political sciences and futures work, to develop more rigorous explicit or formal processes for acknowledging the full range of uncertainties within democratic decision-making. As in previous chapters, our delineation of storylistening provides the conceptual framework to start to put it into practice now, as well as leading to the identification of further types of research needed. For example, there is also a potential research agenda looking historically at the anticipatory roles of stories and changes in public reasoning over time and place, to gather historical evidence on the relationships between storylistening, public reasoning, and behaviours in different contexts. Such enquiry might also consider how the relationship between what narrative evidence might say and the nature of decisions it relates to changes.

Structures of public reasoning are already evolving to include more direct engagement with publics, through public dialogue and deliberative democracy exercises and arrangements.[45] One example of such practice is public dialogue on specific policy-relevant issues involving highly technical and scientific matters such as genetically modified crops, geo-engineering, or AI.[46] Public dialogue of this type typically involves groups of people selected to be representative of a wide range of publics. The selection might mean ensuring members of the groups have different socio-economic, educational, or geographical backgrounds, or that there is representation of groups with potential interests, as well as pre-existing interests (such as those with strongly held value-based views).[47] Across these categories, publics are given the opportunity to engage with experts, in structures that vary from small-scale discussions to permanent institutional arrangements (DeSilvey et al., 2011; Lezaun et al., 2017; Ottinger et al., 2017; Parkhurst, 2017: 151, 162; Wowk et al., 2017; Cohen et al., 2018; Breckon et al., 2019; OECD, 2020b; Ostfeld and Reiner, 2020; Pidgeon, 2020). The output of such dialogue may be evidence about the interests, questions, views, and languages of the groups involved, or it may be evidence of a settled view on a question of public interest. In such instances, the effect of the dialogue will ensure that the settled view is based on deep engagement with the evidence. Such initiatives have been trialled in policy areas from climate change (UK: see Climate Assembly UK, 2020; France: see *Convention Citoyenne pour le Climat*, 2021) to abortion (Republic of Ireland) or tax (USA).[48]

The incorporation of narrative futures methods and storylistening can further enable and facilitate such activities.

Narrative futures methods are of particular value both for creating evidence that can contribute to a pluralistic evidence base, and because they can be used to increase the range of ways in which publics can engage with other evidence, systems, complexity, and uncertainty. (In public dialogue, participants may also create their own stories from the evidence, and those stories can then be debated publicly.) Many dialogue and deliberation initiatives have been driven by an acknowledged need to engage differently with matters of science and health practice, especially ones that are seen as hard for the layperson to grasp. Although expertise in engaging with stories is as important as scientific expertise is for its objects of study, many publics are more comfortable acknowledging their engagement with stories, as creators, tellers, imbibers, sharers, and sheer passive audiences, than they are with science. This is another reason why narrative futures methods can be useful and productive in such contexts. Their adoption opens the way for new forms of public engagement that do not blur expertise and lay forms, but enable greater civic involvement in decision-making, and in reasoning about evidence and creating new narrative evidence.

Evolving the humanities

The development of narrative futures methods has largely been undertaken by academics outside of the discipline that is defined by its engagement with stories – literary studies. Developers of narrative futures methods therefore often lack the rigorous training and professional skill in narrative analysis that academics within literary studies possess. This can weaken the quality of critical engagement with narrative scenarios in FS, both those produced by standard futures methods and those produced by novel narrative methods. In particular, the lack of intersection and interaction between FS and science fiction studies might explain the most underdeveloped narrative futures method – the use of SF stories as anticipatory narrative models. There is a need for literary academics in general, and those specialising in SF in particular, to step outside of their disciplines and engage with futures researchers and practitioners. This is beginning to happen, for example through the activities of the University of Lancaster's Institute for Social Futures (UK) which has been bringing science fiction experts, narrative experts, and futures practitioners in government and industry together, and in Genevieve Liveley, Will Slocombe, and Emily Spires' (2021) work on FLiNT (Futures Literacy through Narrative). But there is more work to be done – for instance, increased participation of literary academics (especially experts in SF) at UNESCO's Futures Literacy summit in December 2020 would have showcased such work as part of the diversity of activities globally that engage with human anticipatory systems and practices.

The skills and methods of literary studies – what academics in this discipline actually do, how they do it, and why their methods of investigation and their results are robust – are not widely understood. Broader engagement by academics not just with lay publics (the predominant mode of contemporary 'public engagement') but with other academic experts (interdisciplinarity) and professional experts (intersectorality) is necessary for that to change. At the same time, literary studies needs to be willing to find new ways to articulate the theory behind its methods, to make explicit what is often implicit, and to continue to expand and evolve its methodologies. Digital humanities offer one potential avenue in this latter direction, but valuable results from such methods invariably rely on their combination with the more established qualitative approaches of the discipline. They are not a quick techno-fix for the validity of the humanities. Avenues to address the former might be to consider explaining literary studies research methods by way of comparison to social science methods, that is, in the languages of other disciplines – what would it mean, for instance, to understand one approach to texts in literary studies as deploying the qualitative approach of constructivist grounded theory?[49]

Evolution is needed not just or even necessarily with regard to what literary academics do, but where and how they do it, with whom, and how they explain what they do to other people. This would lead to deeper societal understanding of the nature and value of literary studies, and the humanities more broadly, and therefore of their importance at all educational levels from primary to tertiary. This speaks to a wider need for literary studies academics, as well as humanities academics in general, to engage in practical, not merely rhetorical, demonstrations of the public value of the humanities.

There is no doubt that independence, and sometimes explicit opposition (for instance to the state, or to university leadership in neoliberal university systems), is necessary. They provide a key demonstration of the public value not just of the humanities in fact, but of academia in general. But they do not and must not exclusively define the position of the humanities. There has to be room for an understanding of the humanities as a valuable site of knowledge production of use to existing structures and institutions of public reasoning and decision-making. There is a need for academic structures and values that support humanities academics willing and able to engage and collaborate with those structures and institutions – for example government and industry – which are equally the very ones that might require or benefit from humanities critique. It is also important to note, as we do in Chapter 1, that to engage is not to relinquish the possibility of critique, although it may provide new insights and understandings that prompt a reconsideration of the beliefs and assumptions underlying the critique. Both independence and engagement (with the potential for critique happening at both sites) are needed. Achieving this is no easy task. The twenty-first-century humanities itself would benefit from engaging in a futures exercise to imagine its own possible, probable, and preferable futures, as well as the multiple pathways it might follow, and even how to survive in an environment of recurrent risk.

Narrative responsibility

In 2020, the SF author Cory Doctorow felt profound guilt as he witnessed the queues for his local gun store as the COVID-19 pandemic hit the USA. The actions of the people queuing were motivated, he concluded, by the story they had told themselves – that in times of crisis, civic structures collapse. Popular narratives, including the disaster stories Doctorow himself has penned, fuel this story, despite historical evidence demonstrating that time and again the opposite is in fact true (Solnit, 2009). Doctorow was experiencing narrative responsibility – the realisation that, as we have explored across the chapters of this book, stories are not 'merely entertainment' but play a fundamental role in how human beings understand and interact with the world and its inhabitants. Doctorow's realisation is part of an individual commitment as a writer to sophisticate his storytelling to eschew easy plots and 'lazy storytelling' and tell stories that work harder to engage with and reflect the complexity of the world. Collective narrative responsibility is also needed: a widespread, open realisation that stories are not 'merely entertainment'; investment in educational and societal structures that equip individuals to engage with stories critically, not be at their mercy (narrative literacy); and institutional structures – within academia, public reasoning, and beyond – that enable stories to be taken seriously (storylistening). The function and effects of dominant stories need to be better understood; the insights and usefulness to public reasoning of less dominant stories need to be highlighted; and new stories need to be created and shared that imagine different pathways, to different possible futures.

The case made in this book for the incorporation of storylistening into decision-making depends on effective and democratic structures of public reasoning already being in place. But if they are not, many of the arguments and ideas we have developed here remain important. Wider narrative literacy to understand how stories are functioning can help people respond to unruly storytelling. Collective storytelling and identifying the importance of diverse stories in terms of topic, tone, and teller can enable wider civic participation within or outwith established structures. In the context of anticipation, narrative literacy goes hand in hand with futures literacy – both can enable people to imagine different futures and perhaps, thereby, offer hope.

Notes

1 Bell (1996) touches on the longer history of connection between SF and futurology, for instance, through works such as Thomas More's *Utopia* and the utopian tradition within SF, as well as H. G. Wells, who authored highly influential fictional and non-fictional futures works.
2 Burnam-Fink (2015: 51) notes that 'a full enumeration of the causes and consequences of this split between scenarios and science fiction is another project'. We have yet to find such a full historical account.
3 See de Jouvenel (2019) on *futuribles*, including the concept's origins, and the philosophy and practices it has led to in the French futures tradition, past and present.
4 These three categories are found in another seminal early work of FS, Alvin Toffler's *Future Shock* (1978: x), which addresses 'new, alternative images of the future – visionary explorations of the possible, systematic investigation of the probable, and moral evaluation of the preferable'. See also Bell (1998).
5 This position is now self-evident in FS, having been stated before Polak by Bertrand de Jouvenel: 'Knowledge of the future is a contradiction in terms' (Jouvenel, 1967:

5, cited in Adam and Groves, 2007: 17). For more recent iterations of the point, see Miller (2006: 4–5, and 2007: 359).

6 See Bell (1993) for a fuller account of the relationship between Lasswell and FS, in which Bell notes a meeting of the Yale Collegium of the Future on 25 September 1967 at which Lasswell presented a mimeographed paper called 'Projecting the future' in which he outlined five tasks of FS, of which the final one is 'The invention, evaluation and selection of policy alternatives (in order to achieve preferred goals)' (Bell, 1993: 808).

7 The case for SF as prediction manifests in moves by early US SF magazine editors (such as Hugo Gernsback and John W. Campbell) to improve the seriousness and standing of the genre (Nevala-Lee, 2018). Suvin's theory and definition of SF still informs some contemporary SF theory and criticism (e.g. Jameson, 2007: xiv), although it has of course been subject to critique (see, e.g., Miéville, 2009; Dillon, 2020).

8 As we also explain in the Glossary, the terms relating to the study and practice of reflection on the future are particularly unstable compared to those in other disciplines and practices, and specific uses are often fiercely promoted by groups and individuals. We have adopted the term 'anticipation' as the broad term for reflective ways of thinking about the future.

9 Bishop et al.'s (2007) synthesis supersedes an early synthesis by McHale and McHale (1976), and more recent ones that they situate themselves in relation to in their overview (Van Notten et al., 2003; Bradfield et al., 2005).

10 Note that scenario development is not the same as scenario planning: 'perhaps the most common confusion when discussing scenarios is equating scenario development with scenario planning. We suggest that "scenario planning" has more to do with a complete foresight study, where scenario development is concerned more specifically with creating actual stories about the future. Scenario planning is a far more comprehensive activity, of which scenario development is one aspect' (Bishop et al., 2007: 6).

11 For early examples of the technique, see Callaghan et al. (2004) and Egerton et al. (2008). More recently, see the papers in the Creative Prototyping Special Section of *Technological Forecasting & Social Change* 84 (2014).

12 Riel Miller (2018: 4) defines anticipatory assumptions in the context of his case for the Futures Literacy Framework (FLF):

AA are the most basic component of anticipatory activities: these assumptions are necessary for all 'uses-of-the-future' because 'imagination' can only be elaborated on the basis of the underlying assumptions. Conscious human AA include choices about what kind of future to anticipate and which methods to use to think about a particular kind of future. AA […] may even be applied to non-conscious anticipation.

13 See, for instance, the early software game created as part of the UK Foresight's scenario-based study of flood risk looking to 2080 (see Government Office for Science, 2004; 'FloodRanger: Educational Flood Management Game', n.d.), or the McKay Carbon Calculator (see Department for Business, Energy & Industrial Strategy, 2020), a single player game in which the player tries to find their preferred set of options for meeting the target of net zero carbon emissions by 2050. Another example of game as futures tool in the policy context is the European Commission Joint Research Centre's Scenario Exploration System, 'a foresight gaming system developed to facilitate the application of futures thinking to policy-making' (Bontoux et al., 2020: 81). For further details, see the Scenario Exploration System website (*European Commission*, [n.d.]). 'Serious games' and 'playful models', informed and constrained by plausible physical, technical, and economic assumptions about the future, can be valuable tools in enabling better intuitive understanding of the potential behaviours of complex systems and in thinking about the future.

14 See a similar argument in 'Speculative Futures' in Liveley, Slocombe, and Spiers (2021: 5–7).

15 In December 2019, Sarah Dillon led one such successful event at the UNESCO Global Futures Literacy Design Forum in Paris (UNESCO, 2019: 13).

16 For earlier work on this interface, see Miles (1990, 1993) and Slaughter (1998).

17 Schwarz (2015: 512) anticipates our arguments in this book when he states that 'literature appears to provide decision makers with a different kind of input, adding to the usual data gathering' and – in a rare prior usage of the term in this context – when he argues that 'organisations should not so much focus on storytelling but rather on *storylistening*'.

18 See Facer (2019) for a compelling case for the need to incorporate futures storytelling and storylistening more widely into education.

19 Although Fergnani and Song do highlight recent initiatives such as the Science Fiction as Foresight conference (April 2020) and the Sci-Fi Futures topic of the 2020 Houston foresight annual spring gathering.

20 Dennis Livingston (1971: 255, 268) enquires into 'the availability and utility of alternative models of the future international political system that may be found in science fiction', and identifies that 'the essential contribution of science fiction consists in its offerings of heuristic, speculative models of social systems that speak to the major issues raised in nonfiction works'. A.H. Louie (2010: 21) notes that models are the vehicles through which humans anticipate, functioning to 'pull the future into the present'.

21 Barbara Adam and Chris Groves' (2007) idea of latent futures in the making (or, emergent futures) mediates to some extent between the idea, on the one hand, that the future is visible based on past-based prediction (closed future) and, on the other, that it is an open site of rigorous imaginings (open future). They note the long-term effects of human activities and the fact that some futures are already irreversibly in progress, even if not yet manifest: 'the contemporary future is always already occupied with the latent outcome of choices, desires, decisions and actions of predecessors and contemporaries' (Adam and Groves, 2007: 36), as well as of course with the laws of the physical and natural world.

22 On the controversial relationship between Ellison's story and *The Terminator* film see Britt (2015).

23 H. Bruce Franklin (2008) also recognises that policy scenarios are narratives, and should be treated as such, and that literary works are narratives and should be treated as such, and that both play a role:

> All such scenarios are dramatic narratives that can be subjected to the kind of critical scrutiny applied to other forms of literature. Many of the most influential, on which our lives could depend, might fail the most basic tests for consistency, depth of consciousness, and psychological accuracy, not to mention ethical content. On the other hand, many works published as science fiction offer insights into our technological, political, economic, and psychological reality, as well as our practical choices, omitted from the scenarios of policymakers.
>
> (Franklin, 2008: 169)

24 For a brief history of nuclear energy, see Office of Nuclear Energy, Science and Technology ([n.d.]). As early as *The World Set Free* (written in 1913; published in 1914), H. G. Wells (1914: 30) imagines a new source of energy derived from the atom:

> The problem which was already being mooted by such scientific men as Ramsay, Rutherford, and Soddy in the very beginning of the twentieth century, the problem of inducing radio-activity in the heavier elements and so tapping the internal energy of atoms, was solved by a wonderful combination of induction, intuition and luck by Holsten so soon as the year 1933.

25 It did not go unnoticed at the time that such celebration was out of kilter with the new reality the bomb brought. Berger (1979: 126) recounts that

> this backslapping led Chandler Davis, a fan as well as an occasional and thoughtful writer for Campbell, to note that many fans were thinking far more about the

justification that the atomic bomb gave science fiction than they were about the implications of the weapon itself: 'The fact that your life is in danger,' he wrote in his mimeographed *Blitherings*, 'seems to interest you less than the fact that Anson MacDonald predicted your life would be in danger'.

(Spring, 1946)

Tens of thousands of lives in Japan were of course not just in danger but already lost.

26 The full details of the investigation are detailed in Berger (1984), who gained access to documents pertaining to the investigation using a Freedom of Information request after they were declassified in April 1983.

27 Another example is Philip Wylie's short story 'The Paradise Crater'. Originally bought for publication in January 1944, the contract was cancelled in January 1945 after an objection from the War Department, and Wylie was placed under house arrest. The story was repurchased and eventually published shortly after the nuclear attacks on Japan, and Wylie went on to become a special consultant to the Federal Civil Defense Administration. See Brians (1987) and Franklin (1984). On Wylie's wide engagement with US government nuclear policy, see Oakes and Grossman (1992), Seed (1999), and Seed (2013).

28 Post-war, SF writers were directly involved in the structures of US public reasoning, for example Benford participated in the Citizens' Advisory Council on National Space Policy (directly connected to the White House through the National Security Advisor), meetings of which were hosted at SF author Larry Niven's house and, in the summer of 1984, attended by Robert Heinlein and Arthur C. Clarke (Benford, 1995).

29 See, for instance, Chandler Davis' 'Nightmare' (1946). Berger (1976: 145) notes that

Along with many of his colleagues, Davis had seen the situation primarily as an insoluble technical one, how to defend against an irresistible weapon, rather than as the essentially political problem faced by Congress and the atomic scientists, the maintenance of peace. Few SF writers thought that war could be prevented.

30 Ursula K. Heise (2016), in discussing extinctions, interestingly reverses the 'narratives are data' argument and includes databases as forms of narrative, along with lists compiled for regulations.

31 See also Bell (1996: 3): 'The future, of course, is still being made. It is what people can shape and design through their purposeful acts'.

32 Miller (2007) argues that the preferable and the probable are subsets of the possible since prioritising probabilities or preferences sets constraints upon possible imaginings. Bell (1996: 14) calls the knowledge gained from anticipations of the future 'surrogate knowledge', recalling our argument in Chapter 3 regarding the surrogative reasoning operating in relation to models.

33 De Sousa Santos' (2014: 22, 21) arguments bear direct relevance to many of those made throughout this book, in particular his case for the need for an 'ecology of knowledges' and his insistence on the need for 'deep listening'. Like us, de Sousa Santos (2014: 22) emphasises the need for both/and, not either/or – different kinds of knowledge are needed for different purposes, and what he calls 'intercultural translation' (in our context, this might be understood also as interdisciplinarity and intersectorality) is needed 'to bring together different knowledges without compromising their specificity'; his case for the need for a 'sociology of absences' (21) bears relevance to our arguments about listening for narrative deficits.

34 Bisht's practice is informed by Ziauddin Sardar's long-standing and significant body of work decolonising futures (see, e.g., his papers collected in Inayatullah and Boxwell, 2003, and Sardar, 2010). For a recent action research initiative focusing on the African context, see the Capacity to Decolonise project (Capacity to Decolonise, 2021; Feukeu et al., 2021).

35 See also Bisht in interview with Niklas Larsen (2020).

36 Genevieve Liveley (2017: 16) proposes that 'exposure to [...] narrative complexity could help to increase our readerly competences, in general, and our anticipatory competences, in particular – both within fictional story worlds and real-world scenarios', but she references here only quantum SF and postmodern novels, not other types of stories such as Jemisin's fantastic temporal sweeps or, for instance, time as experienced in Caribbean writer Rita Indiana's *Tentacle* (2018). Different relationships to time in different cultures are noted in Miller (2006: 4).

37 Whyte (2018: 225) argues: 'Indigenous peoples challenge linear narratives of dreadful futures of climate destabilisation with their own accounts of history that highlight the reality of constant change and emphasize colonialism's role in environmental change'.

38 For an illustration of systemic approaches to recurring risks, this time in public health, see Rutter et al. (2017). For a discussion as to why enabling deliberation to happen downstream (in time) from 'will formation', thereby including what happens afterwards and also widening the range of publics with interest and expertise, see Boswell (2016).

39 The fictional trope of a society living with the vestiges of behaviours designed to combat a risk which materialised in the past, but which has largely been forgotten in the present, occurs in fantasy stories, perhaps because of their potential for extreme narrative tension in which protagonists who strongly anticipate the return of the risk have to operate against an overwhelming apathy from the mainstream. This underlies the 'Winter is coming' thread in *Game of Thrones* (2011-2019), and is found in works such as Anne McCaffrey's *Dragonflight* (1968). That sense of being in possession of knowledge that the world faces disaster, but not being believed, could be considered to have resonance with some of the motivation of campaigners for nuclear disarmament and for early climate change activists and scientists.

40 In the case of climate change, there is ample evidence of extreme variations in the paleoclimate although human activity did not contribute to those changes. In Klinke and Renn's (2001) classification of risks by reference to Greek mythology, these fall into the Cassandra category.

41 For example, Joe Smith (2014: 16) argues that

> one key task [within this] for the research and policy communities is to shift towards explaining climate change research as an immense process of risk assessment, and climate politics as one of humanity's most adventurous attempts at collective risk management.

Drawing on workshops in the UK, the US, and China, Sir David King et al. (2015) provide a series of climate-related risk assessments. These kinds of work would benefit from the incorporation of storylistening.

42 Laurent Bontoux et al. (2020: 83) identify the idea of a safe space as a crucial concept in futures studies and practice, in particular in relation to games: 'The circumstances thus created by a futures-oriented game generate a safe space which is favorable to reflection. This has been referred to under numerous terms such as "the magic circle" (Salen and Zimmerman 2003; Linser et al. 2008), "a ludic architecture" (Walz 2010), and a "recursive space" (Wood 2012). It is a critical function of play in serious game design (Schrage 2000)'.

43 For discussion about the challenges of associating futures thinking with policy analysis as a potential contribution to policy decision-making see, for example, King and Thomas (2007), Craig (2019: 27-44), and van Dorsser et al. (2020). For an illustration of narrative-based anticipation in climate change, see Shepherd (2019).

44 For an illustration of the relationships between levels of proof in public reasoning, policy and law, see the discussion of the Precautionary Principle applied to the application of new technologies, in *Innovation: Managing Risk, Not Avoiding It* (Government Office for Science, 2014).

45 As with FS more generally, this is another area of theory and practice in which language is far from settled.

46 For discussion of the benefits and challenges of public engagement with science, see, for example, Stilgoe et al. (2014).

47 See, for example, HFEA (2013).

48 There are further variations on forms of public engagement outside government, such as 'open strategy-making', in the private sector (Schwarz, 2020).

49 Constructivist grounded theory is a methodology characterised by an inductive approach to research which combines an ongoing process of data collection and analysis with the development of a theory, or explanation, emerging from – 'grounded in' – the data. It differs from deductive approaches designed to test pre-formulated theories or hypotheses. In its original version see Glaser and Strauss ([1967] 2017); in its revised version see Charmaz (2014).

EPILOGUE

When discussing the education of the Guardians in the ideal Republic in Plato's *The Republic*, Socrates proposes that the education of their 'mind and character' (II, 376e7) must include stories, which he separates into two kinds: 'true stories and fiction' (II, 377a1).[1] Socrates first addresses fiction noting that, from the earliest age, stories play a role in educating the mind: 'you know that we begin by telling children stories. These are, in general, fiction, though they contain some truth' (*Republic*, II, 377a4–5). Because stories have such psychological power to influence one's character and beliefs, Socrates proposes a form of censorship, allowing into the Republic only those stories that will mould its future citizens in the correct ways:

> 'Shall we therefore readily allow our children to listen to any stories made up by anyone, and to form opinions that are for the most part the opposite of those we think they should have when they grow up?'
>
> 'We shall not.'
>
> 'Then it seems that our first business is to supervise the production of stories, and choose only those we think suitable, and reject the rest. We shall persuade mothers and nurses to tell our chosen stories to their children, and by means of them to mould their minds and characters which are more important than their bodies. The greater part of the stories current today we shall have to reject.'
>
> *(Republic, II, 377b5–c6)*

Socrates disqualifies the stories of Homer and Hesiod, for instance, on the grounds of failed mimetic modelling – that is, they do not accurately represent the true nature of heroes and gods.

DOI: 10.4324/9780367808426-7

Stories as such are not banned from the Republic; rather, recognising their immense influence, Socrates proposes that stories ought to be controlled by those in power who thus decide which stories are told, by whom, and to whom. He proposes the deployment of stories' persuasive power to the ideal state's own ends, to 'control story-tellers' (*Republic*, III, 386b8) in order to allow the production and dissemination only of stories that convey the state's normative ideals:

> if we are to persuade them that no citizen has ever quarrelled with any other, because it is sinful, our old men and women must tell children stories with this end in view from the first, and we must compel our poets to tell them similar stories when they grow up.
>
> *(Republic, II, 378c7–d3)*

Socrates does not exclude stories from the public sphere but aims to control them and wield their power for the purposes of his imagined state because he recognises that stories are weapons of mass persuasion, and that they engender and fashion the beliefs and characters of the storyimbibers absorbed in them.[2] Socrates identifies certain passages for excision from extant stories not because such passages are badly written but rather, on the contrary, because the better the writing, the more the storyimbiber is absorbed, and the more powerful the story's influence: 'indeed the better they are as poetry the more unsuitable they are for the ears of children or men' (*Republic*, III, 387b3–4).

In *The Republic*, therefore, Plato demonstrates a profound understanding of the persuasive power of stories and the effect of that power on citizens and the public sphere. This does not lead Plato to reject stories, but to seek to control them. However, the persuasive power of stories has contributed to their delegitimisation among the modes and models of rationality that have grounded Western democratic norms of evidence and public reasoning, norms consolidated in the Enlightenment, and rooted in rationalistic, positivist, and empiricist traditions.[3] Again (both/and not either/or), we are not claiming that such a concept of rationality is not important, nor that it does not have its place in public reasoning. But evidence derived from this form of reasoning needs to be complemented by narrative evidence; taking stories seriously requires an expansion of what is considered 'rational' to include interpretation and judgement, as well as calculation and verification.[4] Recently, investigations into public reasoning, decision-making, and the policy process have highlighted this need to reassess the dominant paradigm of reason that informs it, and the types of evidence this determines as useful or relevant (LERU 2012; Brooks, 2014; INGSA, 2018; Brom, 2019; Mair et al., 2019; Kay and King, 2020). Many of these investigations maintain the relevance of, and call for the increased incorporation of, evidence from the humanities. But they do not go further and demonstrate *how* to integrate such evidence into existing systems of decision-making, both structural and conceptual. With the theory and practice of storylistening as presented and elaborated in this book, we present one such way.

We have proposed that stories can constitute an integral part of the evidence base informing public reasoning, and we have provided a framework – storylistening – explaining how they could do so. Stories are not merely vehicles for the communication of science, conduits for knowledge created by other means, and nor are they simply slippery or dangerous entities that threaten reasoning; they have cognitive value in and of themselves, and taking them seriously can provide narrative evidence. We have argued that narrative literacy – understanding how stories function and their effects at individual and collective levels – is necessary in order to engage properly with such evidence.

We have highlighted how decision-makers need to contend with narrative deficits, be they absent stories or the stories hidden in the shadows cast by charismatic stories. We have outlined the importance to storylistening of determining which parts of the system are taken to matter (framing and points of view) and of judging how a single story may, or may not, be relevant to a policy system (scale-up and metonymic legitimacy). We have explored how understanding the craft and science of being an expert is as much of relevance to humanities scholars as it is to scientists, with the former being able to benefit from the hard-won learning of the latter in this respect.

We have considered the cognitive value of stories in understanding collective identities and how storylistening can find different ways to identify and consider publics (through mapping narrative networks). We have proposed that there is a widespread need across all levels of society for greater self-awareness and critical thinking when it comes to listening and telling stories (narrative literacy). We have attended to how power informs the development of dominant stories and behaviours (narrative lock-in), and how stories can play a role in both the re-enforcement and the challenging of group norms.

We have proposed that stories can be understood as narrative models which enable surrogative reasoning about the parts of the target system they represent. Here, storylistening must identify the relevant story or stories to policy issues at hand, identify the target system, and identify the modelling mode of the story (mimetic or anticipatory). We have proposed that stories functioning as narrative models can complement other types of models, especially scientific ones, and that they have great strength when it comes to modelling the particular rather than the general. We therefore advocate for the need for a pluralistic evidence base that takes account of narrative evidence, and requires advisory systems and practices that reach across disciplines. We argue for putting into place structures that enable expert articulation of the state of knowledge within one discipline, or across several (synthesis). We note the structural and personal challenges for academics in working across disciplines while maintaining the need for inter-disciplinarity, and we investigate the need for long-term relationships between academics and those involved in public reasoning, relationships that enable collaboration while keeping space for opposition.

Given that all decision-making is in essence about the future, we have considered the importance of stories in relation to anticipation (and all the terms and practices that we include under that definition, the terminology of the field remaining at present unstable). We have identified the need to evolve structures of public reasoning in order to bring the future into reasoning in new ways, and to evolve the humanities in order to redescribe the boundaries of what it is and does. We highlight the role of storylistening in democratic methods of decision-making such as public dialogue, engaging in co-production of evidence while acknowledging expertise. And we point to the need for increased individual and collective narrative responsibility for stories told and imbibed, and how they impact the world.

It is our intention that the framework of storylistening presented in this book can and should be put into practice. While this book has not shied away from making a rigorous academic case for the cognitive value of stories, and demonstrating that value through performative readings indebted to the discipline of literary studies, many of the elements of storylistening summarised in this conclusion, and explored in detail in the final sections of each chapter, are practical. Storylistening is the theory and practice of gathering narrative evidence to inform decision-making, especially in relation to public reasoning, as part of a pluralistic evidence base. As such, it can be incorporated into established practices for gathering evidence to inform decision-making, as well as highlight the need for expansion or evolution of those practices, and of the structures of academia and its institutions.

Looking beyond the book, immediate practical steps might be for every person or body responsible for providing evidence or scientific advice to audit their disciplinary reach and to begin to experiment with and to develop new ways to include storylistening. For advisory bodies such as standing groups, councils, and committees, the initial task might be to review which of the storylistening functions are most likely to be relevant to the issues with which they are concerned (essentially, to build their own narrative literacy) and then to seek out the most relevant experts or to build structures to create or gather evidence based on those functions. Another step would be to begin to review which shared stories are most dominant in each context, and to seek out evidence about the cognitive value of those stories as well as to consider which less dominant stories might have value and what types of stories might need to be created to fill narrative deficits.

For time-limited projects or working groups tasked with reviewing or synthesising evidence around a particular topic, such as those created by national or local government and Parliament, and by the national academies and international networks of academies, a similar narrative literacy approach would be explicitly to invite relevant experts who could provide evidence, or a starting point to advise on what other forms of expertise might be relevant. For those designing policy-oriented programmes with explicit futures or anticipatory elements, the questions to consider include the role of storylistening in gathering evidence, in the creation and use of narrative futures methods, in the construction of modes of public engagement with evidence and with potential futures, and in deliberation.

Ideally, in all cases there will be space for experimentation, for reflection, and for learning: the most potentially valuable activities will grow further from dialogue between disciplines and between academics and practitioners. Looking more systemically, funders and publishers, and those in leadership positions in the humanities, might also develop new ways to reward and sustain academics who seek to contribute directly to public reasoning and to ensure such engagement does not take place at the expense of their academic progress. Finally, for practitioners the first step is to acknowledge the presence and importance of stories and the practical possibilities for making their cognitive functioning explicit through storylistening.

Our proposal that stories need to be taken seriously in public reasoning is not (only) an assertion that narrative evidence needs to be considered in realms where previously it has not been, but an assertion that stories already function in these environments and yet that functioning has been consistently misunderstood or suppressed. Understanding how and why narrative evidence and storylistening are legitimate and have cognitive value for public reasoning is of crucial contemporary importance. As we made clear from the outset of this book, storylistening is not aligned with post-truth. It is not aligned with the eradication of the importance of scientific evidence. Rather, it is an honest recognition that such evidence is not the only factor in public reasoning. Pretending otherwise does not make stories and their power disappear. Rather, it renders them vulnerable to abuse by those storytellers who recognise and wish to wield their power in ways that do indeed position stories as oppositional to scientific and other forms of essential evidence. In contrast, in this book we have described and evidenced the multiple cognitive functions of stories, showing what those functions are, how they operate in specific policy case studies, and how and why that matters in relation to public reasoning. We have shown that stories can be taken seriously and engaged with in ways that complement, not oppose, other forms of evidence. We have demonstrated that understanding these functions can enable decision-makers not to *tell* appropriate and effective stories, but to *listen* to stories as part of a pluralistic evidence base. This book has therefore not made an explicit case for understanding the power and importance of responsible and informed story*telling* – though that case might be considered implicit and most definitely would be informed by this work. Rather, this book makes a case for understanding the contributions to public reasoning that can be derived from responsible and informed story*listening*. In making this case, we have also indicated important ways in which the structures and practices of public reasoning, and of the humanities, can evolve and adapt in order to better incorporate and convey the insights of narrative evidence. We hope that work will now begin.

Notes

1 Note that the Greek *pseudos*, translated here as 'fiction', 'meant not only "fiction" – stories, tales – but also "what is not true" and so, in suitable contexts, "lies"' (Plato, 2007: 387, n. 2).
2 On narrative persuasion as studied in psychology, see the foundational work of Green and Brock (2000). See Hamby et al. (2018) for a recent effort at a comprehensive

conceptualisation of narrative persuasion. While more research is needed to further identify the mechanisms of narrative persuasion, such as on the role of behavioural modelling or associational learning (Hamby et al., 2018: 123), on the basis of the current evidence, one can propose that narrative persuasion occurs as a result of the mechanisms involved in deictic shift (a shift in perspective from one grounded in the everyday self to one grounded in the narrative) – transportation (Gerrig, 1993) and identification (de Graaf et al., 2012); and the mechanisms involved in deictic return (Hamby et al., 2018) – decoding (Graesser, Singer, and Trabasso, 1994), and externalisation (Larsen and Seilman, 1988).

3 See Walter Fisher (1984, 1989) and what he calls *narrative rationality* for one account of a form of rationality not dependent on propositional logic. Fisher (1985) explains his 'narrative paradigm', his theory that humans are innate storytellers; that reasoning need not be argumentative but can operate according to the logic of good reasons, which has to take into account specificities of historical context, culture, and experience (Fisher, 1978); and that humans naturally assess stories according to narrative probability (a story's coherence) and narrative fidelity (that is, the story's correspondence with lived experience). For an overview of narrative rationality, including disagreement with and extension of Fisher's theory, see Stroud (2016).

4 As Sheila Jasanoff (2012: 13) notes, 'public reasoning, a process that all democratic societies are committed to in avoidance of arbitrary power, depends on prior criteria of what counts as valid reason'. See also Martha Nussbaum (1995: xv), a book written as a result of her identification of the need for 'the investigation and principled defense of a humanistic and multivalued conception of public rationality'. Both Jasanoff and Nussbaum link this concept of rationality to the common-law tradition.

GLOSSARY

This book draws on insights from a wide range of disciplines and practices. Each discipline and practice will have its own precise language, sometimes using words that are not used beyond the discipline, sometimes using the same words as other disciplines but with different meanings, and sometimes using different words to denote overlapping but not identical concepts. As authors, we have also introduced a small number of new words, where to do so was important in the articulation of new ideas and concepts relating to storylistening.

While the *Oxford English Dictionary* remains the final arbiter, this Glossary attempts to help the reader recognise why and how some words are used in the book, and why some words that may be more familiar to them are not used. OED definitions included here are from the *OED Online*, accessed April 2021.

Anticipation   a reflective way of thinking about the future. We use anticipation rather than terms such as futures, foresight, forecasting, or prediction, all of which have wide usage in academic and in practitioner literature. The study and practice of explicit reflection on the future has grown in recent years and the terminology is particularly unstable.

Artificial intelligence (AI)   a set of technologies that enable human-made systems to perform functions typically associated with the human brain. In the twenty-first century, most of what is referred to as AI is based on machine learning approaches although, in its most general and popular uses, the definition is often expanded to include systems based on a wide range of statistical and numerical techniques. Although AI in popular reporting and in stories is often associated with embodied forms, the principle applications are distributed.

Audience   a group who are imbibing the same story, but who are doing so passively and where the fact that they share the imbibing of the story is not of interest for public reasoning purposes.

Charismatic story a compelling story that attracts attention. This may be useful for public discourse (e.g. drawing attention to a system or an element or aspect of that system) or it may be harmful (e.g. distracting attention from the whole, or pointing towards a less valuable element at the expense of a more important one that is less charismatic). A story can be charismatic and not circulate widely, and a widely circulating story (e.g. a blockbuster movie) need not be charismatic.

Complex(ity) a descriptor or attribute of systems or situations in which causality is hard or impossible to determine. Complex systems typically exhibit emergent behaviour. By contrast, a complicated system may be difficult to understand or explain but it should be possible to determine its behaviour given sufficient time, insight, or resource. In formal complexity, the reasons for the complexity are known but the non-linearities in the system mean it has emergent properties that cannot be predicted.

Cognition 'the action or faculty of knowing taken in its widest sense, including sensation, perception, conception, etc., as distinguished from feeling and volition' (OED).

Cognitive empathy see *theory of mind*.

Cognitive value worth, due to having or providing knowledge. Stories have cognitive value and as a result enable *narrative evidence* that can legitimately form part of a pluralistic evidence base. *Evidence* may derive from the storycontent, or it may derive from the relationship between the storycontent and the storyteller(s), storyimbiber(s), or narrative networks associated with the story. In the latter cases, the content of the story may be irrelevant (and may be false).

Dominant story a story that is prevalent within a specific narrative network, a particular area of public reasoning, or prevalent across publics.

Empathy the imagining of, or entering-into, the feelings of another. Discussed at length in Chapter 1. Because of the arguments made therein, we do not use the term elsewhere in the book.

Epistemic 'of or relating to knowledge' (OED).

Evidence 'grounds for belief; facts or observations adduced in support of a conclusion or statement; the available body of information indicating whether an opinion or proposition is true or valid' (OED). The distinctions between different forms of evidence, and the creation of systems for including and for assessing them in public reasoning, are at the heart of the discussions throughout the book.

Evidence synthesis 'the process of bringing together information and knowledge from a range of sources and disciplines to inform debates and decisions on specific issues' (The Royal Society and the Academy of Medical Sciences, 2018: 7).

Expert (noun) 'A person regarded or consulted as an authority on account of special skill, training, or knowledge; a specialist. Also attributive, as in *expert evidence*, *expert witness*, etc.' (OED). All academics are therefore experts in the relevant field, but there are also non-academic experts. The knowledge that experts provide is *evidence.*

Fiction and non-fiction We do not deploy the terms 'fiction' and 'non-fiction' as generic categories in this book since stories move across both. We do, however, deploy a distinction where necessary between *textual* and *non-textual* stories. We do not dispense with distinctions between fact and fiction understood as truth and untruth; rather, we make the case that storylistening enables better understanding of both truths and untruths about a system.

Forecasting, foresight see *anticipation.*

Futures see *anticipation.*

Group an encompassing term. May refer to a collection of individuals which also falls within one or more of the following categories: *audience, network, public.*

Humanities (see, also, Science) refers to the study of literature, art, film, theatre, human cultures, religion, music, history, classics, philosophy, and aspects of other disciplines including anthropology, social and political sciences, and economics. (We note that such a broad definition masks important distinctions between all these fields, but these do not alter this book's arguments.) For the purposes of this book, the definition is intended to include those elements of academic practice which are generally (but not exclusively) not susceptible to experimentation, and where books play a central part in the development, assessment, and recording of knowledge.

Imbibe, imbiber, imbibing see *Storyimbibing.*

Knowledge 'The object of knowing; something known or made known', and 'the fact or condition of knowing something' (OED).

Metonymy (see, also, Metonymic legitimacy) a part standing for a whole, which enables the use of something specific and particular to reason about something more general.

Metonymic legitimacy the extent to which a single story is legitimately representative of a whole, for instance a policy issue or a collective identity.

Mimetic 'representing, picturing, or presenting the real world (esp. in literature, art, etc.)' (OED).

Model structure created to indirectly represent parts of the world in which the model creator or user is interested. An idealised description or conception of a *target system*, which can help perform some cognitive function with respect to that system, yielding knowledge through *surrogative reasoning.*

Narrative taken to be synonymous with *story*, and therefore not used in its noun form in the book (unless in citations or accounts of other's work). Consistently used as an attributive adjective, for example, *narrative evidence, narrative literacy, narrative model*, since more elegant than deploying 'story' as an attributive adjective.

Narrative evidence (see, also, Narrative literacy) the product of the expert act of both direct critical engagement with stories, and critical engagement with others' storyimbibing. Critical engagement means explicit observation, analysis, and reflection. The *evidence* gathered by *storylistening*.

Narrative deficits Narrative deficits are areas in which there is a falling short either in terms of the ability or willingness to take stories seriously, or because there is in fact an (actual or perceived) absence of stories.

Narrative literacy understanding how stories function and their effects at individual and collective levels.

Narrative networks groups whose interactions and hence whose collective identities and behaviours are informed by *storyimbibing* – storytelling, story-sharing, or storycreating. A narrative network may therefore be a *public* or may represent part of a policy system.

Network a group of individuals who are not simply categorised as being in a group because they share characteristics (such as those of an *audience* [who have imbibed the same story], or because they are all from the same age cohort), but are interacting and so creating causal connections in ways that inform their collective identity and behaviours.

Non-textual see *textual*.

Normative 'that constitutes or serves as a norm or standard; implying or derived from a norm; prescriptive' (OED); not purely descriptive.

Policy 'the sum total of government action, from signals of intent to the final outcomes' (Cairney, 2020: 2).

Policymaker generally, anyone who makes decisions that have collective consequences. In this book, specifically, a decision-maker in public office, elected or other.

Policy issue a subject of public interest where there is a point (or points) of contention or significance, and which represents a significant matter for debate and decision-making. Although policy issues are often referred to as challenges, they may concern opportunities as well as risks and problems.

Practitioner a person deliberately engaged in the practice of public reasoning, including individuals working in government, business, or civil organisations, as well as academics seeking to provide expert knowledge.

Prediction see *anticipation*.

Public(s) a public (the slightly awkward term used in some disciplines to avoid inadvertently implying there is such a single entity as 'the public') is a group which is relevant for the immediate purposes of public reasoning but which is assumed not to have direct decision-making powers or specialist expertise relevant to the policy issue at hand.

Public dialogue 'public dialogue is a process during which members of the public interact with scientists, stakeholders (e.g., research funders, businesses and pressure groups) and policy makers to deliberate on issues relevant to future policy decisions' (Sciencewise, 2019: 1).

Public reasoning 'the institutional practices, discourses, techniques and instruments through which modern governments claim legitimacy in an era of limitless risks – physical, political and moral' (Jasanoff, 2012: 5).

Science (see, also, Humanities)   For the purposes of this book, science is the physical, natural, and life sciences, medicine, engineering, mathematics, and the quantitative application of economics and other social sciences. (We note that such a broad definition masks important distinctions between all these fields, but these do not alter this book's arguments.) This definition is intended to include those elements of academic practice which are generally (but not exclusively) susceptible to experimentation, and where knowledge is developed, assessed, and recorded more frequently through peer-reviewed journals than books. (Also applies to the attributive adjective, as in *scientific evidence, scientific models,* etc.)

Story   a causal account of something happening that includes entities with agency, can be distributed or shared, and in which both form and content generate affect and cognition. Stories can be *textual* or *non-textual.*

Storylistening   the theory and practice of gathering narrative evidence to inform decision-making, especially in relation to public reasoning, as part of a pluralistic evidence base.

Storyimbiber   one who imbibes (meaning to absorb, assimilate, or take into one's mind or moral system) a story. Covers the different ways in which people receive stories in different media, as well as acts of story engagement such as embellishment, co-creation, or sharing, not denoted under the more limited term 'reading'. Also used as in *storyimibing* and in, shortened form, *imbibing.* Used instead of audience member, reader, listener, or viewer.

Surrogative reasoning   reasoning about a *model* and its results that enables inferences of *cognitive value* with regard to the *target system.*

System   'a group or set of related or associated things perceived or thought of as a unity or complex whole' (OED). In this book, *system* is used to denote the parts of the world that matter with regard to a specific policy issue. If what is considered to matter changes, so does the definition of the system (and vice versa).

Target system   the parts of the world in which the model creator or user is interested, indirectly represented by a *model.* Ideally, each target system would be modelled in more than one way, including through stories, so that ensembles of models could inform *public reasoning.*

Textual, non-textual   stories can be textual (embedded, embodied, and curated) or non-textual (transient and malleable). Textual stories can circulate without being changed, they have a fixity.

Theory of mind   used as synonymous with *cognitive empathy.* One of two dominant theories that account for the way in which humans are able to interact effectively with other people and in social situations.

BIBLIOGRAPHY

Sources

Abbate, J. 2011. 'True Risks? The Pleasures and Perils of Cyberspace'. In D.L. Ferro and E.S. Swedin (eds.), *Science Fiction and Computing: Essays on Interlinked Domains*, 189–204. London: McFarland.

Adam, B., and Groves, C. 2007. *Future Matters: Action, Knowledge, Ethics*. Leiden: Brill.

Adams, W.M. 2016. 'Do You Speak Lion?' *Science* 353(6302), 867–868. DOI: 10.1126/science.aaf8056

Akerlof, G.A., and Snower, D.J. 2016. 'Bread and Bullets'. *Journal of Economic Behavior & Organization* 126(B), 58–71. DOI: 10.1016/j.jebo.2015.10.021

Albert. 2019. Subtitles to Save the World: Understanding How the Broadcasting Community Is Covering Climate. London: Albert. Accessed 31 October 2020, at: https://wearealbert.org/planet-placement/wp-content/uploads/sites/6/2019/05/Subtitles-to-Save-the-World-Report-FINAL.pdf

Alleyne, B. 2015. *Narrative Networks: Storied Approaches in a Digital Age*. London: SAGE Publications, Inc. DOI: 10.4135/9781473910782

Alvarado, R.C. 2011. 'Science Fiction as Myth: Cultural Logic in Gibson's *Neuromancer*'. In D.L. Ferro and E.S. Swedin (eds.), *Science Fiction and Computing: Essays on Interlinked Domains*, 205–213. London: McFarland.

Andersson, J. 2018. 'Arctic Futures: Expectations, Interests, Claims, and the Making of Arctic Territory'. In J. Beckert and R. Bronk (eds.), *Uncertain Futures: Imaginaries, Narratives, and Calculation in the Economy*, 83–102. Oxford: Oxford University Press.

Aravind, M., and Chung, K.C. 2010. 'Evidence-Based Medicine and Hospital Reform: Tracing Origins Back to Florence Nightingale'. *Plastic and Reconstructive Surgery* 125(1), 403–409. DOI: 10.1097/PRS.0b013e3181c2bb89

ARC. [n.d.]. 'About ARC'. arcworld.org. Accessed 29 September 2020, at: http://www.arcworld.org/about_ARC.asp

ARC. 2007. 'ARC/UNDP Programme Statement on Climate Change'. *arcworld.org*, 7 December 2007. Accessed 29 September 2020, at: www.arcworld.org/news.asp?pageID=207

Archibald, J.A. 2008. *Indigenous Storywork: Educating the Heart, Mind, Body and Spirit*. Vancouver, BC: The University of British Columbia Press.

Arendt, H. 1973. *On Revolution*. Harmondsworth: Penguin.

Astington J. 1990. 'Narrative and the Child's Theory of Mind'. In B.K. Britton and D. Pellegrini (eds.), *Narrative Thought and Narrative Language*, 151–171. Hillsdale, NJ: Erlbaum.

Avin, S. 2019. 'Exploring Artificial Intelligence Futures'. *Journal of Artificial Intelligence Humanities* 2, 169–194.

Bal, P.M., and Veltkamp, M. 2013. 'How Does Fiction Reading Influence Empathy? An Experimental Investigation on the Role of Emotional Transportation'. *PLoS ONE* 8(1), e55341. DOI: 10.1371/journal.pone.0055341

Baldwin, J. 1984. *Notes of a Native Son*. Boston, MA: Beacon Press.

Bamberg, M. 2004. 'Form and Function of "Slut-Bashing" in the Identity Constructions in 15-Year-Old Males'. *Human Development* 47, 331–353. DOI: 10.1159/000081036

Bamberg, M. 2011. '*Who am I?* Narration and Its Contribution to Self and Identity'. *Theory & Psychology* 21(1), 3–24. DOI: 10.1177/0959354309355852

Bamberg, M. 2012. 'Why Narrative?' *Narrative Inquiry* 22(1), 202–210. DOI: 10.1075/ni.22.1.16bam

Bamberg, M. 2016. 'Narrative Inquiry'. In K.B. Jensen, E.W. Rothenbuhler, J.D. Pooley and R.T. Craig (eds.), *The International Encyclopedia of Communication Theory and Philosophy*, 1295–1303. DOI: 10.1002/9781118766804.wbiect239

Bardini, T. 2011. 'A (Brave) New World Is More Than a Few Gizmos Crammed Together: Science Fiction and Cyberculture'. In D.L. Ferro and E.S. Swedin (eds.), *Science Fiction and Computing: Essays on Interlinked Domains*, 167–188. London: McFarland.

Batson, C.D. 1991. *The Altruism Question: Toward a Social-Psychological Answer*. Hillsdale, NJ: Erlbaum.

Batson, C.D. 2009. 'These Things Called Empathy: Eight Related but Distinct Phenomena'. In J. Decety and W. Ickes (eds.), *The Social Neuroscience of Empathy*, 3–15. Cambridge, MA: The MIT Press. DOI: 10.7551/mitpress/9780262012973.003.0002

Batson, C.D. 2014. 'Empathy-Induced Altruism and Morality: No Necessary Connection'. In H. Maibom (ed.), *Empathy and Morality*, 41–58. Oxford: Oxford: University Press.

Batson, C.D., Batson, J.G., Slingsby, J.K., Harrell, K.L., Peekna, H.M., and Todd, R.M. 1991. 'Empathic Joy and the Empathy-Altruism Hypothesis'. *Journal of Personality and Social Psychology* 61(3): 413–426. DOI: 10.1037/0022–3514.61.3.413

Batson, C.D., Batson, J.G., Todd, R.M., Brummet, B.H., Shaw, L.L., and Aldeguer, C.M.R. 1995a. 'Empathy and the Collective Good: Caring for One of the Others in a Social Dilemma'. *Journal of Personality and Social Psychology* 68(4), 619–631. DOI: 10.1037/0022–3514.68.4.619

Batson, C.D., Klein, T.R., Highberger, L., and Shaw, L.L. 1995b. 'Immorality From Empathy-Induced Altruism: When Compassion and Justice Conflict'. *Journal of Personality and Social Psychology* 68(6), 1042–1054. DOI: 10.1037/0022–3514.68.6.1042

Batson, C.D., Lishner, D.A., and Stocks, E.L. 2015. 'The Empathy–Altruism Hypothesis'. In D.A. Schroeder and W.G. Graziano (eds.), *Oxford Library of Psychology: The Oxford Handbook of Prosocial Behavior*, 259–281. Oxford: Oxford University Press. DOI: 10.1093/oxfordhb/9780195399813.013.023

Batson, C.D., and Shaw, L.L. 1991. 'Evidence for Altruism: Toward a Pluralism of Prosocial Motives'. *Psychological Enquiry* 2(2), 107–122. DOI: 10.1207/s15327965pli0202_1

BBC. 2007. 'Robotic Age Poses Ethical Dilemma'. BBC News, 7 March 2007. Accessed 11 November 2020, at: http://news.bbc.co.uk/1/hi/technology/6425927.stm

Bearman, P.S., and Stovel, K. 2000. 'Becoming a Nazi: A Model for Narrative Networks'. *Poetics* 27: 69–90. DOI: 10.1016/S0304-422X(99)00022-4

Beatty, J. 2017. 'Narrative Possibility and Narrative Explanation'. *Studies in History and Philosophy of Science* 62, 31–41. DOI: 10.1016/j.shpsa.2017.03.001

Bechara, A., and Damasio, A.R. 2005. 'The Somatic Marker Hypothesis: A Neural Theory of Economic Decision'. *Games and Economic Behavior* 52(2), 336–372. DOI: 10.1016/j.geb.2004.06.010

Beckert, J., and Bronk, R. (eds.). 2018. *Uncertain Futures: Imaginaries, Narratives, and Calculation in the Economy.* Oxford: Oxford University Press.

Bell, W. 1993. 'H.D. Lasswell and the Futures Field: Facts, Predictions, Values and the Policy Sciences'. *Futures* 25(7), 806–813. DOI: 10.1016/0016-3287(93)90027-Q

Bell, W. 1996. 'What Do We Mean by Futures Studies?' In R.A. Slaughter (ed.), *New Thinking for a New Millennium: The Knowledge Base of Futures Studies*, 3–25. London: Routledge.

Bell, W. 1998. 'Making People Responsible: The Possible, the Probable, and the Preferable'. *American Behavioral Scientist* 42(3), 323–339. DOI: 10.1177/0002764298042003004

Bellamy, E. 1889. 'How I Came to Write "Looking Backward"'. *The Nationalist* 1(1), 1–4.

Bellamy, E. 1937. 'How I Wrote "Looking Backward"'. In M.R. Lester (ed.), *Edward Bellamy Speaks Again! Articles–Public Addresses–Letters*, 217–229. Kansas City, KS: The Peerage Press.

Belton, O., and Dillon, S. 2021. 'Futures of Autonomous Fight: Using a Collaborative Storytelling Game to Assess Anticipatory Assumptions'. *Futures* 128, 1–13. DOI: 10.1016/j.futures.2020.102688

Bendell, J. 2018. 'Deep Adaptation: A Map for Navigating Climate Tragedy'. *Institute for Leadership and Sustainability (IFLAS) Occasional Papers* 2, 27 July 2018. Ambleside: University of Cumbria. Accessed 9 November 2020, at: http://www.lifeworth.com/deepadaptation.pdf

Benford, G. 1995. 'Old Legends'. In G. Bear (ed.), *New Legends*, 270–282. New York: Tor Books.

Benjamin, R. 2019. *Race After Technology: Abolitionist Tools for the New Jim Code.* Cambridge: Polity Press.

Benjamin, W. 2019. *The Storyteller Essays.* Translated by Tess Lewis. Edited by Samuel Titan. New York: The New York Review of Books.

Bennett, B., and Weisskopf, M. 2003. 'The Sum of Two Evils'. *Time*, 25 May. Accessed 9 September 2020, at: http://content.time.com/time/magazine/article/0,9171,454453,00.html#:~:text=After%20months%20of%20recovering%20from,Hussein%2C%20was%20ready%20to%20party

Berger, A.I. 1976. 'The Triumph of Prophecy: Science Fiction and Nuclear Power in the Post-Hiroshima Period'. *Science Fiction Studies* 3(2), 143–150.

Berger, A.I. 1979. 'Nuclear Energy: Science Fiction's Metaphor of Power (*L'énergie nucléaire comme métaphore du pouvoir en science-fiction*)'. *Science Fiction Studies* 6(2), 121–128.

Berger, A.I. 1981. 'Love, Death, and the Atomic Bomb: Sexuality and Community in Science Fiction, 1935–55 (*L'Amour, la mort et la bombe atomique: sexualité et communauté dans la SF de 1935 à 1955*)'. *Science Fiction Studies* 8(3), 280–296.

Berger, A.I. 1984. 'The *Astounding* Investigation: The Manhattan Project's Confrontation with Science Fiction'. *Analog Science Fiction/Science Fact*, 125–137. https://www.gwern.net/docs/radiance/1984-berger.pdf

Berlant, L. (ed.). 2004. *Compassion: The Culture and Politics of an Emotion.* London: Routledge.

Bermúdez, J.L. 1996. 'The Moral Significance of Birth'. *Ethics* 106(2), 378–403. DOI: 10.1086/233622

Bertaux, D. 1981. *Biography and Society: The Life History Approach in the Social Sciences.* Beverly Hills, CA: Sage.

Bertaux, D., and Kohli, M. 1984. 'The Life Story Approach: A Continental View'. *Annual Review of Sociology* 10(1): 215–237. DOI: 10.1146/annurev.so.10.080184.001243

Besley, T., and Hennessy, P. 2009. 'The Global Financial Crisis: Why Didn't Anybody Notice?' *British Academy Review* 14, 8–10.

Biesele, M. 1993. *Women Like Meat: The Folklore and Foraging Ideology of the Kalahari Ju/'hoan*. Bloomington: Indiana University Press.

Billington, M. 2009. 'Interview: Making a Drama Out of the Economic Crisis'. *Guardian*, 14 September 2009. Accessed 14 October 2020, at: https://www.theguardian.com/stage/2009/sep/14/economic-crisis-david-hare-enron

Bina, O., Mateus, S., Pereira, L., and Caffa, A. 2017. 'The Future Imagined: Exploring Fiction as a Means of Reflecting on Today's Grand Societal Challenges and Tomorrow's Options'. *Futures* 86, 166–184. DOI: 10.1016/j.futures.2016.05.009

Binnion, P. 2003. '*Threads* (BBC, 1984)'. *Scope: An Online Journal of Film and Television Studies* May. Accessed 16 September 2020, at: https://www.nottingham.ac.uk/scope/documents/2003/may-2003/film-rev-may-2003.pdf

Bishop, P., Hines, A., and Collins, T. 2007. 'The Current State of Scenario Development: An Overview of Techniques'. *Foresight* 9(1), 5–25. DOI: 10.1108/14636680710727516

Bisht, P. 2017. *Decolonizing Futures: Exploring Storytelling as a Tool for Inclusion in Foresight*. [MRP.] Toronto, ON: OCAD University. http://openresearch.ocadu.ca/id/eprint/2129

Bisht, P. 2020. 'Decolonizing Futures: Finding Voice, and Making Room for Non-Western Ways of Knowing, Being and Doing'. In R. Slaughter and A. Hines (eds.), *The Knowledge Base of Futures Studies 2020*, 216–230. Washington, DC: Association of Professional Futurists.

Bisht, P. 2021. 'Pupul Bisht'. *LinkedIn*. Accessed 21 April 2021, at: https://www.linkedin.com/in/pupulbisht/?originalSubdomain=ca

Bjurström, A., and Polk, M. 2011. 'Physical and Economic Bias in Climate Change Research: A Scientometric Study of IPCC Third Assessment Report'. *Climatic Change* 108, 1–22. DOI: 10.1007/s10584-011-0018-8

Bland, A. 2021. 'How Matt Hancock's Obsession with Matt Damon Film Drove UK's Vaccine Strategy'. *The Guardian*, 2 February. Accessed 28 February 2021, at: https://www.theguardian.com/society/2021/feb/02/how-matt-hancocks-obsession-with-matt-damon-film-inspired-uks-vaccine-strategy

Bland, J., and Westlake, S. 2013. *Don't Stop Thinking About Tomorrow: A Modest Defence of Futurology*. London: nesta. Accessed 6 November 2020, at: https://media.nesta.org.uk/documents/dont_stop_thinking_about_tomorrow.pdf

Blastland, M., and Spiegelhalter, D. 2013. *The Norm Chronicles: Stories and Numbers about Danger*. London: Profile Books.

Blastland, M., Freeman, A.L.J., van der Linden, S., Marteau, T.M., and Spiegelhalter, D. 2020. 'Five Rules for Evidence Communication'. *Nature* 587, 362–364.

Bloom, P. 2016. *Against Empathy: The Case for Rational Compassion*. New York: Ecco Press.

Bloom, P. 2017. 'Empathy and Its Discontents'. *Trends in Cognitive Sciences* 21(1), 24–31. DOI: 10.1016/j.tics.2016.11.004

Bodas-Sagi, D., and Labeaga, J. 2016. 'Using GDELT Data to Evaluate the Confidence on the Spanish Government Energy Policy'. *International Journal of Interactive Multimedia and Artificial Intelligence* 3(6), 38–43. DOI: 10.9781/ijimai.2016.366

Boje, D. 1991. 'The Storytelling Organization: A Study of Story Performance in an Office Supply Firm'. *Administrative Science Quarterly* 36(1), 106–126. DOI: 10.2307/2393432

Bolin, B. 1994. 'Science and Policy Making'. *Ambio* 23(1), 25–29.

Bontoux, L., Sweeney, J.A., Rosa, A.B., Bauer, A., Bengtsson, D., Bock, A.-K., Caspar, B., Charter, M., Christophilopoulos, E., Kupper, F., Macharis, C., Matti, C., Matrisciano, M., Schuijer, J., Szczepanikova, A., van Criekinge, T., and Watson, R. 2020. 'A Game for All Seasons: Lessons and Learnings from the JRC's Scenario Exploration System'. *World Futures Review* 12(1), 81–103. DOI: 10.1177/1946756719890524

Boon, M. and Knuuttila, T. 2008. 'Models as Epistemic Tools in Engineering Sciences: A Pragmatic Approach'. In A. Meijers (ed.), *Handbook of the Philosophy of Science, Volume 9: Philosophy of Technology and Engineering Sciences*, 687–720. Elsevier.

Boswell, J. 2016. 'Deliberating Downstream: Countering Democratic Distortions in the Policy Process'. *Perspectives on Politics*, 14(3), 724–737. DOI: 10.1017/S1537592716001146

Boulding, K. 1973. 'Foreword'. In F. Polak, *The Image of the Future*, v–vi. London: Elsevier Scientific Publishing Company.

Boyd, B. 2009. *On the Origin of Stories: Evolution, Cognition and Fiction*. Cambridge, MA: Harvard University Press.

Boyd, D.R. 2017. *The Rights of Nature: A Legal Revolution that Could Save the World*. Toronto: ECW Press.

Boyd, I. 2013a. 'Point of View: Making Science Count in Government'. *eLife* 2, e010612. DOI: 10.7554/eLife.01061

Boyd, I. 2013b. 'Scientists Do Speak Up, but Politicians Decide Policy'. *The Guardian*, 6 October 2013. Accessed 18 September 2020, at: https://www.theguardian.com/commentisfree/2013/oct/06/scientists-speak-up-politicians-decide-policy

Bradfield, R., Wright, G., Burt, G., Cairns, G., and Van Der Heijden, K. 2005. 'The Origins and Evolution of Scenario Techniques in Long Range Business Planning'. *Futures* 37, 795–812. DOI: 10.1016/j.futures.2005.01.003

Brecht, B. 2001. *Brecht on Theatre*. Translated by John Willett. London: Methuen Drama.

Breckon, J., Hopkins, A., and Rickey, B. 2019. 'Evidence vs Democracy: How "Mini-publics" Can Traverse the Gap Between Citizens, Experts and Evidence'. London: Nesta. Accessed 1 November 2020, at: https://www.alliance4usefulevidence.org/assets/2019/01/Evidence-vs-Democracy-publication.pdf

Brians, P. 1984. 'Nuclear War in Science Fiction, 1945–59 (*La guerre nucléaire en science-fiction, 1945–59*)'. *Science Fiction Studies* 11(3), 253–263.

Brians, P. 1987. *Nuclear Holocausts: Atomic War in Fiction, 1895–1984*. Kent, OH: The Kent State University Press.

Briggs, S.A. 1992. 'Remembering Rachel'. *EPA Journal* 18(2), 62.

British Academy. 2016. *Crossing Paths: Interdisciplinary Institutions, Careers, Education and Applications*. London: British Academy. Accessed 7 November 2020, at: https://www.thebritishacademy.ac.uk/publications/crossing-paths/

Britt, R. 2015. 'Was 1984's *The Terminator* a Harlan Ellison Rip-Off?' *Electric Lit*, 1 July 2015. Accessed 30 October 2020, at: https://electricliterature.com/was-1984s-the-terminator-a-harlan-ellison-rip-off/.

Brom, F. 2019. 'Institutionalizing Applied Humanities: Enabling a Stronger Role for the Humanities in Interdisciplinary Research for Public Policy'. *Palgrave Communications* 5, 72. DOI: 10.1057/s41599-019-0281–2

Brookes, D.E., and Hérbert, L.P. 2006. 'Gender, Race, and Media Representation'. In B.J. Dow and J.T. Wood (eds.), *The SAGE Handbook of Gender and Communication*, 297–318. London: Sage.

Brooks, P., with Jewett, H. (eds.). 2014. *The Humanities and Public Life*. New York: Fordham University Press.

Broome, J. 2014. 'A Philosopher at the IPCC'. *The Philosophers' Magazine* 66, 11–16. DOI: 10.5840/tpm20146673

Broome, J. 2020. 'Philosophy in the IPCC'. In E. Brister and R. Frodeman (eds.), *Philosophy for the Real World: An Introduction to Field Philosophy with Case Studies and Practical Strategies*, 95–110. New York: Routledge.

Brown, A.D. 2006. 'A Narrative Approach to Collective Identities'. *Journal of Management Studies* 43, 731–753. DOI:10.1111/j.1467-6486.2006.00609.x

Brown, L. 2013. 'Storytelling and Ecological Management: Understanding Kinship and Complexity'. *Journal of Sustainability Education* 4. Accessed 29 September 2020, at: http://www.susted.com/wordpress/content/storytelling-and-ecological-management-understanding-kinship-and-complexity_2013_02/

Brown, M. 2020. 'Fiction Readers Have Made Best Leaders in Covid-19 Crisis, says Val McDermid'. *The Guardian*, 16 August 2020: https://www.theguardian.com/books/2020/aug/16/fiction-readers-made-best-leaders-in-covid-19-crisis-val-mcdermid-edinburgh

Brulle, R.J., Carmichael, J., and Jenkins, J.C. 2012. 'Shifting Public Opinion on Climate Change: An Empirical Assessment of Factors Influencing Concern Over Climate Change in the U.S., 2002–2010'. *Climatic Change* 114, 169–188. DOI: 10.1007/s10584-012-0403-y

Bruner, J. 1986. *Actual Minds, Possible Worlds*. Cambridge, MA: Harvard University Press.

Burnam-Fink, M. 2015. 'Creating Narrative Scenarios: Science Fiction Protoyping at Emerge'. *Futures* 70, 48–55. DOI: 10.1016/j.futures.2014.12.005

Burnham, D. 1979. 'Nuclear Experts Debate "The China Syndrome"'. *The New York Times*, 18 March 1979, D1.

Burns, J. 2009. *Goddess of the Market: Ayn Rand and the American Right*. New York: Oxford University Press.

Cairney, P. 2015. 'Policy Concepts in 1000 Words: Framing'. *Paul Cairney: Politics & Public Policy* [online]. 2 November 2015. Accessed 24 September 2020, at: https://paulcairney.wordpress.com/2015/11/02/policy-concepts-in-1000-words-framing/

Cairney, P. 2016. *The Politics of Evidence-Based Policy Making*. London: Palgrave Macmillan.

Cairney, P. 2018. 'Three Habits of Successful Policy Entrepreneurs'. *Policy & Politics* 46(2), 199–215. DOI: 10.1332/030557318X15230056771696

Cairney, P. 2020. *Understanding Public Policy: Theories and Issues*. 2nd edn. London: Red Globe Press.

Cairney, P., and Kwiatkowski, R. 2017. 'How to Communicate Effectively with Policymakers: Combine Insights from Psychology and Policy Studies'. *Palgrave Communications* 3, 37. DOI: 10.1057/s41599-017-0046-8

Cairney, P., and Oliver, K. 2020. 'How Should Academics Engage in Policymaking to Achieve Impact?' *Political Studies Review* 18(2), 228–244. DOI: 10.1177/1478929918807714

Cairney, P., and Weible, C.M. 2015. 'Comparing and Contrasting Peter Hall's Paradigms and Ideas with the Advocacy Coalition Framework'. In J. Hogan and M. Howlett (eds.), *Policy Paradigms in Theory and Practice: Studies in the Political Economy of Public Policy*, 83–99. London: Palgrave Macmillan. DOI: 10.1057/9781137434043_5

Calder, M., Craig, C., Culley, D., de Cani, R., Donnelly, C.A., Douglas, R., Edmonds, B., Gascoigne, J., Gilbert, N., Hargrove, C., Hinds, D., Lane, D.C., Mitchell, D., Pavey, G., Robertson, D., Rosewell, B., Sherwin, S., Walport, M., and Wilson, A. 2018. 'Computational Modelling for Decision-making: Where, Why, What, Who and How'. *Royal Society Open Science* 5, 172096. DOI: 10.1098/rsos.172096

Callaghan, V., Clarke, G., and Chin, J. 2004. 'Pervasive Computing and Urban Development: Issues for the individual and Society'. *United Nations World Urban Forum (Habitat), Cities: Crossroads of Cultures, Inclusiveness and Integration?* Barcelona, 13–17 September 2004. Accessed 29 October 2020, at: http://victor.callaghan.info/publications/2004_UN_Habitat04(PervasiveComputing).pdf

Campbell, A. 2016. 'Why Bankers Should Have to Join Book Clubs'. *The Irish Times*, 6 June 2016. Accessed 30 October 2020, at: https://www-irishtimes-com.ezp.lib.cam.ac.uk/opinion/aifric-campbell-why-bankers-should-have-to-join-book-clubs-1.2673650

Candy, S. 2018. 'Gaming Futures Literacy: The Thing from the Future'. In R. Miller (ed.), *Transforming the Future: Anticipation in the 21st Century*, 233–246. London: Routledge.

Capacity to Decolonise. 2021. 'Purpose of Project'. *Capacity to Decolonise*. Accessed 21 April 2021, at: http://foresightfordevelopment.org/c2d/

Cash, D., Clark, W.C., Alcock, F., Dickson, N.M., Eckley, N., and Jäger, J. 2003. 'Salience, Credibility, Legitimacy and Boundaries: Linking Research, Assessment and Decision Making'. *KSG Working Papers Series*. Accessed 17 April 2021, at: http://nrs.harvard.edu/urn-3:HUL.InstRepos:32067415

Cartwright, N. 2007. *Hunting Causes and Using Them: Approaches in Philosophy and Economics*. Cambridge: Cambridge University Press.

Cartwright, N., and Hardie, J. 2012. *Evidence-Based Policy: A Practical Guide to Doing It Better*. Oxford: Oxford University Press.

Carvalho, A., and Burgess, J. 2005. 'Cultural Circuits of Climate Change in U.K. Broadsheet Newspapers, 1985–2003'. *Risk Analysis* 25, 1457–1469. DOI: 10.1111/j.1539–6924.2005.00692.x

Castellani, T., Valente, A., Cori, L., and Bianchi, F. 2016. 'Detecting the Use of Evidence in a Meta-Policy'. *Evidence & Policy: A Journal of Research, Debate and Practice* 12(1), 91–107. DOI: 10.1332/174426415X14430152798949

Cave, S., Dihal, K., and Dillon, S. (eds.). 2020. *AI Narratives: A History of Imaginative Thinking about Intelligent Machines*. Oxford: Oxford University Press.

Cavallo, G., and Chartier, R. 1999. 'Introduction'. In G. Cavallo and R. Chartier (eds.), *A History of Reading in the West*, 1–36. Amherst, MA: University of Massachusetts Press.

Ceruzzi, P.E. 2011. 'Manned Space Flight and Artificial Intelligence: "Natural" Trajectories of Technology'. In D.L. Ferro and E.S. Swedin (eds.), *Science Fiction and Computing: Essays on Interlinked Domains*, 95–116. London: McFarland.

Chabay, I., Koch, L., Martinez, G., and Scholz, G. 2019. 'Influence of Narratives of Vision and Identity on Collective Behavior Change'. *Sustainability* 11, 5680. DOI: 10.3390/su11205680

Chait, J. 2009. 'Wealthcare: Ayn Rand and the Invincible Cult of Selfishness on the American Right'. *The New Republic*, 14 September 2009. Accessed 27 September 2020, at: https://newrepublic.com/article/69239/wealthcare-0

Chapman, J. 2006. 'The BBC and the Censorship of *The War Game*'. *Journal of Contemporary History* 41(1), 75–94. DOI: 10.1177/0022009406058675

Charmaz, K. 2014. *Constructing Grounded Theory*. 2nd edn. London: SAGE Publishing.

Chartier, R. 1995. *Forms and Meanings: Texts, Performances, and Audiences from Codex to Computer*. Philadelphia: University of Pennsylvania Press.

Chatman, S. 1980. *Story and Discourse: Narrative Structure in Fiction and Film*. London: Cornell University Press.

Chow, R. 1995. *Primitive Passions: Visuality, Sexuality, Ethnography, and Contemporary Chinese Cinema*. New York: Columbia University Press.

Christensen, J., Cox, C., and Szabo-Jones, L. (eds.). 2018. *Activating the Heart: Storytelling, Knowledge Sharing, and Relationship*. Waterloo, ON: Wilfrid Laurier University Press.

Climate Assembly UK. 2020. *The Path to Net Zero*. London: House of Commons. Accessed 21 April 2021, at: https://www.climateassembly.uk/report/read/final-report.pdf

Cohen, S., Demeritt, D., Robinson, J., and Rothman, D. 1998. 'Climate Change and Sustainable Development: Towards Dialogue'. *Global Environmental Change* 8(4), 341–371. DOI: 10.1016/S0959-3780(98)00017-X

Cohen, T., Stilgoe, J., and Cavoli, C. 2018. 'Reframing the Governance of Automotive Automation: Insights from UK Stakeholder Workshops'. *Journal of Responsible Innovation* 5, 257–279. DOI: 10.1080/23299460.2018.1495030

Collins, H. 2014. *Are We All Scientific Experts Now?* Cambridge: Polity.

Collins, H., Evans, R., and Weinel, M. 2017. 'STS as Science or Politics?' *Social Studies of Science* 47(4), 580–586. DOI: 10.1177/0306312717710131

Contessa, G. 2010. 'Introduction'. *Synthese* 172, 193–195. DOI: 10.1007/s11229-009-9501-4

Convention Citoyenne pour le Climat. 2021. *Avis de la convention citoyenne pour le climat sur les réponses apportées par le gouvernement à ses propositions.* Paris: Conseil Économique, Social et Environnemental. Accessed 21 April 2021, at: https://www.convention-citoyennepourleclimat.fr/wp-content/uploads/2021/03/CCC-rapport_Session8_GR-1.pdf

Cooke, J. 2017. 'Violations of Empathy'. *New Formations* 89/90, 153–169. DOI: 10.3898/NEWF:89/90.09.2016

Cooper, A.C.G. 2016. 'Exploring the Scope of Science Advice: Social Sciences in the UK Government'. *Palgrave Communications* 2, 16044. DOI: 10.1057/palcomms.2016.44

Coplan, A. 2004. 'Empathic Engagement with Narrative Fictions'. *The Journal of Aesthetics and Art Criticism* 62(2), 141–152. DOI: 10.1111/j.1540-594X.2004.00147.x

Coplan, A. 2011. 'Will the Real Empathy Please Stand Up? A Case for a Narrow Conceptualization'. *The Southern Journal of Philosophy* 49(1), 40–65. DOI: 10.1111/j.2041-6962.2011.00056.x

Corbera, E., Calvet-Mir, L., Hughes, H., and Paterson, M. 2016. 'Patterns of Authorship in the IPCC Working Group III Report'. *Nature Climate Change* 6, 94–99. DOI: 10.1038/nclimate2782

Cornell S. 2000. 'That's the Story of Our Life'. In P. Spickard and W.J. Burroughs (eds.), *We Are a People: Narrative and Multiplicity in Constructing Ethnic Identity*, 41–53. Philadelphia, PA: Temple University Press.

Corner, A., and Clarke, J. 2017. *Talking Climate: From Research to Practice in Public Engagement.* London: Palgrave Macmillan.

Corner, A., and Groves, C. 2014. 'Breaking the Climate Change Communication Deadlock'. *Nature Climate Change* 4, 743–745. DOI: 10.1038/nclimate2348

Cosmides, L., and Tooby, J. 2005. 'Neurocognitive Adaptations Designed for Social Exchange'. In D. Buss (ed.), *The Handbook of Evolutionary Psychology*, 584–627. Hoboken, NJ: Wiley.

Coupland, C. 2001. 'Accounting for Change: A Discourse Analysis of Graduate Trainees' Talk of Adjustment'. *Journal of Management Studies* 38, 1103–1119. DOI: 10.1111/1467–6486.00274

Craig, C. 2019. *How Does Government Listen to Scientists?* Cham: Palgrave Macmillan.

Crist, E., and Rinker, H.B. (eds.). 2009. *Gaia in Turmoil: Climate Change, Biodepletion and Earth Ethics in an Age of Crisis.* Cambridge, MA: The MIT Press.

Csibra, G., Bíró, S., Koós, O., and Gergely, G. 2003. 'One-Year-Old Infants Use Teleological Representations of Actions Productively'. *Cognitive Science* 27, 111–133. DOI: 10.1016/S0364-0213(02)00112-X

Cuneo, J. 2011. '"Hello, Computer": The Interplay of *Star Trek* and Modern Computing'. In D.L. Ferro and E.S. Swedin (eds.), *Science Fiction and Computing: Essays on Interlinked Domains*, 131–147. London: McFarland.

Cunliffe, A.L. 2001. 'Managers as Practical Authors: Reconstructing our Understanding of Management Practice'. *Journal of Management Studies*, 38: 351–371. DOI: 10.1111/1467-6486.00240

Currie, A., and Sterelny, K. 2017. 'In Defence of Story-Telling'. *Studies in History and Philosophy of Science* 62, 14–21. DOI: 10.1016/j.shpsa.2017.03.003

Currie, G. 2010. *Narrative and Narrators: A Philosophy of Stories*. Oxford: Oxford University Press.

Darnton, R. 1982. 'What Is the History of Books?' *Daedalus* 111(3), 65–83.

Dator, J. 2017. 'Editorial: Time, the Future, and Other Fantasies'. *World Futures Review* 9(1), 5–16. DOI: 10.1177/1946756716687488.

Davies, P. 2008. 'Making Policy Evidence-Based: The UK Experience'. *Regional Impact Evaluation Workshop*. World Bank Middle East and North Africa Region, Cairo: 13–17 January 2008.

Davies, S., Selin, C., Gano, G., and Guimaraes Pereira, A. 2011. 'Citizen Engagement and Urban Change: Three Case Studies of Material Deliberation'. *Cities* 29(6), 351–357. DOI: 10.1016/j.cities.2011.11.012

Davis, M.H. 1996. *Empathy: A Social Psychological Approach*. Madison, WI: Brown & Benchmark.

Delgado, R. 1996. 'Rodrigo's Eleventh Chronicle: Empathy and False Empathy'. *California Law Review* 84, 61–100. DOI: 10.2307/3480903

Department for Business, Energy & Industrial Strategy. 2020. 'Carbon Calculator'. *Gov. uk*, 3 December 2020. Accessed 18 March 2021, at: https://www.gov.uk/guidance/carbon-calculator

DeSilvey, C., Naylor, D., and Sackett, C. (eds.). 2011. *Anticipatory History*. Axminster: Uniformbooks.

Díaz, S., Demissew, S., Carabias, J., Joly, C., Lonsdale, M., Ash, N., Larigauderie, A., Adhikari, J.R., Arico, S., Báldi, A., Bartuska, A., Baste, I.A., Bilgin, A., Brondizio, E., Chan, K.M.A., Figueroa, V.E., Duraiappah, A., Fischer, M., Hill, R., Koetz, T., Leadley, P., Lyver, P., Mace, G.M., Martin-Lopez, B., Okumura, M., Pacheco, D., Pascual, U., Pérez, E.S., Reyers, B., Roth, E., Saito, O., Scholes, R.S., Sharma, N., Tallis, H., Thaman, R., Watson, R., Yahara, T., Hamid, Z.A., Akosim, C., Al-Hafedh, Y., Allahverdiyev, R., Amankwah, E., Asah, S.T., Asfaw, Z., Bartus, G., Brooks, L.A., Caillaux, J., Dalle, G., Darnaedi, D., Driver, A., Erpul, G., Escobar-Eyzaguirre, P., Failler, P., Mokhtar Fouda, A.M., Fu, B., Gundimeda, H., Hashimoto, S., Homer, F., Lavore, S., Lichtenstein, G., Mala, A.M., Mandivenyi, W., Matczak, P., Mbizvo, C., Mehrdadi, M., Metzger, J.P., Mikissa, J.B., Moller, H., Mooney, H.A., Mumby, P., Nagendra, H., Nesshover, C., Oteng-Yeboah, A.A., Pataki, G., Roué, M., Rubis, J., Schultz, M., Smith, P., Sumaila, R., Takeuchi, K., Thomas, S., Verma, M., Yeo-Chang, Y., and Zlatanova, D. 2015. 'The IPBES Conceptual Framework – Connecting Nature and People'. *Current Opinion in Environmental Sustainability* 14(1), 1–16. DOI: 10.1016/j.cosust.2014.11.002

Dibdin, E. 2020. 'Experts Break Down How Real "Contagion" Is Following a Surge in Viewers'. *Bustle*, 12 March 2020. Accessed 19 October 2020, at: https://www.bustle.com/p/how-accurate-is-contagion-3-experts-break-down-the-2011-film-22618201?utm_source=twitter&utm_medium=owned&utm_campaign=bustle

van Dijck, J., and Rieder, B. (eds.). 2019. 'Special Issue: Transnational Materialities'. *Internet Policy Review* 8(2). DOI: 10.14763/2019.2.1418

Dillon, G.L. 2012. *Walking the Clouds: An Anthology of Indigenous Science Fiction*. Tucson: University of Arizona Press.

Dillon, G.L. 2016. 'Native Slipstream: Blackfeet Physics in *The Fast Red Road*'. In B. Stratton (ed.), *The Fictions of Stephen Graham: A Critical Companion*, 345–355. Albuquerque: University of New Mexico Press.

Dillon, S. 2015. 'Literary Equivocation: Reproductive Futurism and *The Ice People*'. In S. Dillon and C. Edwards (eds.), *Maggie Gee: Critical Essays*, 101–132. Canterbury: Glyphi.

Dillon, S. 2018. 'English and the Public Good'. In R. Eaglestone and G. Marshall (eds.), *English: Shared Futures*, 194–201. Martlesham: Boydell and Brewer.

Dillon, S. 2020. 'Who Rules the World? Reimagining the Contemporary Feminist Dystopia'. In J. Cooke (ed.), *New Feminist Literary Studies*, 169–181. Cambridge: Cambridge University Press.

Dillon, S. [Forthcoming a]. 'The Deictic Humanities: Towards a Taxonomy of Interdiciplinarities'.

Dillon, S. [Forthcoming b]. 'On the Politics of Adaptation: *Cloud Atlas* and Narrative Evolution'.

Dillon, S., and Schaffer, J. [Forthcoming]. 'What AI Researchers Read: The Role of Stories in Artificial Intelligence Research'.

Dilthey, W. 1988. 'The Understanding of Other Persons and Their Life-Expressions'. In K. Mueller-Vollmer (ed.), *The Hermeneutics Reader*, 152–164. New York: Continuum.

Djikic, M., Oatley, K., and Moldoveanu, M.C. 2013. 'Reading Other Minds: Effects of Literature on Empathy'. *Scientific Study of Literature* 3(1), 28–47. DOI: 10.1075/ssol.3.1.06dji

Doctorow, C. 2020. 'The Dangers of Cynical Sci-Fi Disaster Stories'. *Slate*, 13 October 2020. Accessed 1 November 2020, at: https://slate.com/technology/2020/10/cory-docotorow-sci-fi-intuition-pumps.html

Donald, D. 2009. 'Forts, Curriculum, and Indigenous Métissage: Imagining Decolonization of Aboriginal-Canadian Relations in Educational Contexts'. *First Nations Perspectives* 2(1): 1–24.

Donnelly, C.A., Boyd, I., Campbell, P., Craig, C., Vallance, P., Walport, M., Whitty, C.J.M., Woods, E., and Wormald, C. 2018. 'Four Principles to Make Evidence Synthesis More Useful for Policy'. *Nature* 558 (21 June 2018), 361–364. DOI: 10.1038/d41586-018-05414-4

van Dorsser, C., and Taneja, P. 2020. 'An Integrated Three-Layered Foresight Framework'. *Foresight* 22(2), 250–272. DOI: 10.1108/FS-05-2019-0039

van Dorsser, C., Tanejaa, P., Walker, W., and Marchau, V. 2020. 'An Integrated Framework for Anticipating the Future and Dealing with Uncertainty in Policymaking'. *Futures* 124, 102594. DOI: 10.1016/j.futures.2020.102594

Douglas, A. 1986. 'Introduction: The Art of Controversy'. In H. Beecher Stowe, *Uncle Tom's Cabin or, Life Among the Lowly*, 7–36. London: Penguin.

Douglas, H. 2012. 'Weighing Complex Evidence in a Democratic Society'. *Kennedy Institute of Ethics Journal* 22(2), 139–162. DOI: 10.1353/ken.2012.0009

Douglas, H. 2015. 'Politics and Science: Untangling Values, Ideologies, and Reasons'. *The ANNALS of the American Academy of Political and Social Science* 658(1), 296–306. DOI: 10.1177/0002716214557237

Dovidio, J.F., Piliavin, J.A., Schroeder, D.A., and Penner, L.A. 2006. *The Social Psychology of Prosocial Behavior*. Hillsdale, NJ: Erlbaum.

Drukman, J.N., and Lupia, A. 2017. 'Using Framing to Make Scientific Communication More Effective'. In K.H. Jamieson, D.M. Kahan, and D.A. Scheufele (eds.), *The Oxford Handbook of the Science of Science Communication*, 351–360. Oxford: Oxford University Press.

Ducarme, F., Luque, G.M., and Courchamp, F. 2013. 'What Are "Charismatic Species" for Conservation Biologists?' *Ecole Normale Supérieure de Lyon BioSciences Master Reviews* (July 2013). Accessed 17 April 2021, at: http://biologie.ens-lyon.fr/ressources/bibliographies/pdf/m1-11-12-biosci-reviews-ducarme-f-2c-m.pdf?lang=fr

Ducheyne, S. 2008. 'Towards an Ontology of Scientific Models'. *Metaphysica* 9(1), 119–127. DOI: 10.1007/s12133-008-0026-y

Dunn, J. 1988. *The Beginnings of Social Understanding*. Cambridge, MA: Harvard University Press.

Dunn, J. 1991. 'Understanding Others: Evidence from Naturalistic Studies of Children'. In A. Whiten (ed.), *Natural Theories of Mind: Evolution, Development and Simulation of Everyday Mindreading*, 51–61. Oxford: Basil Blackwell.

Economic and Social Research Council. [n.d.]. 'Research Syntheses'. Accessed 19 October 2020, at: http://www.esrc.ac.uk/public-engagement/public-dialogues/research-syntheses/

Edelman, L. 2004. *No Future: Queer Theory and the Death Drive*. Durham, NC: Duke University Press.

Eder, K. 2009. 'A Theory of Collective Identity: Making Sense of the Debate on a "European Identity"'. *European Journal of Social Theory* 12(4), 427–447. DOI: 10.1177/1368431009345050

Editors, The. 1984. 'Three Minutes to Midnight', *Bulletin of the Atomic Scientists* 40(1), 2.

Egeland, G.M., Yohannes, S., Okalik, L., Kilabuk, J., Racicot, C., Wilcke, M., Kuluguqtuq, J., and Kisa, S. 2013. 'The Value of Inuit Elders' Storytelling to Health Promotion During Times of Rapid Climate Change and Uncertain Food Security'. In H.V. Kuhnlein, B. Erasmus, D. Spigelski, and B. Burlingame (eds.), *Indigenous Peoples' Food Systems and Well-Being: Interventions and Policies for Healthy Communities*, 141–157. Rome: Food and Agriculture Organization of the United Nations, Centre for Indigenous Peoples' Nutrition and Environment.

Egerton, S., Callaghan, V., and Clark, G. 2008. 'Using Multiple Personas in Service Robots to Improve Exploration Strategies When Mapping New Environments'. *4th International Conference on Intelligent Environments*. University of Washington, Seattle, 21–22 July.

Eisenberg, N., and Miller, P.A. 1987. 'The Relation of Empathy to Prosocial and Related Behaviors.' *Psychological Bulletin* 101(1), 91–119. DOI: 10.1037/0033-2909.101.1.91

Eisenberg, N., and Strayer, J. (eds.). 1987. *Empathy and its Development*. Cambridge: Cambridge University Press.

Eisenstein, M. 2017. 'How Social Scientists Can Help to Shape Climate Policy'. *Nature* 551 (29 November 2017), 142–144. DOI: 10.1038/d41586-017-07418-y

Ehrlich, P.R. 1979. 'Paul Ehrlich Reconsiders Silent Spring'. *Bulletin of the Atomic Scientists* 35, 34–36.

Elkins, C. 1979. 'Science Fiction versus Futurology: Dramatic versus Rational Models'. *Science Fiction Studies* 6(1), 20–31.

English, J.F. 2010a. 'Everywhere and Nowhere: The Sociology of Literature After "the Sociology of Literature"'. *New Literary History* 41(2), v–xxiii. DOI: 10.1353/nlh.2010.0005

English, J.F. (ed.). 2010b. Special Issue: *New Sociologies of Literature*, *New Literary History* 41(2).

Erlich, V. 1955. *Russian Formalism: History, Doctrine*. The Hague: Mouton and Co.

Eubanks, V. 2019. *Automating Inequality: How High-Tech Tools Profile, Police, and Punish the Poor*. London: Picador.

European Commission. [n.d.]. 'The Scenario Exploration System (SES)'. *European Commission*. Accessed 3 March 2021, at: https://knowledge4policy.ec.europa.eu/foresight/tool/scenario-exploration-system-ses_en

European Parliament, European Union. 2017. European Parliament resolution of 16 February 2017 with recommendations to the Commission on Civil Law Rules on Robotics (2015/2103[INL]). Accessed 16 September 2020, at: https://www.europarl.europa.eu/doceo/document/TA-8-2017-0051_EN.html?redirect#title2

Facer, K. 2019. 'Storytelling in Troubled Time: What is the Role for Educators in the Deep Crises of the 21st Century?' *Literacy* 53(1), 3–13. DOI: 10.1111/lit.12176

Fazey, I., Moug, P., Allen, S., Beckmann, K., Blackwood, D., Bonaventura, M., Burnett, K., Danson, M., Falconer, R., Gagnon, A.S., Harkness, R., Hodgson, A., Holm, L., Irvine, K.N., Low, R., Lyon, C., Moss, A., Moran, C., Naylor, L., O'Brien, K., Russell, S., Skerratt, S., Rao-Williams, J., and Wolstenholme, R. 2018. 'Transformation in a Changing Climate: A Research Agenda'. *Climate and Development* 10(3), 197–217. DOI: 10.1080/17565529.2017.1

Fazey, I., Wise, R.M., Lyon, C., Câmpeanu, C., Moug, P., and Davies, T.E. 2016. 'Past and Future Adaptation Pathways'. *Climate and Development* 8(1), 26–44. DOI: 10.1080/17565529.2014.989192

Feenberg, A. 1977. 'An End to History: Science Fiction in the Nuclear Age'. *The Johns Hopkins Magazine*, March, 12–22.

Feldman, C.F., Bruner, J., Renderer, B., and Spitzer, S. 1990. 'Narrative comprehension'. In B.K. Britton and D. Pellegrini (eds.), *Narrative Thought and Narrative Language*, 1–78. Hillsdale, NJ: Erlbaum.

Felski, R. 2008. *Uses of Literature*. Oxford: Blackwell Publishing.

Felt, U., Fouché, R., Miller, C.A., and Smith-Doerr, L. (eds.). 2017. *The Handbook of Science and Technology Studies*. Cambridge, MA: The MIT Press.

Fergnani, A., and Song, Z. 2020. 'The Six Scenario Archetypes Framework: A Systematic Investigation of Science Fiction Films Set in the Future'. *Futures* 124, 102645. DOI: 10.1016/j.futures.2020.102645

Fernández-Llamazares, Á., and Cabeza, M. 2018. 'Rediscovering the Potential of Indigenous Storytelling for Conservation Practice'. *Conservation Letters* 11, e12398. DOI: 10.1111/conl.12398

Ferro, D., and Swedin, E. 2009. 'Computer Fiction: "A Logic Named Joe"'. In J. Impagliazzo, T. Järvi, and P. Paju (eds.), *History of Nordic Computing 2: Second IFIP WG 9.7 Conference, HiNC 2, Turku, Finland, August 21–23, 2007, Revised Selected Papers*, 84–94. Berlin: Springer. DOI: 10.1007/978-3-642-03757-3_9

Ferro, D.L. 2011. 'Introduction'. In D.L. Ferro and E.S. Swedin (eds.), *Science Fiction and Computing: Essays on Interlinked Domains*, 1–12. London: McFarland.

Feukeu, K.E., Ajilore, B., Bourgeois, R., Miller, R., Carden, F., and Karuri-Sebina, G. 2021. 'The Capacity to Decolonise: Building Futures Literacy in Africa'. *Capacity to Decolonise* [working paper]. Accessed 21 April 2021, at: http://foresightfordevelopment.org/c2d/wp-content/uploads/2021/03/C2D-Research-Paper-March-2021.pdf

Fischer, M. 2017. 'Literature and Empathy'. *Philosophy and Literature* 41(2), 431–464. DOI: 10.1353/phl.2017.0050

Fischoff, M. 2015. 'What to Expect When You're Engaging: Tips for Academic Outreach'. *Network for Business Sustainability*, 27 May 2015. Accessed 7 November 2020, at: https://www.nbs.net/articles/what-to-expect-when-youre-engaging-tips-for-academic-outreach

Fisher, W.R. 1978. 'Toward a Logic of Good Reasons'. *Quarterly Journal of Speech* 64(4), 376–384. DOI: 10.1080/00335637809383443

Fisher, W.R. 1984. 'Narration as a Human Communication Paradigm: The Case of Public Moral Argument'. *Communication Monographs* 51(1), 1–22. DOI: 10.1080/03637758409390180

Fisher, W.R. 1985. 'The Narrative Paradigm: In the Beginning'. *Journal of Communication* 35(4), 74–89. DOI: 10.1111/j.1460-2466.1985.tb02974.x

Fisher, W.R. 1989. 'Clarifying the Narrative Paradigm'. *Communication Monographs* 56(1), 55–58. DOI: 10.1080/03637758909390249

Fishkin, J., and Luskin, R. 1999. 'Bringing Deliberation to the Democratic Dialogue'. In M. McCombs and A. Reynolds (eds.), *A Poll with a Human Face: The National Issues Convention Experiment in Political Communication*, 3–38. Mahwah, NJ: Lawrence Erlbaum.

Fishkin, J., and Luskin, R. 2005. 'Experimenting with a Democratic Ideal: Deliberative Polling and Public Opinion'. *Acta Politica* 40, 284–298. DOI: 10.1057/palgrave.ap.5500121

Flanagan, K., Clarke, S., Agar, J., Edgerton, D., and Craig, C. 2019. *Lessons from the History of UK Science Policy*. London: The British Academy.

Fleischmann, K.R., and Templeton, T.C. 2008. 'Past Futures and Technoscientific Innovation: The Mutual Shaping of Science Fiction and Science Fact'. *Proceedings of the American Society for Information Science and Technology* 45, 1–11. DOI: 10.1002/meet.2008.1450450345

Flood, A. 2020. 'Publishers Report Sales Boom in Novels about Fictional Epidemics'. *The Guardian*, 5 March. Accessed 19 October 2020, at: https://www.theguardian.com/books/2020/mar/05/publishers-report-sales-boom-in-novels-about-fictional-epidemics-camus-the-plague-dean-koontz

'FloodRanger: Educational Flood Management Game'. [n.d.] *Discovery Software*. Accessed 18 March 2021, at: http://www.discoverysoftware.co.uk/FloodRanger.htm

Fong, K., Mullin, J.B., and Mar, R. 2013. 'What You Read Matters: The Role of Fiction Genre in Predicting Interpersonal Sensitivity'. *Psychology of Aesthetics, Creativity, and the Arts* 7(4), 370–376. DOI: 10.1037/a0034084

Ford, J., Cameron, L., Rubis, J., Maillet, M., Nakashima, D., Willox, A.C., and Pearce, T. 2016. 'Including Indigenous Knowledge and Experience in IPCC Assessment Reports'. *Nature Climate Change* 6, 349–353. DOI: 10.1038/nclimate2954

Ford, J.D., Vanderbilt, W., and Berrang-Ford, L. 2012. 'Authorship in IPCC AR5 and Its Implications for Content: Climate Change and Indigenous Populations in WGII'. *Climatic Change* 113, 201–213. DOI: 10.1007/s10584-011-0350-z

Foucault, M. 1970. *The Order of Things: An Archaeology of the Human Sciences*. London: Tavistock.

Foucault, M. 1972. *The Archaeology of Knowledge*. London: Tavistock.

Foucault, M. 1979. 'Power and Norms'. In M. Morris and P. Patton (eds.), *Power, Truth, and Strategy*, 59–66. Sydney: Feral Publications.

Foucault, M. 1980. *Power/ Knowledge: Selected Interviews and Other Writings 1972–77*. Brighton: Harvester.

Foucault, M. 1984. 'The Order of Discourse'. In M. Shapiro (ed.), *Language and Politics*, 108–138. Oxford: Blackwell.

Foucault, M. 2000. *Power: The Essential Works of Michel Foucault, 1954–1984*, vol. 3. Edited by James D. Faubion. Translated by Robert Hurley and Others. London: Allen Lane.

Foucault, M. 2007. *Security, Territory, Population: Lectures at the Collège de France 977–1978*. Translated by Graham Burchell. Basingstoke: Palgrave Macmillan.

Francis. 2015. Encyclical Letter Laudato Si': Of the Holy Father Francis on Care for Our Common Home. *The Holy See*, 24 May. Accessed 15 September 2020, at: http://www.vatican.va/content/francesco/en/encyclicals/documents/papa-francesco_20150524_enciclica-laudato-si.html

Franklin, H.B. 1984. *Countdown to Midnight: Twelve Great Stories about Nuclear War*. New York: Dutton.

Franklin, H.B. 2008. *War Stars: The Superweapon and the American Imagination*. Amherst: University of Massachusetts Press.

Franklin, J.H. 1938. 'Edward Bellamy and the Nationalist Movement'. *The New England Quarterly* 11, 739–772.

Freedman, L. 2017. *The Future of War: A History*. New York: PublicAffairs.

Freeman, M. 1984. 'History, Narrative, and Life-Span Developmental Knowledge'. *Human Development* 27, 1–19. DOI: 10.1159/000272899

Frenkel, J. (ed.). 2001. True Names *by Victor Vinge and* The Opening of the Cyberspace Frontier. New York: Tom Doherty Associates.

Frigg, R. 2006. 'Scientific Representation and the Semantic View of Theories'. *Theoria* 55, 49–65. DOI: theoria200621125

Frigg, R. 2010. 'Fiction in Science'. In J. Woods (ed.), *Fictions and Models: New Essays*, 247–287. Munich: Philiosophia Verlag.

Frigg, R., and Hartmann, S. 2020. 'Models in Science'. *The Stanford Encyclopedia of Philosophy* (Spring 2020 Edition), Edward N. Zalta (ed.). Accessed 21 February 2021, at: https://plato.stanford.edu/archives/spr2020/entries/models-science/

Frigg, R., and Nguyen, J. 2016. 'The Fiction View of Models Reloaded'. *The Monist* 99(3), 225–242. DOI: 10.1093/monist/onw002

Frigg, R., and Nguyen, J. 2020a. *Modelling Nature: An Opinionated Introduction to Scientific Representation*. Cham: Springer.

Frigg, R., and Nguyen, J. 2020b. 'Scientific Representation'. *The Stanford Encyclopedia of Philosophy* (Spring 2020 Edition), Edward N. Zalta (ed.). Accessed 13 October 2020, at: https://plato.stanford.edu/archives/spr2020/entries/scientific-representation/

Fromm, E. 1960. 'Foreword'. In E. Bellamy (Ed.), *Looking Backward: 2000–1887*, v–xx. New York: New American Library.

'Front Row'. 2021. *BBC Sounds*, 6 April 2021. Accessed 20 April 2021, at: https://www.bbc.co.uk/sounds/play/m000tt9r

Galafassi, D., Daw, T.M., Thyresson, M., Rosendo, S., Chaigneau, T., Bandeira, S., Munyi, L. Gabrielsson, I., and Brown, K. 2018. 'Stories in Social-Ecological Knowledge Cocreation'. *Ecology and Society* 23(1), 23. DOI: 10.5751/ES-09932-230123

Galinsky, A.D., and Moskowitz, G.B. 2000. 'Perspective-Taking: Decreasing Stereotype Expression, Stereotype Accessibility, and In-Group Favoritism'. *Journal of Personality and Social Psychology* 78(4), 708–724. DOI: 10.1037/0022-3514.78.4.708

Galison, P., and Stump, D.J. 1996. *The Disunity of Science: Boundaries, Contexts, and Power*. Stanford, CA: Stanford University Press.

Gallagher, S. 1996. 'The Moral Significance of Primitive Self-Consciousness: A Response to Bermúdez'. *Ethics* 107(1), 129–140. DOI: 10.1086/233699

Gallagher, S. 2001. 'The Practice of Mind: Theory, Simulation or Primary Interaction?' *Journal of Consciousness Studies* 8(5–7), 83–108.

Gallagher, S. 2004. 'Understanding Interpersonal Problems in Autism: Interaction Theory as An Alternative to Theory of Mind.' *Philosophy, Psychiatry, & Psychology* 11(3): 199–217. DOI: 10.1353/ppp.2004.0063

Gallagher, S. 2006. *How the Body Shapes the Mind*. Oxford: Clarendon Press.

Gallagher, S. 2007a. 'Logical and Phenomenological Arguments Against Simulation Theory'. In D.D. Hutto and M.M. Ratcliffe (eds.), *Folk Psychology Re-Assessed*, 63–78. Dordrecht: Springer.

Gallagher, S. 2007b. 'Simulation Trouble', *Social Neuroscience* 2(3–4), 353–365. DOI: 10.1080/17470910601183549

Gallagher, S. 2008. 'Inference or Interaction: Social Cognition Without Precursors'. *Philosophical Explorations* 11(3), 163–174. DOI: 10.1080/13869790802239227

Gallagher, S., and Hutto, D.D. 2008. 'Understanding Others Through Primary Interaction and Narrative Practice'. In J. Zlatev, T.P. Racine, C. Sinha, and E. Itkonen (eds.), *The Shared Mind: Perspectives on Intersubjectivity*, 17–38. Philadelphia, PA: John Benjamins Publishing Co.

Gallagher, S., and Meltzoff, A. 1996. 'The Earliest Sense of Self and Others: Merleau-Ponty and Recent Developmental Studies'. *Philosophical Psychology* 9(2), 211–233. DOI: 10.1080/09515089608573181

Galtung, J., and Inayatullah, S. 1997. *Macrohistory and Macrohistorians: Perspectives on Individual, Social and Civilizational Change*. Westport, CT: Praeger.

GDELT Project, The. 2020. 'Intro: Watching Our World'. *The GDELT Project*. Accessed 20 July 2021, at: https://www.gdeltproject.org

Gelfert, A. 2016. *How to Do Science with Models: A Philosophical Primer*. Dordrecht: Springer.

Genette, G. 1972. *Figures III*. Paris: Éditions du Seuil.

Genette, G. 1980. *Narrative Discourse: An Essay in Method*. Translated by Jane E. Lewin. Ithaca, NY: Cornell University Press.

Georgakopoulou, A. 2007. *Small Stories, Interaction and Identities*. Amsterdam: John Benjamins Publishing Company. DOI: 10.1075/sin.8

Geraci, R.M. 2010. *Apocalyptic AI: Visions of Heaven in Robotics, Artificial Intelligence, and Virtual Reality*. New York: Oxford University Press.

Gerbner, G., and Gross, L. 1976. 'Living with Television: The Violence Profile'. *Journal of Communication* 76(2), 173–199. DOI: 10.1111/j.1460-2466.1976.tb01397.x

Gerrig, R.J. 1993. *Experiencing Narrative Worlds: On the Psychological Activities of Reading*. New Haven, CT: Yale University Press.

Geschke, D., Lorenz, J., and Holtz, P. 2019. 'The Triple-filter Bubble: Using Agent-based Modelling to Test a Meta-theoretical Framework for the Emergence of Filter Bubbles and Echo Chambers'. *The British Journal of Social Psychology*, 58(1), 129–149. DOI: 10.1111/bjso.12286

Gessen, M. 2019. 'What HBO's "Chernobyl" Got Right, and What It Got Terribly Wrong'. *The New Yorker*, 4 June 2019. Accessed 28 September 2020, at: https://www.newyorker.com/news/our-columnists/what-hbos-chernobyl-got-right-and-what-it-got-terribly-wrong

Ghorashi, H. 2008. 'Giving Silence a Chance: The Importance of Life Stories for Research on Refugees'. *Journal of Refugee Studies* 21(1), 117–132. DOI: 10.1093/jrs/fem033

Ghosh, A. 2016. *The Great Derangement: Climate Change and the Unthinkable*. Chicago, IL: University of Chicago Press.

Gibbard, A., and Varian, H.R. 1978. 'Economic Models'. *The Journal of Philosophy* 75(11), 664–677.

Gibson, R., and Zillmann, D. 1994. 'Exaggerated Versus Representative Exemplification in News Reports: Perception of Issues and Personal Consequences'. *Communication Research* 21(5), 603–624. DOI: 10.1177/009365094021005003

Glaser, B.G., and Strauss, A.L. 2017. *The Discovery of Grounded Theory: Strategies for Qualitative Research*. London: Routledge.

Gleick, P.H. 2020. 'Book Review: Bad Science and Bad Arguments Abound in "Apocalypse Never" by Michael Shellenberger'. *Yale Climate Connections*, 15 July 2020. Accessed 29 September 2020, at: https://yaleclimateconnections.org/2020/07/review-bad-science-and-bad-arguments-abound-in-apocalypse-never/

Gluckman, P. 2014. 'The Art of Science Advice to Government'. *Nature* 507, 163–165. DOI: 10.1038/507163a

Goertzel, B. 2011. 'Who Coined the Term "AGI"?' *goertzel.org*, 28 August 2011. Accessed 12 November 2020, at: https://goertzel.org/who-coined-the-term-agi/

Godfrey-Smith, P. 2006. 'The Strategy of Model-Based Science'. *Biology and Philosophy* 21, 725–740. DOI: 10.1007/s10539-006-9054-6

Goldman, A.I. 1989. 'Interpretation Psychologized'. *Mind and Language* 4, 161–185. DOI: 10.1111/j.1468-0017.1989.tb00249.x

Goodbody, A., and Johns-Putra, A. (eds.). 2018. *Cli-Fi: A Companion*. Oxford: Peter Lang.

Gopnik, A., and Meltzoff, A. 1993. 'Imitation, Cultural Learning and the Origins of "Theory of Mind"'. *Behavioral and Brain Sciences* 16(3), 521–523. DOI: 10.1017/S0140525X00031368

Gordon, R.M. 1986. 'Folk Psychology as Simulation'. *Mind and Language* 1, 158–171. DOI: 10.1111/j.1468-0017.1986.tb00324.x

Government Office for Science. 2004. *Foresight: Future Flooding*. London: Office of Science and Technology. Accessed 1 November 2020, at: https://www.gov.uk/government/publications/future-flooding

Government Office for Science. 2005. *Foresight: Drugs Futures 2025*. London: Office of Science and Technology. Accessed 18 September 2020, at: https://www.gov.uk/government/publications/drugs-futures-2025

Government Office for Science. 2012. *Blackett Review of High Impact Low Probability Risks*. London: Office of Science and Technology. Accessed 20 April 2021, at: https://assets.publishing.service.gov.uk/government/uploads/system/uploads/attachment_data/file/278526/12-519-blackett-review-high-impact-low-probability-risks.pdf

Government Office for Science. 2013. *Foresight Future Identities: Changing Identities in the UK, the Next 10 Years*. London: The Government Office for Science. Accessed 9 October 2020, at: https://assets.publishing.service.gov.uk/government/uploads/system/uploads/attachment_data/file/273966/13-523-future-identities-changing-identities-report.pdf

Government Office for Science. 2014. *Annual Report of the Government Chief Scientific Adviser 2014. Innovation: Managing Risk, Not Avoiding It. Evidence and Case Studies*. London: The Government Office for Science. Accessed 15 March 2021, at: https://assets.publishing.service.gov.uk/government/uploads/system/uploads/attachment_data/file/381906/14-1190b-innovation-managing-risk-evidence.pdf

Government Office for Science. 2016. *Future of Cities: Foresight for Cities*. London: The Government Office for Science. Accessed 17 April 2021, at: https://assets.publishing.service.gov.uk/government/uploads/system/uploads/attachment_data/file/516443/gs-16-5-future-cities-foresight-for-cities.pdf

Government Office for Science. 2018. *Computational Modelling: Technological Futures*. London: The Government Office for Science. Accessed 19 October 2020, at: https://assets.publishing.service.gov.uk/government/uploads/system/uploads/attachment_data/file/682579/computational-modelling-blackett-review.pdf

de Graaf, A., Hoeken, H., Sanders, J., and Beentjes, J. 2009. 'The Role of Dimensions of Narrative Engagement in Narrative Persuasion'. *Communications* 34(4), 385–405. DOI: 10.1515/COMM.2009.024

de Graaf, A., Hoeken, H., Sanders, J., Beentjes, J.W.J. 2012. 'Identification as a Mechanism of Narrative Persuasion'. *Communication Research* 39(6), 802–823. DOI: 10.1177/0093650211408594

Graesser, A.C., Singer, M., and Trabasso, T. 1994. 'Constructing Inferences During Narrative Text Comprehension'. *Psychological Review* 101(3), 371–395.

Grafton-Green, P. 2021. 'Matt Hancock tells LBC How Film Contagion Alerted Him to Global Vaccine Scramble'. *LBC*, 3 February 2021. Accessed 28 February 2021, at: https://www.lbc.co.uk/news/matt-hancock-tells-lbc-how-film-contagion-alerted-him-to-global-vaccine-scramble/

Graham, G., Greenhill, A., and Callaghan, V. 2014. 'Technological Forecasting and Social Change Special Section: Creative Prototyping'. *Technological Forecasting & Social Change* 84, 1–4. DOI: 10.1016/j.techfore.2013.11.007

Graham, G., and Mehmood, R. 2014. 'The Strategic Prototype "Crime-Sourcing" and the Science/Science Fiction Behind It'. *Technological Forecasting & Social Change* 84, 86–92. DOI: 10.1016/j.techfore.2013.10.026

Green, M.C., and Brock, T.C. 2000. 'The Role of Transportation in the Persuasiveness of Public Narratives'. *Journal of Personality and Social Psychology* 79(5), 701–721. DOI: 10.1037/0022–3514.79.5.701

Greene, N. [n.d.]. 'The First Successful Case of the Rights of Nature Implementation in Ecuador'. *Global Alliance for the Rights of Nature* [online, n.d.], http://therightsofnature.org/first-ron-case-ecuador/

Gregory, W.L., Cialdini, R.B., and Carpenter, K.M. 1982. 'Self-Relevant Scenarios as Mediators of Likelihood Estimates and Compliance: Does Imagining Make It So?' *Journal of Personality and Social Psychology* 43(1), 89–99. DOI: 10.1037/0022-3514.43.1.89

Griswold, E. 2012. 'How "Silent Spring" Ignited the Environmental Movement'. *The New York Times*, 21 September 2012. Accessed 9 November 2020, at: https://www.nytimes.com/2012/09/23/magazine/how-silent-spring-ignited-the-environmental-movement.html

Griswold, W. 2000. *Bearing Witness: Readers, Writers, and the Novel in Nigeria*. Princeton, NJ: Princeton University Press.

Gross, P.R., and Levitt, N. 1994. *Higher Superstition: The Academic Left and Its Quarrels with Science*. Baltimore, MD: The Johns Hopkins University Press.

Gubrium, J.F., and Holstein, J.A. 2008. 'Narrative Ethnography'. In S. Nagy Hesse-Biber and P. Leavy (eds.), *Handbook of Emergent Methods*, 241–264. New York: The Guilford Press.

Guldi, J., and Armitage, D. 2014. *The History Manifesto*. Cambridge: Cambridge University Press.

Ha, T.-H. 2017. 'US Republican Leaders Love Ayn Rand's Controversial Philosophy—and Are Increasingly Misinterpreting It'. *Quartz*, 19 January 2017. Accessed 28 September 2020, at: https://qz.com/882493/donald-trump-paul-ryan-and-andy-puzder-say-they-love-ayn-rands-controversial-philosophy-heres-what-us-republicans-keep-getting-wrong-about-it/

Habermas, J. 1989. *The Structural Transformation of the Public Sphere: An Inquiry into a Category of Bourgeois Society*. Translated by Thomas Burger with Frederick Lawrence. Cambridge: Polity Press.

Habermas, T., and Köber, C. 2014. 'Autobiographical Reasoning is Constitutive for Narrative Identity: The Role of the Life Story for Personal Continuity'. In K.C. McLean and M. Syed (eds.), *The Oxford Handbook of Identity Development*. Oxford: Oxford University Press. DOI: 10.1093/oxfordhb/9780199936564.013.010

Hacking, I. 1999. *The Social Construction of What?* Cambridge, MA: Harvard University Press.

Halden, G. 2017. *Three Mile Island: The Meltdown Crisis and Nuclear Power in American Popular Culture*. London: Routledge.

Halliwell, S. 2002. *The Aesthetics of Mimesis: Ancient Texts and Modern Problems*. Princeton, NJ: Princeton University Press.

Hamby, A., Brinberg, D., and Jaccard, J. 2018. 'A Conceptual Framework of Narrative Persuasion'. *Journal of Media Psychology: Theories, Methods, and Applications* 30(3), 113–124. DOI: 10.1027/1864-1105/a000187

Hammond, M.M., and Kim, S.J. (eds.). 2014. *Rethinking Empathy through Literature*. New York: Routledge.

Harcourt, R., de Bruin, W.B., Dessai, S., and Taylor, A. 2020. 'What Adaptation Stories are UK Newspapers Telling? A Narrative Analysis'. *Environmental Communication* 14(8), 1061–1078. DOI: 10.1080/17524032.2020.1767672

Hartmann, S. 1995. 'Models as a Tool for Theory Construction: Some Strategies of Preliminary Physics'. In W. Herfel, W. Krajewski, I. Niiniluoto, and R. Wojcicki (eds.), *Theories and Models in Scientific Process*, 49–67. Amsterdam: Rodopi.

Hassan, I.H. 1998. 'Queries for Postcolonial Studies'. *Philosophy and Literature* 22(2): 328–342. DOI: 10.1353/phl.1998.0043

Hays, S.P. 1987. *Beauty, Health, and Permanence: Environmental Politics in the United States, 1955–1985*. Cambridge: Cambridge University Press.

Heikkila, T., and Cairney, P. 2018. 'Comparison of Theories of the Policy Process'. In C. Weible and P. Sabatier (eds.), *Theories of the Policy Process*, 301–327. Boulder, CO: Westview Press.

Hein, G., Silani, G., Preuschoff, K., Batson, C.D., and Singer, T. 2010. 'Neural Responses to Ingroup and Outgroup Members' Suffering Predict Individual Differences in Costly Helping'. *Neuron* 68(1), 149–160. DOI: 10.1016/j.neuron.2010.09.003

Heise, U.K. 2008. *Sense of Place and Sense of Planet: The Environmental Imagination of the Global*. Oxford: Oxford University Press.

Heise, U.K. 2016. *Imagining Extinction: The Cultural Meanings of Endangered Species*. Chicago, IL: University of Chicago Press.

Heller, A.C. 2009. *Ayn Rand and the World She Made*. New York: Nan A. Talese.

HFEA. 2013. *Mitochondria Replacement Consultation: Advice to Government*. London: Human Fertilisation and Embryology Authority. Accessed 15 March 2021, at: https://www.hfea.gov.uk/media/2618/mitochondria_replacement_consultation_-_advice_for_government.pdf

Hilborn, R., and Mangel, M. 1997. *The Ecological Detective: Confronting Models with Data (MPB-28)*. Oxford: Princeton University Press.

Hillebrecht, A.L.T., and Berros, M.V. (eds.). 2017. 'Can Nature Have Rights? Legal and Political Insights'. *RCC Perspectives: Transformations in Environment and Society* 2017(6). DOI: 10.5282/rcc/8164

Hiramatsu, A., Mimura, N., and Sumi, A. 2008. 'A Mapping of Global Warming Research Based on IPCC AR4'. *Sustainability Science* 3, 201–213. DOI: 10.1007/s11625-008-0058-9

Hoffman, M.L. 1981. 'The Development of Empathy'. In J. Rushton and R. Sorrentino (eds.), *Altruism and Helping Behavior: Social, Personality, and Developmental Perspectives*, 41–63. Hillsdale, NJ: Lawrence Erlbaum Associates.

Hoffman, M.L. 1996. 'Empathy and Moral Development'. *The Annual Report of Educational Psychology in Japan* 35, 157–162.

Hoffman, M.L. 2000. *Empathy and Moral Development: Implications for Caring and Justice.* Cambridge: Cambridge University Press.

Horn, L. 2018. 'Future Incorporated?' In W. Davies (ed.), *Economic Science Fictions*, 41–58. London: Goldsmiths Press.

Hornstein, H.A. 1978. 'Promotive Tension and Prosocial Behavior: A Lewinian Analysis'. In L. Wispe (ed.), *Altruism, Sympathy, and Helping: Psychological and Sociological Principles*, 177–207. New York: Academic Press.

Hornyak, T.N. 2006. *Loving the Machine: The Art and Science of Japanese Robotics.* New York: Kodansha International.

House of Commons. 1965. 'BBC Film Censored? Parliamentary question asked in the House of Commons by William Hamilton MP about the TV film "The War Game"', 2 December 1965. *The National Archives* (CAB 21/5808). Accessed 16 September 2020, at: https://www-nationalarchives-gov-uk.ezp.lib.cam.ac.uk/education/resources/sixties-britain/bbc-film-censored/

Howe, J.P. 2014. *Behind the Curve: Science and the Politics of Global Warming.* Seattle: University of Washington Press.

Hughes, H.R., and Paterson, M. 2017. 'Narrowing the Climate Field: The Symbolic Power of Authors in the IPCC's Assessment of Mitigation'. *Review of Policy Research* 34, 744–766. DOI: 10.1111/ropr.12255

Huisman, D. 2014. 'Telling a Family Culture: Storytelling, Family Identity, and Cultural Membership'. *Interpersona: An International Journal on Personal Relationships* 8(2), 144–158. DOI: 10.5964/ijpr.v8i2.152

Hulme, M. 2009. *Why We Disagree about Climate Change: Understanding Controversy, Inaction and Opportunity.* Cambridge: Cambridge University Press.

Hulme, M. 2011. 'Meet the Humanities'. *Nature Climate Change* 1, 177–179. DOI: 10.1038/nclimate1150

Hulme, M., and Mahony, M. 2010. 'Climate Change: What Do We Know About the IPCC?' *Progress in Physical Geography: Earth and Environment* 34(5), 705–718. DOI: 10.1177/0309133310373719

Humphreys, M., and Brown, A.D. 2002. 'Narratives of Organizational Identity and Identification: A Case Study of Hegemony and Resistance'. *Organization Studies* 23(3), 421–447. DOI: 10.1177/0170840602233005

Hunt, S. 2014. 'Ontologies of Indigeneity: The Politics of Embodying a Concept'. *Cultural Geographies* 21(1), 27–32. DOI: 10.1177/1474474013500226

Hutto, D.D. 2004. 'The Limits of Spectatorial Folk Psychology'. *Mind & Language* 19, 548–573. DOI: 10.1111/j.0268-1064.2004.00272.x

Hutto, D.D. 2005. 'Knowing What? Radical Versus Conservative Enactivism'. *Phenomenology and the Cognitive Sciences* 4, 389–405. DOI: 10.1007/s11097-005-9001-z

Hutto, D.D. 2006. 'Narrative Practice and Understanding Reasons: Reply to Gallagher'. In R.A. Menary (ed.), *Radical Enactivism Intentionality, Phenomenology, and Narrative: Focus on the Philosophy of Daniel D. Hutto*, 231–247. Amsterdam: J. Benjamins Publishing Co.

Hutto, D.D. 2007a. 'Folk Psychology without Theory or Simulation'. In D.D. Hutto and M.M. Ratcliffe (eds.), *Folk Psychology Re-Assessed*, 115–135. Dordrecht: Springer.

Hutto, D.D. 2007b. 'The Narrative Practice Hypothesis: Origins and Applications of Folk Psychology'. *Royal Institute of Philosophy Supplement* 60, 43–68. DOI: 10.1017/S1358246107000033

Hutto, D.D. 2008. *Folk Psychological Narratives: The Sociocultural Basis of Understanding Reasons.* Cambridge, MA: The MIT Press.

Hynes, H.P. 1989. *The Recurring Silent Spring*. New York: Pergamon.

Iandoli, L., Klein, M., and Zollo, G. 2009. 'Enabling On-Line Deliberation and Collective Decision-Making through Large- Scale Argumentation'. *International Journal of Decision Support System Technology* 1(1), 69–92. DOI: 10.4018/jdsst.2009010105

Inayatullah, S. 2017. 'Macrohistory and Timing the Future as Practice'. *World Futures Review* 9(1), 26–33. DOI: 10.1177/1946756716686788

Inayatullah, S., and Boxwell, G. (eds.) 2003. *Islam, Postmodernism and Other Futures: A Ziauddin Sardar Reader*. London: Pluto Press.

Ingham, L. 2018. 'Making Asimov's Psychohistory a Reality: Using Big Data to Predict the Future'. *Factor* Spring. Accessed 16 September 2020, at: https://magazine.factor-tech. com/factor_spring_2018/making_asimov_s_psychohistory_a_reality_using_big_ data_to_predict_the_future

Ingrao, B. 2001. 'Economic Life in Nineteenth-Century Novels: What Economists Might Learn from Literature'. In G. Erreygers (ed.), *Economics and Interdisciplinary Exchange*, 7–40. London: Routledge.

INGSA. 2018. 'The INGSA Manifesto for 2030: Scientific Advice for the Global Goals'. *International Network for Government Science Advice*. https://www.ingsa.org/manifesto/

IPCC. 2018. *Global Warming of 1.5°C*. Geneva: IPCC. [In Press.] Accessed 6 November 2020, at: https://www.ipcc.ch/sr15/

Iseke, J. 2013. 'Indigenous Storytelling as Research'. *International Review of Qualitative Research* 6(4), 559–577. DOI: 10.1525/irqr.2013.6.4.559

Iyengar, S. 1990. 'Framing Responsibility for Political Issues: The Case of Poverty'. *Political Behavior* 12, 19–40. DOI: 10.1007/BF00992330

Iyengar, S. 1991. *Is Anyone Responsible? How Television Frames Political Issues*. Chicago, IL: University of Chicago Press.

Iyengar, S., and Kinder, D.R. 1987. *News That Matters: Television and American Opinion*. Chicago, IL: University of Chicago Press.

Jameson, F. 1981. *The Political Unconscious: Narrative as a Socially Symbolic Act*. London: Routledge.

Jameson, F. 2007. *Archaeologies of the Future: The Desire Called Utopia and Other Science Fictions*. London: Verso.

Janofsky, M.K. 2005. 'Michael Crichton, Novelist, Becomes Senate Witness'. *The New York Times*, 29 September 2005, E1.

Jasanoff, S. (ed.). 2006. *States of Knowledge: The Co-production of Science and the Social Order*. London: Routledge.

Jasanoff, S. 2007. *Designs on Nature: Science and Democracy in Europe and the United States*. Oxford: Princeton University Press.

Jasanoff, S. 2008. 'Speaking Honestly to Power'. *American Scientist* 96(3), 240–243.

Jasanoff, S. 2011. 'Cosmopolitan Knowledge: Climate Science and Global Civic Epistemology'. In J.S. Dryzek, R.B. Norgaard, and D. Schlosberg (eds.), *The Oxford Handbook of Climate Change and Society*. Oxford: Oxford University Press. DOI: 10.1093/ oxfordhb/9780199566600.003.0009

Jasanoff, S. 2012. *Science and Public Reason*. London: Routledge.

Jasanoff, S. n.d. 'Civic Epistemologies'. *Sheila Jasanoff: Pforzheimer Professor of Science and Technology Studies, Harvard Kennedy School*. Accessed 17 April 2021, at: https://sheilajasanoff. org/research/civic-epistemologies/#:~:text=Civic%20epistemologies%20are%20the%20 stylized,put%20to%20use%20in%20decisionmaking.&text=%E2%80%9CRestoring%20 Reason%3A%20Causal%20Narratives%20and, Political%20Culture%2C%E2%80%9D% 20in%20B

Jasanoff, S., and Kim, S.-H. (eds.). 2015. *Dreamscapes of Modernity: Sociotechnical Imaginaries and the Fabrication of Power*. London: The University of Chicago Press.

Jasanoff, S., and Simmet, H.R. 2017. 'No Funeral Bells: Public Reason in a "Post-Truth" Age'. *Social Studies of Science* 47(5), 751–770. DOI: 10.1177/0306312717731936

JDD. 2019. 'Emmanuel Macron touché par "Les Misérables"'. *Le Journal du Dimanche*, 17 November 2019. Accessed 16 September 2020, at: https://www.lejdd.fr/Politique/emmanuel-macron-touche-par-les-miserables-3931762?popSuccess=1&hcnx_id=-2t1YKvAUoIvcgXvJ7yE4821pOcPfs76H&status=failure&step=&reason=&hmac=a81a7dd6671099ea9db6d566ca38b75b

Jeevanjee, N., Hassanzadeh, P., Hill, S., and Sheshadri, A. 2017. 'A Perspective on Climate Model Hierarchies'. *Journal of Advances in Modeling Earth Systems* 9, 1760–1771, DOI: 10.1002/2017MS001038

Jeffries, S. 2020. 'Ladj Ly on Shocking President Macron with His Paris Riot Film: "How Could He Not Know?"'. *The Guardian*, 20 August. Accessed 16 September 2020, at: https://www.theguardian.com/film/2020/aug/20/ladj-ly-shocking-president-macron-paris-riot-film-les-miserables-la-haine

Jenkins, H. 1992. *Textual Poachers: Television Fans and Participatory Culture*. London Routledge.

Jenkins, H., Ford, S., and Green, J. 2013. *Spreadable Media: Creating Value and Meaning in a Networked Culture*. New York: New York University Press.

Jenni, K., and Loewenstein, G. 1997. 'Explaining the Identifiable Victim Effect'. *Journal of Risk and Uncertainty* 14, 235–257. DOI: 10.1023/A:1007740225484

Johns-Putra, A. 2019a. *Climate Change and the Contemporary Novel*. Cambridge: Cambridge University Press.

Johns-Putra, A. (ed.). 2019b. *Climate and Literature*. Cambridge: Cambridge University Press.

Johnson, B.D. 2011. *Science Fiction Prototyping: Designing the Future with Science Fiction*. San Rafael, CA: Morgan & Claypool.

Johnson, D.R. 2012. 'Transportation Into a Story Increases Empathy, Prosocial Behaviour, and Perceptual Bias Toward Fearful Expressions'. *Personality and Individual Differences* 52(2), 150–155. DOI: 10.1016/j.paid.2011.10.005

Jones, B.F. 2009. 'The Burden of Knowledge and the "Death of the Renaissance Man": Is Innovation Getting Harder?'. *Review of Economic Studies* 76, 283–317. DOI:10.1111/j.1467-937X.2008.00531.x

Jordan, M.R., Amir, D., and Bloom, P. 2016. 'Are Empathy and Concern Psychologically Distinct?' *Emotion* 16(8), 1107–1116. DOI: 10.1037/emo0000228

de Jouvenel, H. 2019. 'Futuribles: Origins, Philosophy, and Practices—Anticipation for Action'. *World Futures Review* 11(1), 8–18. DOI: 10.1177/1946756718777490

Joy, B. 2000. 'Why the Future Doesn't Need Us'. *Wired*, 1 April 2000. Accessed 30 September 2020, at: https://www.wired.com/2000/04/joy-2/

Kaestle, C.F., Damon-Moore, H., Stedman, L.C., Tinsley, K., and Trollinger, Jr., W.V. 1991. *Literacy in the United States: Readers and Reading since 1880*. New Haven, CT: Yale University Press.

Kahan, D.M., Braman, D., Gastil, J., Slovic, P., and Mertz, C.K. 2007. 'Culture and Identity-Protective Cognition: Explaining the White-Male Effect in Risk Perception'. *Journal of Empirical Legal Studies* 4, 465–505. DOI: 10.1111/j.1740-1461.2007.00097.x

Kahn, H. 1960. *On Thermonuclear War*. Princeton, NJ: Princeton University Press.

Kaplan, F. 2015. 'A Map for Big Data Research in Digital Humanities'. *Frontiers in Digital Humanities* 2, 1. DOI: 10.3389/fdigh.2015.00001

Karylowski, J. 1982. 'Two Types of Altruistic Behavior: Doing Good to Feel Good or to Make the Other Feel Good'. In V.J. Deriega and J. Grzelak (eds.), *Cooperation and Helping Behavior: Theories and Research*, 397–413. New York: Academic Press.

Kasperson, R.E., and Kasperson, J.X. 1996. 'The Social Amplification and Attenuation of Risk'. *The ANNALS of the American Academy of Political and Social Science* 545(1), 95–105. DOI: 10.1177/0002716296545001010

Katz, P.A., and Zalk, S.R. 1978. 'Modification of Children's Racial Attitudes'. *Developmental Psychology* 14(5), 447–461. DOI: 10.1037/0012-1649.14.5.447

Kaufman, W. 2006. *The Civil War in American Culture*. Edinburgh: Edinburgh University Press.

Kay, J., and King, M. 2020. *Radical Uncertainty: Decision-Making for an Unknowable Future*. London: W.W. Norton.

Keen, S. 2006. 'A Theory of Narrative Empathy'. *Narrative* 14(3), 207–236.

Keen, S. 2007. *Empathy and the Novel*. Oxford: Oxford University Press.

Kidd, D.C., and Castano, E. 2013. 'Reading Literary Fiction Improves Theory of Mind'. *Science*, 18 October, 377–380. DOI: 10.1126/science.1239918

Killingsworth, M.J., and Palmer, J.S. 1995. 'The Discourse of "Environmentalist Hysteria"'. *Quarterly Journal of Speech* 81, 1–19. DOI: 10.1080/00335639509384094

King, D., Schrag, D., Dadi, Z., Ye, Q., and Ghosh, A. 2015. *Climate Change: A Risk Assessment*. Cambridge: Centre for Science and Policy. Accessed 13 November 2020, at: http://www.csap.cam.ac.uk/projects/climate-change-risk-assessment/

King, D.A., and Thomas, S.M. 2007. 'Taking Science Out of the Box: Foresight Recast'. *Science* 316(5832), 1701–1702. DOI: 10.1126/science.1146051

Kirby, D.A. 2011. 'Creating a Techno-Mythology for a New Age: The Production History of *The Lawnmower Man*'. In D.L. Ferro and E.S. Swedin (eds.), *Science Fiction and Computing: Essays on Interlinked Domains*, 214–229. London: McFarland.

Klimecki, O.M., Leiberg, S., Ricard, M., and Singer, T. 2014. 'Differential Pattern of Functional Brain Plasticity after Compassion and Empathy Training'. *Social Cognitive and Affective Neuroscience* 9(6), 873–879. DOI: 10.1093/scan/nst060

Klinke, A., and Renn, O. 2001. 'Precautionary Principle and Discursive Strategies: Classifying and Managing Risks'. *Journal of Risk Research* 4(2), 159–173. DOI: 10.1080/136698701750128105

Kluger, J. 2015. 'Senator Throws Snowball! Climate Change Disproven!' *Time*, 27 February. Accessed 20 April 2021, at: https://time.com/3725994/inhofe-snowball-climate/

Kofman, A. 2018. 'Bruno Latour, the Post-Truth Philosopher, Mounts a Defense of Science'. *The New York Times Magazine*, 25 October. Accessed 18 April 2021, at: https://www.nytimes.com/2018/10/25/magazine/bruno-latour-post-truth-philosopher-science.html

Kogut, T., and Ritov, I. 2005a. 'The "Identified Victim" Effect: An Identified group, or Just a Single Individual?' *Journal of Behavioral Decision Making* 18(3), 157–167. DOI: 10.1002/bdm.492

Kogut, T., and Ritov, I. 2005b. 'The Singularity of Identified Victims in Separate and Joint Evaluations'. *Organizational Behavior and Human Decision Processes* 97(2), 106–116. DOI: 10.1016/j.obhdp.2005.02.003

Koopman, E.M. 2015. 'Empathic Reactions After Reading: The Role of Genre, Personal Factors and Affective Responses'. *Poetics* 50, 62–79. DOI: 10.1016/j.poetic.2015.02.008

Koopman, E.M., and Hakemulder, F. 2015. 'Effects of Literature on Empathy and Self-Reflection: A Theoretical-Empirical Framework'. *Journal of Literary Theory* 9(1), 79–111. DOI: 10.1515/jlt-2015-0005

Kovach, M. 2009. *Indigenous Methodologies: Characteristics, Conversations and Contexts.* Toronto: University of Toronto Press.

Krause, M., and Robinson, K. 2017. 'Charismatic Species and Beyond: How Cultural Schemas and Organisational Routines shape Conservation'. *Conservation & Society* 15(3), 313–321. DOI: 10.4103/cs.cs_16_63

Krebs, D. 1975. 'Empathy and Altruism'. *Journal of Personality and Social Psychology* 32(6), 1134–1146. DOI: 10.1037/0022-3514.32.6.1134

Kruger, D.J. 2003. 'Evolution and Altruism: Combining Psychological Mediators with Naturally Selected Tendencies'. *Evolution and Human Behavior* 24(2), 118–125. DOI: 10.1016/S1090–5138(02)00156-3

Kuzmičová, A., Mangen, A., Støle, H., Begnum, A.C., and Whiteley, S. 2017. 'Literature and Readers' Empathy: A Qualitative Text Manipulation Study'. *Language and Literature* 26(2), 137–152. DOI: 10.1177/0963947017704729

Lamarque, P. 2003. 'Fiction'. In J. Levinson (ed.), *The Oxford Handbook of Aesthetics*, 377–391. Oxford: Oxford University Press.

Lampe, C., Zube, P., Lee, J., Park, C.H., and Johnston, E. 2014. 'Crowdsourcing Civility: A Natural Experiment Examining the Effects of Distributed Moderation in Online Forums'. *Government Information Quarterly* 32(4), 317–326. DOI: 10.1016/j.giq.2013.11.005

Langellier, K.M., and Peterson, E.E. 2004. *Storytelling in Daily Life: Performing Narrative.* Philadelphia, PA: Temple University Press.

Langellier, K.M., and Peterson, E.E. 2006. 'Narrative Performance Theory: Telling Stories, Doing Family'. In D.O. Braithwaite and L.A. Baxter (eds.), *Engaging Theories in Family Communication: Multiple Perspectives*, 99–114. London: Sage Publications.

Larsen, N. 2020. 'Decolonising Futures'. *Medium*, 10 December 2020. Accessed 3 March 2021, at: https://medium.com/copenhagen-institute-for-futures-studies/decolonising-futures-with-pupul-bisht-b1245ac416ff

Larsen, S., and Seilman, U. 1988. 'Personal Remindings while Reading Literature'. *Text* 8, 411–429. DOI: 10.1515/text.1.1988.8.4.411

Latour, B., and Woolgar, S. 1986. *Laboratory Life: The Construction of Scientific Facts.* Princeton, NJ: Princeton University Press.

Lawrence, R.L., and Paige, D.S. 2016. 'What Our Ancestors Knew: Teaching and Learning Through Storytelling'. In C.R. Nanton (ed.), *Tectonic Boundaries: Negotiating Convergent Forces in Adult Education*, 63–72. San Francisco, CA: Wiley Periodicals.

Leach, M., Sterling A.C., and Scoones I. 2010. *Dynamic Sustainabilities: Technology, Environment, Social Justice.* London: Earthscan.

Leake, E. 2014. 'Humanising the Inhumane: The Value of Difficult Empathy'. In M.M. Hammond and S.J. Kim (eds.), *Rethinking Empathy Through Literature*, 175–186. London: Routledge.

Lees, R. 2017. *Centre for Science and Policy Final Report: An Overview of UK Policy Priorities and How the Arts and Humanities Can Help to Address Them.* Cambridge: Centre for Science and Policy. Accessed 7 April 2021, at: https://www.csap.cam.ac.uk/media/uploads/files/1/an-overview-of-uk-policy-priorities-and-how-the-arts-and-humanities-can-help-to-address-them.pdf

Leetaru, K. 2011. 'Culturomics 2.0: Forecasting Large-Scale Human Behavior Using Global News Media Tone in Time And Space'. *First Monday* 16(9). DOI: 10.5210/fm.v16i9.3663

Leiserowitz, A.A. 2004. 'Before and After *The Day After Tomorrow*: A U.S. Study of Climate Change Risk Perception'. *Environment* 46(9), 23–44.

Lemos, M.C., and Morehouse, B.J. 2005. 'The Co-Production of Science and Policy in Integrated Climate Assessments'. *Global Environmental Change* 15(1), 57–68. DOI: 10.1016/j.gloenvcha.2004.09.004

Leplin, J. 1980. 'The Role of Models in Theory Construction'. In T. Nickles (ed.), *Scientific Discovery, Logic, and Rationality*, 267–283. Dordrecht: Springer Netherlands. DOI: 10.1007/978-94-009-8986-3_12

Leopold, A. 1949. *A Sand County Almanac: And Other Sketches Here and There*. Oxford: Oxford University Press.

LERU. 2012. *Social Sciences and Humanities: Essential Fields for European Research and in Horizon 2020*. Leuven: LERU Publications. https://www.leru.org/files/Social-Sciences-and-Humanities-Essential-Fields-for-European-Research-and-Horizon-2020-Full-paper.pdf

Leslie, A.M. 1987. 'Pretense and Representation: The Origins of "Theory of Mind"'. *Psychological Review* 94(4), 412–426. DOI: 10.1037/0033–295X.94.4.412

Levy, A. 2012. 'Models, Fictions, and Realism: Two Packages'. *Philosophy of Science* 79, 738–748. DOI: 10.1086/667992

Levy, A. 2015. 'Modeling Without Models'. *Philosophical Studies* 152, 781–798. DOI: 10.1007/s11098-014-0333-9

Lewis C. 1994. 'Episodes, Events and Narratives in the Child's Understanding of Mind'. In C. Lewis and P. Mitchell (ed.), *Children's Early Understanding of the Mind*, 457–480. Hillsdale, NJ: Erlbaum.

Lewis C., Freeman, N.H., Hagestadt, C., and Douglas, H. 1994. 'Narrative Access and Production in Preschooler's False Belief Reasoning'. *Cognitive Development* 9(4), 397–424. DOI: 10.1016/0885-2014(94)90013-2

Lezaun, J., Marres, N., and Tironi, M. 2017. 'Experiments in Participation'. In U. Felt, R. Fouché, C.A. Miller, and L. Smith-Doerr (eds.), *The Handbook of Science and Technology Studies*, 195–222. Cambridge, MA: The MIT Press.

Lieblich, A., and Josselson, R. (eds.). 1994. *Exploring Identity and Gender: The Narrative Study of Lives*. Thousand Oaks, CA: Sage.

Lifton, R.J. 1967. *Death in Life: Survivors of Hiroshima*. New York: Random House.

Linde, C. 1986. 'Private Stories in Public Discourse: Narrative Analysis in the Social Sciences'. *Poetics* 15(1–2), 183–202. DOI: 10.1016/0304-422X(86)90039-2

Linde, C. 2001. 'Narrative and Social Tacit Knowledge'. *Journal of Knowledge Management* 5(2), 160–170. DOI: 10.1108/13673270110393202

Lindhé, A. 2016. 'The Paradox of Narrative Empathy and the Form of the Novel, or What George Eliot Knew'. *Studies in the Novel* 48(1), 19–42. DOI: 10.1353/sdn.2016.0011

Linser, R., Lindstad, N.R., and Vold, T. 2008. 'The Magic Circle: Game Design Principles and Online Role-Play Simulations'. In J. Luca and E. Weippl, *Proceedings of the ED-MEDIA 2008—World Conference on Educational Multimedia, Hypermedia & Telecommunications*, 5290–5297. Vienna: Association for the Advancement of Computing in Education.

Litcher, J.H., and Johnson, D.W. 1969. 'Changes in Attitudes Toward Negroes of White Elementary School Students After Use of Multiethnic Readers'. *Journal of Educational Psychology* 60(2), 148–152. DOI: 10.1037/h0027081

Liveley, G. 2017. 'Anticipation and Narratology'. In R. Poli (ed.), *Handbook of Anticipation*, 1–20. Basel: Springer International Publishing. DOI: 10.1007/978-3-319–31737-3_7-1

Liveley, G., Slocombe, W., and Spiers, E. 2021. 'Futures Literacy Through Narrative'. *Futures* 125, 102663. DOI: 10.1016/j.futures.2020.102663

Livingston, D. 1971. 'Science Fiction Models of Future World Order Systems'. *International Organization* 25(2), 254–270. DOI: 10.1017/S002081830001763X

Livingstone, S. 2005. 'On the Relation Between Audiences and Publics'. In S. Living-stone, *Audiences and Publics: When Cultural Engagement Matters for the Public Sphere*, 17–42. Bristol: Intellect Ltd.

Lloyd, E.A., and Oreskes, N. 2018. 'Climate Change Attribution: When Is It Appropriate to Accept New Methods?' *Earth's Future* 6, 311– 325. DOI: 10.1002/2017EF000665

Lloyd, E.A., and Shepherd, T.G. 2020. 'Environmental Catastrophes, Climate Change, and Attribution'. *Annals of the New York Academy of Sciences* 1469, 105–124. DOI: 10.1111/nyas.14308

Long, E. 1993. 'Textual Interpretation as Collective Action'. In J. Boyarin (ed.), *The Ethnography of Reading*, 180–211. Oxford: University of California Press.

Longino, H.E. 2002. *The Fate of Knowledge*. Princeton, NJ: Princeton University Press.

Louie, A.H. 2010. 'Robert Rosen's Anticipatory Systems'. *Foresight* 12(3), 18–29. DOI: 10.1108/14636681011049848

Lovelock, J. 1979. *Gaia: A New Look at Life on Earth*. Oxford: Oxford University Press.

Lovelock, J. 1988. *The Ages of Gaia: A Biography of Our Living Earth*. New York: W.W. Norton & Company, Inc.

Lovelock, J. 1991. *Healing Gaia: Practical Medicine for the Planet*. New York: Harmony Books.

Lovelock, J. 2006. *The Revenge of Gaia: Earth's Climate Crisis and the Fate of Humanity*. New York: Basic Books.

Lowe, T., Brown, K., Dessai, S., de França Doria, M., Haynes, K., and Vincent, K. 2006. 'Does Tomorrow Ever Come? Disaster Narrative and Public Perceptions of Climate Change'. *Public Understanding of Science* 15(4), 435–457. DOI: 10.1177/0963662506063796

Lynam, T., and Walker I. 2016. 'Making Sense of Climate Change: Orientations to Adaptation' *Ecology and Society* 21(4), 17. DOI: 10.5751/ES-08886-210417

MacDonald, J. 1998. *The Arctic Sky: Inuit Astronomy, Star Lore, and Legend*. Toronto: The Royal Ontario Museum and the Nunavut Research Institute.

Macfarlane, R. 2005. 'The Burning Question'. *The Guardian*, 24 September. Accessed 14 October 2020, at: https://www.theguardian.com/books/2005/sep/24/featuresreviews.guardianreview29

MacIntyre, A.C. 1981. *After Virtue: A Study in Moral Theory*. London: Duckworth.

Mahasneh, R.A., Romanowski, M.H., and Dajani, R.B. 2017. 'Reading Social Stories in the Community: A Promising Intervention for Promoting Children's Environmental Knowledge and Behavior in Jordan'. *The Journal of Environmental Education* 48(5), 334–346. DOI: 10.1080/00958964.2017.1319789

Mahr, B. 2012. 'On the Epistemology of Models'. In G. Abel and J. Conant (eds.), *Rethinking Epistemology*, vol. 1, 301–352. Berlin: De Gruyter.

Mair, D., Smillie, L., La Placa, G., Schwendinger, F., Raykovska, M., Pasztor, Z., and Van Bavel, R. 2019. *Understanding Our Political Nature: How to put knowledge and reason at the heart of political decision-making*. Luxembourg: Publications Office of the European Union. DOI: 10.2760/374191

Mäki, U. 2009. 'MISSing the World: Models as Isolations and Credible Surrogate Systems'. *Erkenntnis* 70(1), 29–43. DOI: 10.1007/s10670-008-9135-9

Malmsheimer, L.M. 1986. 'Three Mile Island: Fact, Frame, and Fiction'. *American Quarterly* 38(1), 35–52. DOI: 10.2307/2712592

Malone, E.L., and Rayner, S.F. 2001. 'Role of the Research Standpoint in Integrating Global-Scale and Local-Scale Research'. *Climate Research* 19(2), 173–178. DOI: 10.3354/cr019173

Manthorpe, R. 2021. 'COVID-19: Rejected Contracts and a Hollywood Movie – How UK Struck Deal to Guarantee Vaccine Supply'. *Sky News*, 1 February 2021. Accessed 28 February 2021, at: https://news.sky.com/story/covid-19-rejected-contracts-and-a-hollywood-movie-how-uk-struck-deal-to-guarantee-vaccine-supply-12204044

Mar, R., Oatley, K., Hirsch, J., de la Paz, J., and Peterson, J.B. 2006a. 'Bookworms Versus Nerds: Exposure to Fiction Versus Non-Fiction, Divergent Associations with Social Abilities, and the Simulation of Fictional Social Worlds'. *Journal of Research in Personality* 40(5), 694–712. DOI: 10.1016/j.jrp.2005.08.002

Mar, R.A., DeYoung, C.G., Higgins, D.M., and Peterson, J.B. 2006b. 'Self-Liking and Self-Competence Separate Self-Evaluation From Self-Deception: Associations With Personality, Ability, and Achievement'. *Journal of Personality* 74(4), 1047–1078. DOI: 10.1111/j.1467-6494.2006.00402.x

Mar, R.A., and Oatley, K. 2008. 'The Function of Fiction is the Abstraction and Simulation of Social Experience'. *Perspectives on Psychological Science* 3(3), 173–192. DOI: 10.1111/j.1745-6924.2008.00073.x

Mar, R., Oatley, K., and Peterson, J.B. 2009. 'Exploring the Link Between Reading Fiction and Empathy: Ruling Out Individual Differences and Examining Outcomes'. *Communications* 34(4), 407–428. DOI: 10.1515/COMM.2009.025

Margulis, L. 1998. *Symbiotic Planet: A New Look at Evolution.* New York: Basic Books.

Marnell, B. 2018. 'U.K. Wants to Use Isaac Asimov Style Rules to Protect Us from Rogue A.I.'. *SyFyWire*, 18 April 2018. Accessed 11 November 2020, at: https://www.syfy.com/syfywire/uk-wants-to-use-isaac-asimov-style-rules-to-protect-us-from-rogue-ai

Marsh, N. 2016. '"Paradise Falls: A Land Lost in Time": Representing Credit, Debt and Work after the Crisis'. In R. Colesworthy and P. Nicholls (eds.), *How Abstract is It? Thinking Capital Now*, 13–30. London: Routledge.

Marshall, N., Adger, N., Attwood, S., Brown, K., Crissman, C., Cvitanovic, C., De Young, C., Gooch, M., James, C., Jessen, S., Johnson, D., Marshall, P., Park, S., Wachenfeld, D., and Wrigley, D. 2017. 'Empirically Derived Guidance for Social Scientists to Influence Environmental Policy'. *PLoS ONE* 12(3), e0171950. DOI: 10.1371/journal.pone.0171950

Martin, K. 2012. *Stories in a New Skin: Approaches to Inuit Literature.* Winnipeg: University of Manitoba Press.

Mauch, C. 2019. 'Slow Hope: Rethinking Ecologies of Crisis and Fear'. *RCC Perspectives: Transformations in Environment and Society* 2019(1). DOI: 10.5282/rcc/8556

Mayumi, K., Solomon, S.D., and Chang, J. 2005. 'The Ecological and Consumption Themes of the Films of Hayao Miyazaki'. *Ecological Economics* 54(1), 1–7. DOI: 10.1016/j.ecolecon.2005.03.012

McAdams, D.P., and McLean, K.C. 2013. 'Narrative Identity'. *Current Directions in Psychological Science* 22(3), 233–238. DOI: 10.1177/0963721413475622.

McCauley, L. 2007. 'AI Armageddon and the Three Laws of Robotics'. *Ethics and Information Technology* 9, 153–164 (2007). DOI: 10.1007/s10676-007-9138-2

McCloskey, D.N. 1990a. 'Storytelling in Economics'. In D. Lavoie (ed.), *Economics and Hermeneutics*, 61–75. London: Routledge.

McCloskey, D.N. 1990b. *If You're So Smart: The Narrative of Economic Expertise.* Chicago, IL: University of Chicago Press.

McCloskey, D.N. 1994. *Knowledge and Persuasion in Economics.* New York: Cambridge University Press.

McCloskey, D.N. 2021. *Bettering Humanomics: A New, and Old, Approach to Economic Science.* London: The University of Chicago Press.

McElwee, P.D. 2020. 'The Social Lives of Climate Reports'. *Anthropology News*, 22 April. DOI: 10.1111/AN.1391

McEwan, I. 2001. 'Only Love and Then Oblivion. Love Was All They Had to Set Against Their Murderers'. *The Guardian*, 15 September. Accessed 9 September 2020: https://www.theguardian.com/world/2001/sep/15/september11.politicsphilosophyandsociety2

McHale, J., and McHale, M.C. 1976. 'An Assessment of Futures Studies World Wide'. *Futures* 8, 135–145. DOI: 10.1016/0016-3287(76)90063-X

McPherson, J.M. 1988. *Battle Cry of Freedom: The Civil War Era*. Oxford: Oxford University Press.

Meckling, J., and Allan, B.B. 2020. 'The Evolution of Ideas in Global Climate Policy'. *Nature Climate Change* 10, 434–438 (2020). DOI: 10.1038/s41558-020-0739-7

Merideth, R. 1993. *The Environmentalist's Bookshelf: A Guide to the Best Books*. New York: Hall.

Merrie, A., Keys, P., Metiana, M., and Österblom, H. 2018. 'Radical Ocean Futures-Scenario Development Using Science Fiction Prototyping'. *Futures* 95, 22–32. DOI: 10.1016/j.futures.2017.09.005

Miéville, C. 2009. 'Cognition as Ideology: A Dialectic of SF Theory'. In M. Bould and C. Miéville (eds.), *Red Planets: Marxism and Science Fiction*, 231–248. London: Pluto Press.

Miles, I. 1990. 'Fiction and Forecasting'. *Futures* 22(1), 83–91. DOI: 10.1016/0016-3287(90)90099-4

Miles, I. 1993. 'Stranger than Fiction: How Important is Science Fiction for Futures Studies?' *Futures* 25(3), 315–321. DOI: 10.1016/0016-3287(93)90139-K

Miller, C., and Bennett, I. 2008. 'Thinking Longer Term about Technology: Is There Value in Science Fiction-Inspired Approaches to Constructing Futures?' *Science and Public Policy* 35(8), 597–606. DOI: 10.3152/030234208X370666

Miller, C.A., O'Leary, J., Graffy, E., Stechel, E.B., and Dirks, G. 2015. 'Narrative Futures and the Governance of Energy Transitions'. *Futures* 70, 65–74. DOI: 10.1016/j.futures.2014.12.001

Miller, R. 2006. 'From Trends to Futures Literacy: Reclaiming the Future'. *Centre For Strategic Education, Seminar Series Paper No. 160*, December 2006. Jolimont: Centre For Strategic Education.

Miller, R. 2007. 'Futures Literacy: A Hybrid Strategic Scenario Method'. *Futures* 39, 341–362. DOI: 10.1016/j.futures.2006.12.001

Miller, R. 2011. 'Futures Literacy: Embracing Complexity and Using the Future'. *ETHOS* 10, 23–28.

Miller, R. (ed.). 2018. *Transforming the Future: Anticipation in the 21st Century*. London: Routledge.

Milne, S. 2015. '*Pinkoes and Traitors* by Jean Seaton Review: My Father, the BBC and a Very British Coup'. *The Guardian*, 27 February. Accessed 16 September 2020, at: https://www.theguardian.com/books/2015/feb/27/seumas-milne-on-pinkoes-and-traitors-by-jean-seaton-review-my-father-the-bbc-and-a-very-british-coup

Milner, A., and Burgmann, J.R. 2020. *Science Fiction and Climate Change: A Sociological Approach*. Liverpool: Liverpool University Press.

Milojević, I., and Izgarjan, A. 2014. 'Creating Alternative Futures through Storytelling: A Case Study from Serbia'. *Futures* 57, 51–61. DOI: 10.1016/j.futures.2013.12.001

Mink, L. 1978. 'Narrative Form as Cognitive Instrument'. In R.H. Canary and H. Koziciki (ed.), *The Writing of History: Literary Form and Historical Understanding*, 129–149. Madison: University of Wisconsin Press.

Mitchell, W.J.T. (ed.). 1981. *On Narrative*. Chicago, IL: University of Chicago Press.

Moore, O. 2007. 'Inuit Leader Nominated for Nobel'. *The Globe and Mail*, 2 February. Accessed 11 November 2020, at: https://www.theglobeandmail.com/news/national/inuit-leader-nominated-for-nobel/article20392724/

Morgan, M.S. 2001. 'Models, Stories and the Economic World'. *Journal of Economic Methodology* 8(3), 361–384. DOI: 10.1080/13501780110078972

Morgan, M.S. 2012. *The World in the Model: How Economists Work and Think*. Cambridge: Cambridge University Press.

Morgan, M.S., Hajek, K.M., and Berry, D.J. [Forthcoming]. *Narrative Science: Reasoning, Representing and Knowing since 1800*. Cambridge: Cambridge University Press.

Morgan, M.S., and Wise, M.N. 2017. 'Narrative Science and Narrative Knowing: Introduction to Special Issue on Narrative Science'. *Studies in History and Philosophy of Science* 62, 1–5. DOI: 10.1016/j.shpsa.2017.03.005

Morley, D., and Brunsdon, C. 1999. *The Nationwide Television Studies*. London: Routledge

Morson, G.S., and Schapiro, M. 2018. *Cents and Sensibility: What Economics Can Learn from the Humanities*. Oxford: Princeton University Press.

Mulgan, G. 2020. 'The Imaginary Crisis (and how we might quicken social and public imagination)'. *Demos Helsinki*, April 2020. Accessed 20 April 2021, at: https://demoshelsinki.fi/wp-content/uploads/2020/04/the-imaginary-crisis-web.pdf

Murgia, M. 2017. 'From Autonomous Drones to Fake News Generators, Military Researchers Seek to Weaponise AI'. *Financial Times*, 3 May 2017. Accessed 11 November 2020, at: https://www.ft.com/content/566ee806-0fea-11e7-a88c-50ba212dce4d

Nabokov, P. 2006. *Where the Lightning Strikes: The Lives of American Indian Sacred Places*. New York: Viking.

Naqvi, I. 2018. 'There Is No Psychohistory, and There Never Will Be'. *Scatterplot*, 22 February 2018. Accessed 16 September 2020, at: https://scatter.wordpress.com/2018/02/22/there-is-no-psychohistory-and-there-never-will-be/#_ftn1

National Academies of Sciences, Engineering, and Medicine. 2016. *Attribution of Extreme Weather Events in the Context of Climate Change*. Washington, DC: The National Academies Press. DOI: 10.17226/21852.

Ndalianis, A. 2013. 'Astro Boy, Science-fictionality and Japanese Robotics'. *Deletion*, 20 August 2013. Accessed 29 September 2020, at: https://www.deletionscifi.org/episodes/episode-1/astro-boy-science-fictionality-and-japanese-robotics/

Nelson K. 2007. *Young Minds in Social Worlds*. Cambridge, MA: Harvard University Press.

Nersessian, N.J. 1999. 'Model-Based Reasoning in Conceptual Change'. In L. Magnani, N.J. Nersessian, and P. Thagard (eds.), *Model-Based Reasoning in Scientific Discovery*, 5–22. Boston, MA: Springer US. DOI: 10.1007/978-1-4615-4813-3_1

Nersessian, N.J. 2010. *Creating Scientific Concepts*. Cambridge, MA: The MIT Press.

Nevala-Lee, A. 2018. *Astounding: John W. Campbell, Isaac Asimov, Robert A. Heinlein, L. Ron Hubbard, and the Golden Age of Science Fiction*. New York: Dey Street Books.

Newby, H. 1993. Global Environmental Change and the Social Sciences: Retrospect and Prospect. Paper presented to the IGFA Preparatory meeting, Noordwijk, the Netherlands. (Unpublished)

Newman, J. 2017. 'Debating the Politics of Evidence-Based Policy'. *Public Administration* 95, 1107–1112. DOI: 10.1111/padm.12373

Noble, S.U. 2018. *Algorithms of Oppression: How Search Engines Reinforce Racism*. New York: NYU Press.

Nussbaum, M.C. 1995. *Poetic Justice: The Literary Imagination and Public Life*. Boston, MA: Beacon Press.

Nussbaum, M.C. 1997. *Cultivating Humanity: A Classical Defense of Reform in Liberal Education*. London: Harvard University Press.

Nussbaum, M.C. 2013. *Political Emotions: Why Love Matters For Justice*. London: Belknap Press.

Oakes, G., and Grossman, A. 1992. 'Managing Nuclear Terror: The Genesis of American Civil Defense Strategy'. *International Journal of Politics, Culture, and Society* 5(3), 361–403. DOI: 10.1007/BF01423899

Oatley, K. 1999. 'Why Fiction May be Twice as True as Fact: Fiction as Cognitive and Emotional Simulation'. *Review of General Psychology* 3(2), 101–117. DOI: 10.1037/1089-2680.3.2.101

O'Barr, W.M., and Conley, J.M. 1992. *Fortune and Folly: The Wealth and Power of Institutional Investing*. New York: McGraw-Hill.

Ochs, E., and Capps, L. 2001. *Living Narrative: Creating Lives in Everyday Storytelling*. Cambridge, MA: Harvard University Press.

Ochs, E., and Taylor, C. 1995. 'The "Father Knows Best" Dynamic in Dinnertime Narratives'. In K. Hall and M. Bucholtz (eds.), *Gender Articulated: Language and the Socially Constructed Self*, 97–120. London: Routledge.

Ochsner, M., Hug, S.E., and Daniel, H.D. 2016. 'Humanities Scholars' Conceptions of Research Quality'. In M. Ochsner, S. Hug, and H.D. Daniel (eds.), *Research Assessment in the Humanities*, 43–69. Cham: Springer. DOI: 10.1007/978-3-319-29016-4_5

OECD. 2020a. 'Addressing Societal Challenges Using Transdisciplinary Research'. *OECD Science, Technology and Industry Policy Papers* 88. Paris: OECD Publishing. DOI: 10.1787/0ca0ca45-en

OECD. 2020b. *Innovative Citizen Participation and New Democratic Institutions: Catching the Deliberative Wave*. Paris: OECD Publishing. DOI: 10.1787/339306da-en

Office of Nuclear Energy, Science and Technology. [n.d.] *The History of Nuclear Energy*. Washington, DC: U.S. Department of Energy. Accessed 2 March 2021, at: https://www.energy.gov/sites/prod/files/The%20History%20of%20Nuclear%20Energy_0.pdf

Oliver, K., and Cairney, P. 2019. 'The Dos and Donts of Influencing Policy: A Systematic Review of Advice to Academics'. *Palgrave Communications*, 5. DOI: 10.1057/s41599-019-0232-y

Oliver, K., and Faul, M.V. 2018. 'Networks and Network Analysis in Evidence, Policy and Practice'. *Evidence & Policy: A Journal of Research, Debate and Practice* 14(3), 369–379. DOI: 10.1332/174426418X15314037224597

O'Neil, C. 2017. *Weapons of Math Destruction: How Big Data Increases Inequality and Threatens Democracy*. London: Penguin Books.

O'Reilly, J. 2015. 'Glacial Dramas: Typos, Projections, and Peer Review in the Fourth Assessment of the Intergovernmental Panel on Climate Change'. In J. Barnes and M.R. Dove (eds.), *Climate Cultures: Anthropological Perspectives on Climate Change*, 107–126. New Haven, CT: Yale University Press. DOI: 10.12987/9780300213577-006

Oreskes, N., and Conway, E.M. 2014. *The Collapse of Western Civilization: A View From the Future*. New York: Columbia University Press.

Ostfeld, R., and Reiner, D.M. 2020. 'Public Views of Scotland's Path to Decarbonization: Evidence from Citizens' Juries and Focus Groups'. *Energy Policy* 140, 111332. DOI: 10.1016/j.enpol.2020.111332

Ottinger, G., Barandiarán, J., and Kimura, A.H. 2017. 'Environmental Justice: Knowledge, Technology, and Expertise'. In U. Felt, R. Fouché, C.A. Miller, L. Smith-Doerr (eds.), *The Handbook of Science and Technology Studies*, 1029–1058. Cambridge, MA: The MIT Press.

Owens, S. 2015. *Knowledge, Policy, and Expertise: The UK Royal Commission on Environmental Pollution 1970–2011.* Oxford: Oxford University Press.

Owens, S. 2018. 'Trust in Experts? Knowledge, Advice and Influence in Environmental Policy'. In *Science in Times of Challenged Trust and Expertise*, 10–19. ALLEA General Assembly, 16 May 2018, Bulgarian Academy of Sciences, Sofia.

Paluck, E.L. 2009. 'Reducing Intergroup Prejudice and Conflict Using the Media: A Field Experiment in Rwanda'. *Journal of Personality and Social Psychology* 96(3), 574–587. DOI: 10.1037/a0011989

Panero, M.E., Weisberg, D.S., Black, J., Goldstein, T.R., Barnes, J.L., Brownell, H., and Winner, E. 2016. 'Does Reading a Single Passage of Literary Fiction Really Improve Theory of Mind? An Attempt at Replication'. *Journal of Personality and Social Psychology* 111(5), e46–e54. DOI: 10.1037/pspa0000064

Parkhurst, J. 2017. *The Politics of Evidence: From Evidence-Based Policy to the Good Governance of Evidence.* London: Routledge.

Parkinson, J. 2006. *Deliberating in the Real World: Problems of Legitimacy in Deliberative Democracy.* Oxford: Oxford University Press.

Paschen, J.-A., and Ison, R. 2014. 'Narrative Research in Climate Change Adaptation: Exploring a Complementary Paradigm for Research and Governance'. *Research Policy* 43(6), 1083–1092. DOI: 10.1016/j.respol.2013.12.006

Pawley, C. 2002. 'Seeking "Significance": Actual Readers, Specific Reading Communities'. *Book History* 5(1), 143–160. DOI: 10.1353/bh.2002.0013

Penner, L.A., Dovidio, J.F., Piliavin, J.A., and Schroeder, D.A. 2005. 'Prosocial Behavior: Multilevel Perspectives'. *Annual Review of Psychology* 56, 365–392. DOI: 10.1146/annurev.psych.56.091103.070141

Pennington, N., and Hastie, R. 1988. 'Explanation-based Decision Making: Effects of Memory Structure on Judgment'. *Journal of Experimental Psychology: Learning, Memory, and Cognition* 14, 521–533. DOI: 10.1037/0278-7393.14.3.521

Pérez-Soba, M., and Maas, R. 2015. 'Scenarios: Tools for Coping with Complexity and Future Uncertainty?' In A.J. Jordan and J.R. Turnpenny, *The Tools of Policy Formulation: Actors, Capacities, Venues and Effects*, 52–75. Cheltenham: Edward Elgar Publishing.

Perloff, M. 2004. *Differentials: Poetry, Poetics, Pedagogy.* Tuscaloosa: University of Alabama Press.

Peschard, I. 2011. 'Making Sense of Modeling: Beyond Representation'. *European Journal for Philosophy of Science* 1(3), 335–352. DOI: 10.1007/s13194-011-0032-8

Peterson, C., and McCabe, A. 1994. 'A Social Interactionist Account of Developing Decontextualised Narrative Skill'. *Developmental Psychology* 30(6), 937–948.

Phoenix, C., and Sparkes, A.C. 2009. 'Being Fred: Big Stories, Small Stories and the Accomplishment of a Positive Ageing Identity'. *Qualitative Research* 9(2), 219–236. DOI: 10.1177/1468794108099322.

Pidgeon, N. 2020. 'Engaging Publics About Environmental and Technology Risks: Frames, Values and Deliberation'. *Journal of Risk Research* [published online, 17 April 2020]. DOI: 10.1080/13669877.2020.1749118

Pidgeon, N., and Fischhoff, B. 2011. 'The Role of Social and Decision Sciences in Communicating Uncertain Climate Risks'. *Nature Climate Change* 1, 35–41. DOI: 10.1038/nclimate1080

Pielke, Jr., R. 2015. 'Five Modes of Science Engagement'. *Roger Pielke Jr.'s Blog: Science, Innovation, Politics*, 19 January. Accessed 18 April 2021, at: http://rogerpielkejr.blogspot.com/2015/01/five-modes-of-science-engagement.html

Pielke, Jr., R.A. 2007. *The Honest Broker: Making Sense of Science in Policy and Politics.* Cambridge: Cambridge University Press.

Pierce, A. 2013. 'If Corporations Have Rights, Why Doesn't Nature?' *Pachamama Alliance*, 11 January. Accessed 15 September 2020, at: http://www.pachamama.org/blog/if-corporations-have-rights-why-doesnt-nature

Pihkala, P. 2019. *Climate Anxiety*. Translated by Minna Andersén. Helsinki: MIELI Mental Health Finland.

Piliavin, J.A., Dovidio, J.F., Gaertner, S.L., and Clark, R.D. 1981. *Emergency Intervention*. New York: Academic Press.

Piliavin, J.A., Dovidio, J.F., Gaertner, S.L., and Clark, R.D. 1982. 'Responsive Bystanders: The Process of Intervention'. In V.J. Derlega and J. Grzelak (eds.), *Cooperation and Helping Behavior: Theories and Research*, 279–304. New York: Academic Press.

Piliavin, J.A., and Piliavin, I.M. 1973. 'The Good Samaritan: Why Does He Help?' Madison, WI: University of Wisconsin–Madison. Unpublished manuscript.

Plato. 2007. *The Republic*. Translated by Desmon Lee. London: Penguin Classics.

Plummer, K. 2001. *Documents of Life 2: An Invitation to a Critical Humanism*. London: Sage.

Plummer, K. 2019. *Narrative Power: The Struggle for Human Value*. Cambridge: Polity.

Pohl, F. 2012. 'The Future's Mine'. In N. Harkaway (ed.), *Arc 1.2: Posthuman Conditions*, [n.p.]. London: Reed Business Information Ltd. Kindle DX Edition.

Polanyi, L. 1985. *Telling the American Story: A Structural and Cultural Analysis of Conversational Storytelling*. Norwood, NJ: Ablex Publishing.

Polletta, F. 2006. *It Was Like a Fever: Storytelling in Protest and Politics*. Chicago, IL: University of Chicago Press.

Polletta, F., Chen, P.C.B., Gardner, B.G., and Motes, A. 2011. 'The Sociology of Storytelling'. *Annual Review of Sociology* 37, 109–130. DOI: 10.1146/annurev-soc-081309-150106

Polletta, F., and Jasper, J.M. 2001. 'Collective Identity and Social Movements'. *Annual Review of Sociology* 27, 283–305. DOI: 10.1146/annurev.soc.27.1.283

Poovey, M. 2008. *Genres of the Credit Economy: Mediating Value in Eighteenth- and Nineteenth-Century Britain*. Chicago, IL: The University of Chicago Press.

Pope, C. 2005. 'An In-Depth Response to "The Death of Environmentalism"'. *Grist*, 14 January. Accessed 29 September 2020, at: https://grist.org/article/pope-reprint/

Prentice, D.A., Gerrig, R.J., and Bailis, D.S. 1997. 'What Readers Bring to the Processing of Fictional Texts'. *Psychonomic Bulletin & Review* 4, 416–420. DOI: 10.3758/BF03210803

Prinz, J.J. 2011. 'Is Empathy Necessary for Morality?' In A. Coplan and P. Goldie (eds.), *Empathy: Philosophical and Psychological Perspectives*, 211–229. Oxford: Oxford University Press.

Qiao, F., Li, P., Zhang, X., Ding, Z., Cheng, J., and Wang, H. 2017. 'Predicting Social Unrest Events with Hidden Markov Models Using GDELT'. *Discrete Dynamics in Nature and Society*, 8180272. DOI: 10.1155/2017/8180272

Qitsualik, R. 1998. 'Word and Will—Part Two: Words and the Substance of Life'. *Nunatsiaq News*, 12 November. Accessed 27 September 2015, at: http://www.nunatsiaqonline.ca/archives/nunavut981130/ nvt81113_09.html

Quong, J. 2018. 'Public Reason'. In Edward N. Zalta (ed.), *The Stanford Encyclopedia of Philosophy* (Spring 2018 edition). Accessed 9 November 2020, at: https://plato.stanford.edu/archives/spr2018/entries/public-reason/

Radin, J. 2019. 'Alternative Facts and States of Fear: Reality and STS in an Age of Climate Fictions'. *Minerva* 57, 411–431. DOI: 10.1007/s11024-019-09374-5

Radway, J. 1984. *Reading the Romance: Women, Patriarchy, and Popular Literature*. Chapel Hill: The University of North Carolina Press.

Rapley, C., and De Meyer, K. 2014. 'Climate Science Reconsidered'. *Nature Climate Change* 4, 745–746. DOI: 10.1038/nclimate2352

Rapley, C.G., De Meyer, K., Carney, J., Clarke, R., Howarth, C., Smith, N., Stilgoe, J., Youngs, S., Brierley, C., Haugvaldstad, A., Lotto, B., Michie, S., Shipworth, M., and Tuckett, D. 2014. *Time for Change? Climate Science Reconsidered: Report of the UCL Policy Commission on Communicating Climate Science, 2014.* London: UCL Policy Commission on Communicating Climate Science, University College London.

Raven, P.G., and Elahi, S. 2015. 'The New Narrative: Applying Narratology to the Shaping of Futures Outputs'. *Futures* 74, 45–61. DOI: 10.1016/j.futures.2015.09.003

Ravenscroft, A. 2012. *The Postcolonial Eye: White Australian Desire and the Visual Field of Race.* Farnham: Ashgate Publishing.

Rawls, J. 1971. *A Theory of Justice.* Cambridge, MA: Harvard University Press.

Rayner, S. 2017. 'Wicked Problems'. In D. Richardson, N. Castree, M.F. Goodchild, A. Kobayashi, W. Liu, and R.A. Marston (eds.), *International Encyclopedia of Geography: People, the Earth, Environment and Technology.* DOI: 10.1002/9781118786352.wbieg0048

Reason, M., and Heinemeyer, C. 2016. 'Storytelling, Story-Retelling, Storyknowing: Towards a Participatory Practice of Storytelling'. *Research in Drama Education: The Journal of Applied Theatre and Performance* 21(4), 558–573. DOI: 10.1080/13569783.2016.1220247

Recchia, G. 2020. 'The Fall and Rise of AI: Investigating AI Narratives with Computational Methods'. In S. Cave, K. Dihal, and S. Dillon (eds.), *AI Narratives: A History of Imaginative Thinking about Intelligent Machines*, 382–407. Oxford: Oxford University Press.

Ricoeur, P. 1979. 'The Human Experience of Time and Narrative'. *Research in Phenomenology* 9, 17–34.

Ricoeur, P. 1984–1988. *Time and Narrative*, 3 vols. Translated by Kathleen McLaughlin and David Pellauer. Chicago, IL: University of Chicago Press.

Riedl, M.O., and Harrison, B. 2015. 'Using Stories to Teach Human Values to Artificial Agents'. *Association for the Advancement of Artificial Intelligence.* Accessed 9 November 2020, at: https://www.cc.gatech.edu/~riedl/pubs/aaai-ethics16.pdf

The Rights of Nature: A Global Movement. 2018. Directed by Issac Goeckeritz, Hal Crimmel, and María Valeria Berros. USA: IG Films.

Riner, R.D. 1987. 'Doing Futures Research—Anthropologically'. *Futures* 19(3), 311–328. DOI: 10.1016/0016-3287(87)90022-X

Ritivoi, A.D. 2016. 'Reading Stories, Reading (Others') Lives: Empathy, Intersubjectivity, and Narrative Understanding'. *Storyworlds: A Journal of Narrative Studies* 8(1): 51–75. DOI: 10.5250/storyworlds.8.1.0051

Rittel, H.W.J., and Webber, M.M. 1973. 'Dilemmas in a General Theory of Planning. *Policy Sciences* 4, 155–169. DOI: 10.1007/BF01405730

Robbins, B. 2020. Microscope explorer. *Lame mage productions.* http://www.lamemage.com/microscope/

Robinson, J.A., and Hawpe, L. 1986. In T.R. Sarbin (ed.), *Narrative Psychology: The Storied Nature of Human Conduct*, 111–125. New York: Praeger Publishers.

Rockström, J., Steffen, W., Noone, K., Lambin, E., Lenton, T.M., Scheffer, M., Folke, C., Schellnhuber, H.J., de Wit, C.A., Hughes, T., van der Leeuw, S., Rodhe, H., Sörlin, S., Snyder, P.K., Costanza, R., Svedin, U., Falkenmark, M., Karlberg, L., Corell, R.W., Fabry, V.J., Hansen, J., Walker, B., Liverman, D., Richardson, K., Crutzen, P., and Foley, J. 2009. 'Planetary Boundaries: Exploring the Safe Operating Space for Humanity'. *Ecology and Society* 14(2), 32. http://www.ecologyandsociety.org/vol14/iss2/art32/

Roscoe, P. 2016. 'Method, Measurement, and Management in IPCC Climate Modeling'. *Human Ecology* 44, 655–664. DOI: 10.1007/s10745-016-9867-0

Rosen, M. 2015. 'Ethnographies of Reading: Beyond Literacy and Books'. *Anthropological Quarterly* 88(4), 1059–1083. DOI: 10.1353/anq.2015.0049

The Royal Society. 2017. *Machine Learning: The Power and Promise of Computers that Learn by Example*. London: The Royal Society. Accessed 24 September 2020, at https://royalsociety.org/topics-policy/projects/machine-learning/

The Royal Society. 2018. *Portrayals and Perceptions of AI and Why They Matter*. London: The Royal Society. Accessed 3 November 2020, at: https://royalsociety.org/-/media/policy/projects/ai-narratives/AI-narratives-workshop-findings.pdf

The Royal Society and the Academy of Medical Sciences. 2018. *Evidence Synthesis for Policy: A Statement of Principles*. Accessed 3 November 2020, at: https://royalsociety.org/-/media/policy/projects/evidence-synthesis/evidence-synthesis-statement-principles.pdf

Rueckert, W. 1996. 'Literature and Ecology: An Experiment in Ecocriticism'. In C. Glotfelty and H. Fromm (eds.), *The Ecocriticism Reader: Landmarks in Literary Ecology*, 105–123. Athens: University of Georgia Press.

Russell, E. 2017. 'Why *Princess Mononoke* is Even More Relevant 20 Years Later'. *Dazed*, 12 July. Accessed 14 October 2020, at: https://www.dazeddigital.com/life-culture/article/36735/1/why-princess-mononoke-is-even-more-relevant-20-years-later

Russell, S. 2019. *Human Compatible: AI and the Problem of Control*. London: Allen Lane.

Rutter, H., Savona, N., Glonti, K., Bibby, J., Cummins, S., Finegood, D.T., Greaves, F., Harper, L., Hawe, P., Moore, L., Petticrew, M., Rehfuess, E., Shiell, A., Thomas, J., and White, M. 2017. 'The Need for a Complex Systems Model of Evidence for Public Health'. *The Lancet* 390(10112), 9 December, 2602–2604. DOI: 10.1016/S0140-6736(17)31267-9

Sabatier, P.A., and Jenkins-Smith H.C. (eds.). 1993. *Policy Change and Learning: An Advocacy Coalition Approach*. Boulder, CO: Westview Press.

Saha, A., and van Lente, S. 2020. *Rethinking 'Diversity' in Publishing*. London: Goldsmiths Press. Accessed 1 October 2020, at: https://www.spreadtheword.org.uk/wp-content/uploads/2020/06/Rethinking_diversity_in-publishing_WEB.pdf

Salen, K., and Zimmerman, E. 2003. *Rules of Play: Game Design Fundamentals*. Cambridge: The MIT Press.

Samra-Fredericks, D. 2003. 'Strategizing as Lived Experience and Strategists' Everyday Efforts to Shape Strategic Direction'. *Journal of Management Studies* 40, 141–174. DOI: 10.1111/1467-6486.t01-1-00007

SAPEA. 2019. *Making Sense of Science for Policy under Conditions of Complexity and Uncertainty*. Berlin: SAPEA. DOI: 10.26356/MASOS

Sardar, Z. 2010. 'The Namesake: Futures; Futures Studies; Futurology; Futuristic; Foresight—What's in a name?' *Futures* 42, 177–184. DOI: 10.1016/j.futures.2009.11.001

Saunders, T. 2018. 'Common Futures: People Talk About the Future of Work and How They Feel About It'. *nesta*, 15 June. Accessed 31 October 2020, at: https://www.nesta.org.uk/blog/common-futures-people-talk-about-future-work-and-how-they-feel-about-it/

Sawyer, R.J. 2007. 'Robot Ethics'. *Science* 318(5853), 1037. DOI: 10.1126/science.1151606

Scalise Sugiyama, M. 2005. 'Reverse-Engineering Narrative: Evidence of Special Design'. In J. Gottschall and D.S. Wilson (eds.), *The Literary Animal*, 177–196. Chicago, IL: Northwestern University Press.

Scalise Sugiyama, M. 2011. 'The Forager Oral Tradition and the Evolution of Prolonged Juvenility'. *Frontiers in Evolutionary Psychology* 2, 133. DOI: 10.3389/fpsyg.2011.00133

Scalise Sugiyama, M. 2016. 'Narrative'. In T.K. Shackelford and V.A. Weekes-Shackelford (eds.), *Encyclopedia of Evolutionary Psychological Science*. Basel: Springer International Publishing. DOI: 10.1007/978-3-319-16999-6_3316-1

Scarry, E. 1996. 'The Difficulty of Imagining Other People'. In M.C. Nussbaum and J. Cohen (eds.), *For Love of Country: Debating the Limits of Patriotism*, 98–110. Boston, MA: Beacon Press.

Schank, R.C., and Abelson, R.P. 1977. *Scripts, Plans, Goals and Understanding: An Inquiry into Human Knowledge Structures.* Hillsdale, NJ: Lawrence Erlbaum Associates.

Schelling, T.C. 1968. 'The Life You Save May Be Your Own'. In S.B. Chase (ed.), *Problems in Public Expenditure Analysis*, 127–162. Washington, DC: Brookings Institution.

Schiffrin, D., De Fina, A., and Nylund, A. 2010. *Telling Stories: Language, Narrative, and Social Life.* Washington, DC: Georgetown University Press.

Scholes, R., and R. Kellogg. 1966. *The Nature of Narrative.* Oxford: Oxford University Press.

Schrage, M. 2000. *Serious Play: How the World's Best Companies Simulate to Innovate.* Boston, MA: Harvard Business School Press.

Schroeder, D.A., Penner, L.A., Dovidio, J.F., and Piliavin, J.A. 1995. *The Psychology of Helping and Altruism: Problems and Puzzles.* New York: McGraw Hill.

Schwarz, J.O. 2015. 'The "Narrative Turn" in Developing Foresight: Assessing How Cultural Products Can Assist Organisations in Detecting Trends'. *Technological Forecasting and Social Change* 90(B), 510–513. DOI: 10.1016/j.techfore.2014.02.024

Schwarz, J.O. 2020. 'Revisiting Scenario Planning and Business Wargaming from an Open Strategy Perspective'. *World Futures Review* 12(3), 291–303. DOI: 10.1177/1946756720953182

Schwarz, J.O., Kroehl, R., and von der Gracht, H.A. 2014. 'Novels and Novelty in Trend Research: Using Novels to Perceive Weak Signals and Transfer Frames of Reference'. *Technological Forecasting and Social Change* 84, 66–73. DOI: 10.1016/j.techfore.2013.09.007

Sciencewise. 2019. 'The Government's Approach to Public Dialogue on Science and Technology'. June. Accessed 13 November 2020, at: https://sciencewise.org.uk/wp-content/uploads/2019/11/Guiding-Principles.pdf

Seed, D. 1999. *American Science Fiction and the Cold War: Literature and Film.* Edinburgh: Edinburgh University Press.

Seed, D. 2013. *Under the Shadow: The Atomic Bomb and Cold War Narratives.* Kent, OH: The Kent State University Press.

Select Committee on Artificial Intelligence. 2018. *AI in the UK: Ready, Willing, and Able?'* (No. HL 100 2017–19). Available from House of Lords: https://publications.parliament.uk/pa/ld201719/ldselect/ldai/100/100.pdf

SFE. 2018. 'Cli-Fi'. *SFE: The Encyclopedia of Science Fiction*, 7 January. Accessed 14 October 2020, at: http://www.sf-encyclopedia.com/entry/cli-fi

Shackley and Skodvin, 1995. 'IPCC Gazing and the Interpretative Social Sciences'. *Global Environmental Change* 5(3), 175–180. DOI: 10.1016/0959-3780(95)00021-F

Shah, H. 2020. 'Global Problems Need Social Science'. *Nature* 577 (16 January 2020), 295. DOI: 10.1038/d41586-020-00064-x

Shaw, A., Sheppard, S., Burch, S., Flanders, D., Wiek, A., Carmichael, J., Robinson, J., and Cohen, S. 2009. 'Making Local Futures Tangible: Synthesizing, Downscaling, and Visualizing Climate Change Scenarios For Participatory Capacity Building'. *Global Environmental Change* 19(4), 447–463. DOI: 10.1016/j.gloenvcha.2009.04.002

Shaw, K. 2015. *Crunch Lit.* London: Bloomsbury.

Sheldon, R. 2016. *The Child to Come: Life after the Human Catastrophe.* Minneapolis: University of Minnesota Press.

Shellenberger, M. 2020. *Apocalypse Never: Why Environmental Alarmism Hurts Us All.* New York: HarperCollins.

Shellenberger, M., and Nordhaus, T. 2004. *The Death of Environmentalism: Global Warming Politics in a Post-Environmental World* [online]. Accessed 29 September 2020, at: https://s3.us-east-2.amazonaws.com/uploads.thebreakthrough.org/legacy/images/Death_of_Environmentalism.pdf

Shepherd, T.G. 2016. 'A Common Framework for Approaches to Extreme Event Attribution'. *Current Climate Change Reports* 2, 28–38. DOI: 10.1007/s40641-016-0033-y

Shepherd, T.G. 2019. 'Storyline Approach to the Construction of Regional Climate Change Information'. *Proceeding of the Royal Society A: Mathematical, Physical and Engineering Sciences* 475, 20190013. DOI: 10.1098/rspa.2019.0013

Shepherd, T.G., Boyd, E., Calel, R.A., Chapman, S.C., Dessai, S., Dima-West, I.M., Fowler, H.J., James, R., Maraun, D., Martius, O., Senior, C.A., Sobel, A.H., Stainforth, D.A., Tett, S.F.B., Trenberth, K.E., van den Hurk, B.J J.M., Watkins, N.W., Wilby, R.L., and Zenghelis, D.A. 2018. 'Storylines: An Alternative Approach to Representing Uncertainty in Physical Aspects of Climate Change'. *Climatic Change* 151, 555–571. DOI: 10.1007/s10584-018-2317-9

Shepherd, T.G., and Sobel, A.H. 2020. 'Localness in Climate Change'. *Comparative Studies of South Asia, Africa and the Middle East* 40(1), 7–16. DOI: 10.1215/1089201X-8185983

Shiller, R.J. 2019. *Narrative Economics: How Stories Go Viral and Drive Major Economic Events*. Princeton, NJ: Princeton University Press.

Shuman, A. 2005. *Other People's Stories: Entitlement Claims and the Critique of Empathy*. Champaign, IL: University of Illinois.

Simas, E.N., Clifford, S., and Kirkland, J.H. 2020. 'How Empathic Concern Fuels Political Polarization'. *American Political Science Review* 114(1), 258–269. DOI: 10.1017/S0003055419000534

Simon, H. 1987. 'Making Management Decisions: The Role of Intuition and Emotion'. *The Academy of Management Executive* 1(1), 57–64. DOI: 10.5465/ame.1987.4275905

Singer, J.A. 2004. 'Narrative Identity and Meaning Making Across the Adult Lifespan: An Introduction'. *Journal of Personality* 72(3), 437–460. DOI: 10.1111/j.0022-3506.2004.00268.x

Sismondo, S. 2017. 'Post-Truth?' *Social Studies of Science* 47(1), 3–6. DOI: 10.1177/0306312717692076

Slagle, M. 2007. 'A Robot Made to Look Like a Boy'. *The Mercury News*, 13 September. Accessed 29 September 2020, at: https://www.pressreader.com/usa/the-mercury-news/20070913/282273840984769

Slaughter, R.A. 1998. 'Futures Beyond Dystopia'. *Futures* 30(10), 993–1002. DOI: 10.4324/9780203465158

Slocombe, W. 2020. 'Machine Visions: Artificial Intelligence, Society, and Control'. In S. Cave, K. Dihal, and S. Dillon (eds.), *AI Narratives: A History of Imaginative Thinking about Intelligent Machines*, 213–236. Oxford: Oxford University Press.

Slovic, P. 2007a. '"If I Look at the Mass I Will Never act": Psychic Numbing and Genocide'. *Judgment and Decision Making* 2(2), 79–95.

Slovic, P. 2007b. 'Science Briefs: Psychic Numbing and Genocide'. *Psychological Science Agenda* 21(10). https://www.apa.org/science/about/psa/2007/11/slovic

Smith, A. 2010. *The Theory of Moral Sentiments*. London: Penguin.

Smith, B. 2014. 'Words After Things: Narrating the Ends of Worlds'. In J. Smith, R. Tyszczuk, and R. Butler (eds.), *Culture and Climate Change: Narratives*, 58–68. Cambridge: Shed.

Smith, J. 2014. 'From Truth War to a Game of Risk'. In J. Smith, R. Tyszczuk, and R. Butler (eds.), *Culture and Climate Change: Narratives*, 15–24. Cambridge: Shed.

Smith, K., and Stewart, E. 2017. 'We Need to Talk about Impact: Why Social Policy Academics Need to Engage with the UK's Research Impact Agenda'. *Journal of Social Policy* 46(1), 109–127. DOI: 10.1017/S0047279416000283

Snow, C.P. 1959. *The Two Cultures and the Scientific Revolution*. Cambridge: Cambridge University Press.

Solnit, R. 2009. *A Paradise Built in Hell: The Extraordinary Communities That Arise in Disaster*. London: Viking Books.

Somers, M.R. 1992. 'Narrativity, Narrative Identity, and Social Action: Rethinking English Working-Class Formation'. *Social Science History* 16(4), 591–630. DOI: 10.1017/S0145553200016679

Somers, M.R. 1994. 'The Narrative Constitution of Identity: A Relational and Network Approach'. *Theory and Society* 23(5), 605–649. DOI: 10.1007/BF00992905

Sous, A., and Wesolowsky, T. 2019. 'Belarusian Nobel Laureate Says HBO Series Has "Completely Changed Perception" of Chernobyl'. *RadioFreeEurope RadioLiberty*, 13 June 2019. Accessed 28 September 2020, at: https://www.rferl.org/a/belarusian-nobel-laureate-says-hbo-series-has-completely-changed-perception-of-chernobyl/29997496.html

de Sousa Santos, B. 2014. *Epistemologies of the South: Justice Against Epistemicide*. London: Routledge.

de Sousa Santos, B. 2016. 'Epistemologies of the South and the future'. *From the European South: A Transdisciplinary Journal of Postcolonial Humanities* 1, 17–29. http://europeansouth.postcolonialitalia.it/journal/2016-1/3.2016-1.Santos.pdf

Sperling, A. (ed.). 2020a. 'Special Issue: Climate Fictions', *Paradoxa* 31.

Sperling, A. 2020b. 'Climate Fictions: Introduction', *Paradoxa* 31, 7–21.

Sperling, N. 2020. '"Contagion," Steven Soderbergh's 2011 Thriller, Is Climbing Up the Charts'. *The New York Times*, 4 March. Accessed 19 October 2020, at: https://www.nytimes.com/2020/03/04/business/media/coronavirus-contagion-movie.html

Steffen, W., Richardson, K., Rockstrom, J., Cornell, S.E., Fetzer, I., Bennett, E.M., Biggs, R., Carpenter, S.R., de Vries, W., de Wit, C.A., Folke, C., Gerten, D., Heinke, J., Mace, G.M., Persson, L.M., Ramanathan, V., Reyers, B., and Sörlin, S. 2015. 'Planetary Boundaries: Guiding Human Development on a Changing Planet'. *Science* 347(6223), 1259855. DOI: 10.1126/science.1259855

Steinmetz, G. 1992. 'Reflections on the Role of Social Narratives in Working-Class Formation: Narrative Theory in the Social Sciences'. *Social Science History* 16(3), 489–516. DOI: 10.1017/S014555320001659X

Stilgoe, J. 2014. *The Road Ahead: Public Dialogue on Science and Technology*. London: Sciencewise Expert Resource Centre. Accessed 6 November 2020, at: https://sciencewise.org.uk/wp-content/uploads/2018/12/the_road_ahead.pdf

Stilgoe, J., Lock, S.J., and Wilsdon, J. (ed.). 2014. Special Issue: Public Engagement in Science. *Public Understanding of Science* 23(1), 4–120.

Stirling, A., and Mitchell, C. 2018. 'Evaluate Power and Bias in Synthesizing Evidence for Policy'. *Nature* 561, 33. DOI: 10.1038/d41586-018-06128-3

Stocks, E.L., Lishner, D.A. and Decker, S.K. 2009. 'Altruism or Psychological Escape: Why Does Empathy Promote Prosocial Behavior?' *European Journal of Social Psychology* 39(5), 649–665. DOI: 10.1002/ejsp.561

Stone, A.R. 1991. 'Will the Real Body Please Stand Up? Boundary Stories about Virtual Cultures'. In M. Benedikt (ed.), *Cyberspace: First Steps*, 81–118. Cambridge, MA: The MIT Press.

Stone, C.D. 1972. *Should Trees Have Standing? Law, Morality, and the Environment*. Oxford: Oxford University Press.

Stone, D. 2011. *Policy Paradox: The Art of Political Decision Making*. New York: Norton.

Stone, E. 1988. *Black Sheep and Kissing Cousins: How Our Family Stories Shape Us*. New York: Times Books.

Stork, D.G. (ed.). 1997. *HAL's Legacy: 2001's Computer as Dream and Reality*. Cambridge, MA: The MIT Press.

Strange, J.J., and Leung, C.C. 1999. 'How Anecdotal Accounts in News and in Fiction Can Influence Judgments of a Social Problem's Urgency, Causes, and Cures'. *Personality and Social Psychology Bulletin* 25(4), 436–449. DOI: 10.1177/0146167299025004004

Strauss, L.L. 1954. 'Remarks Prepared by Lewis L. Strauss, Chairman, United States Atomic Energy Commission, For Delivery At The Founders' Day Dinner, National Association of Science Writers, on Thursday, September 16, 1954, New York, New York'. [document] *https://www.nrc.gov/docs/ML1613/ML16131A120.pdf*

Streeby, S. 2018. *Imagining the Future of Climate Change: World-Making through Science Fiction and Activism*. Berkeley: University of California Press.

Stroud, N.J. 2008. 'Media Use and Political Predispositions: Revisiting the Concept of Selective Exposure'. *Political Behavior* 30(3), 341–366. DOI: 10.1007/s11109-007-9050-9

Stroud, S.R. 2016. 'Narrative Rationality'. In K.B. Jensen, E.W. Rothenbuhler, J.D. Pooley, and R.T. Craig (eds.), *The International Encyclopedia of Communication Theory and Philosophy*. New York: Wiley. DOI: 10.1002/9781118766804.wbiect050

Stutts, N.B., and Barker, R.T. 1999. 'The Use of Narrative Paradigm Theory in Assessing Audience Value Conflict in Image Advertising'. *Management Communication Quarterly* 13(2), 209–244. DOI: 10.1177/0893318999132002

Sundberg, J. 2014. 'Decolonizing Posthumanist Geographies'. *Cultural Geographies* 21(1), 33–47. DOI: 10.1177/1474474013486067

'Survey: Peering Round the Corner'. 2001. *The Economist* 360(8235), 13 October, 6.

Sutherland, W.J., and Burgman, M.A. 2015. 'Use Experts Wisely'. *Nature* 526 (15 October 2015), 317–318. DOI: 10.1038/526317a

Suvin, D. 1979. *Metamorphoses of Science Fiction: On the Poetics and History of a Literary Genre*. New Haven, CT: Yale University Press.

Svoboda, M. 2014. 'The Long Melt: The Lingering Influence of "The Day After Tomorrow"'. *Yale Climate Connections*, 5 November 2014. Accessed 11 November 2020, at: https://yaleclimateconnections.org/2014/11/the-long-melt-the-lingering-influence-of-the-day-after-tomorrow/#:~:text=The%20film%20unquestionably%20increased%20the, of%20the%202001%20IPCC%20report.%E2%80%9D

Swain, D., Ceballos, G., Francis, J., Emanuel, K., Sriver, R., Doerr, S., and Hausfather, Z. 2020. 'Article by Michael Shellenberger Mixes Accurate and Inaccurate Claims in Support of a Misleading and Overly Simplistic Argumentation About Climate Change'. *Climate Feedback*, 6 July 2020. Accessed 29 September 2020, at: https://climatefeedback.org/evaluation/article-by-michael-shellenberger-mixes-accurate-and-inaccurate-claims-in-support-of-a-misleading-and-overly-simplistic-argumentation-about-climate-change/

Swirski, P. 2006. *Of Literature and Knowledge: Explorations in Narrative Thought Experiments, Evolution and Game Theory*. London: Routledge.

Swoyer, C. 1991. 'Structural Representation and Surrogative Reasoning'. *Synthese* 87, 449–508. DOI: 10.1007/BF00499820

Taber, C.S. and Lodge, M. 2006. 'Motivated Skepticism in the Evaluation of Political Beliefs'. *American Journal of Political Science* 50, 755–769. DOI: 10.1111/j.1540-5907.2006.00214.x

Tengö, M., Hill, R., Malmer, P., Raymond, C.M., Spierenburg, M., Danielsen, F., Elmqvist, T., and Folke, C. 2017. 'Weaving Knowledge Systems in IPBES, CBD and Beyond—Lessons Learned for Sustainability'. *Current Opinion in Environmental Sustainability* 26–27, 17–25. DOI: 10.1016/j.cosust.2016.12.005

Tett, G. 2010. *Fool's Gold: How Unrestrained Greed Corrupted a Dream, Shattered Global Markets and Unleashed a Catastrophe*. London: Abacus.

Thompson, B.S., and Rog, S.M. 2019. 'Beyond Ecosystem Services: Using Charismatic Megafauna as Flagship Species for Mangrove Forest Conservation'. *Environmental Science & Policy* 102, 9–17. DOI: 10.1016/j.envsci.2019.09.009

Tilly, C. 2002. *Stories, Identities, and Political Change*. Lanham, MD: Rowman and Littlefield.

Titchener, E.B. 1909. *Lectures on the Experimental Psychology of the Thought Processes*. New York: The Macmillan Company.

Todd, Z. 2016. 'An Indigenous Feminist's Take on the Ontological Turn: "Ontology" Is Just Another Word For Colonialism'. *Journal of Historical Sociology* 29(1), 4–22. DOI: 10.1111/johs.12124

Toffler, A. 1978. 'Foreword'. In M. Maruyama and A.M. Harkins (eds.), *Cultures of the Future*, ix–xvi. The Hague: Mouton.

Topel, F. 2019. '"Chernobyl" Creator Craig Mazin on His New HBO Miniseries and the Debt We Owe to the Truth (Interview)'. *slashfilm.com*, 6 May 2019. Accessed 9 November 2020, at: https://www.slashfilm.com/craig-mazin-interview-chernobyl/

Topp, L., Mair, D., Smillie, L., and Cairney, P. 2018. 'Knowledge Management for Policy Impact: The Case of the European Commission's Joint Research Centre'. *Palgrave Communications* 4, 87. DOI: 10.1057/s41599-018-0143-3

Trenberth, K., Fasullo, J., and Shepherd, T. 2015. 'Attribution of Climate Extreme Events'. *Nature Climate Change* 5, 725–730. DOI: 10.1038/nclimate2657

Trexler, A. 2016. *Anthropocene Fictions: The Novel in a Time of Climate Change*. Charlottesville: University of Virginia Press.

Tuchman, G., Kaplan Daniels, A., Benet, J. 1978. *Hearth and Home: Images of Women in the Mass Media*. New York: Oxford University Press.

Tuhiwai-Smith, L.1999. *Decolonizing Methodologies: Research and Indigenous Peoples*. London: Zed Books.

Turner, S.P. 2014. *The Politics of Expertise*. London and New York: Routledge.

Turney, J. 1998. *Frankenstein's Footsteps: Science, Genetics and Popular Culture*. New Haven, CT: Yale University Press.

Tversky, A., and Kahneman, D. 1974. 'Judgment under Uncertainty: Heuristics and Biases'. *Science* 185(4157), 1124–1131. DOI: 10.1126/science.185.4157.1124

UKRI. [n.d.] 'Principles of Robotics'. *UKRI: Engineering and Physical Sciences Research Council*. Accessed 11 November 2020, at: https://epsrc.ukri.org/research/ourportfolio/themes/engineering/activities/principlesofrobotics/

UNESCO. 2019. *Global Futures Literacy Design Conference*, 16 December. UNESCO Headquarters, Paris: Catalogue of Learning-by-doing Labs.

Van Notten, P.W.F., Rotmans, J., van Asselt, M., and Rothman, D. 2003. 'An Updated Scenario Typology'. *Futures* 35, 423–443. DOI: 10.1016/S0016-3287(02)00090-3

Venturini, T., De Pryck, K., and Ackland, R. 2020. 'Bridging in Network Organisations the Case of International Panel on Climate Change (IPCC)'. *SSRN Electronic Journal*, 24 June. DOI: 10.2139/ssrn.3636924

Victor, D.G. 2015. 'Embed the Social Sciences in Climate Policy'. *Nature* 520, 27–29. DOI: 10.1038/520027a

Vollaro, D.R. 2009. 'Lincoln, Stowe, and the "Little Woman/Great War" Story: The Making, and Breaking, of a Great American Anecdote'. *Journal of the Abraham Lincoln Association* 30(1), 18–34.

Walz, S.P. (ed.). 2010. *Toward a Ludic Architecture: The Space of Play and Games*. Pittsburgh: ETC Press.

Watts, V. 2013. 'Indigenous Place-Thought and Agency Amongst Humans and Non Humans (First Woman and Sky Woman Go On a European World Tour!)'. *Decolonization: Indigeneity, Education & Society* 2(1), 20–34.

Weart, S.R. 2012. *The Rise of Nuclear Fear*. Cambridge, MA: Harvard University Press.

Weinstein, C. 2004. 'Introduction'. In C. Weinstein (ed.), *The Cambridge Companion to Harriet Beecher Stowe*, 1–14. Cambridge: Cambridge University Press.

Wells, H.G. 1914. *The World Set Free: A Story of Mankind*. London: Macmillan & Co., Limited.

Wheare, K.C. 1955. *Government by Committee: An Essay on the British Constitution*. Oxford: The Clarendon Press.

Wheeler, C., Green, M.C., and Brock, T.C. 1999. 'Fictional Narratives Change Beliefs: Replications of Prentice, Gerrig, and Bailis (1997) with Mixed Corroboration'. *Psychonomic Bulletin & Review* 6, 136–141. DOI: 10.3758/BF03210821

White, R. 2017. 'Walter Benjamin: "The Storyteller" and the Possibility of Wisdom'. *Journal of Aesthetic Education* 51(1), 1–14. DOI: 10.5406/jaesteduc.51.1.0001

Whitty, C.J.M. 2015. 'What Makes an Academic Paper Useful for Health Policy?' *BMC Medicine* 13, 301. DOI: 10.1186/s12916-015-0544-8

Whyte, K.P. 2018. 'Indigenous Science (Fiction) for the Anthropocene: Ancestral Dystopias and Fantasies of Climate Change Crises'. *Environment and Planning E: Nature and Space* 1(1–2), 224–242. DOI: 10.1177/2514848618777621

Wiegand, W.A. 1998. 'Introduction', In J.P. Danky and W.A. Wiegand (eds.), *Print Culture in a Diverse America*, 1–13. Urbana, IL: University of Illinois Press.

Williams, R. 1983. *Culture and Society, 1780–1950*. New York: Columbia University Press.

Wilson, G.M. 2003. 'Narrative'. In J. Levinson (ed.), *The Oxford Handbook of Aesthetics*, 392–407. Oxford: Oxford University Press.

Wilson, S. 2008. *Research is Ceremony: Indigenous Research Methods*. Halifax: Fernwood.

Winstead, A. 2017. 'Beyond Persuasion: Margaret Atwood's Speculative Politics'. *Studies in the Novel* 49(2), 228–249. DOI: 10.1353/sdn.2017.0018

Wittgenstein, L. 1953. *Philosophical Investigations*. Oxford: Blackwell.

Wood, A. 2012. 'Recursive Space: Play and Creating Space'. *Games and Culture* 7(1), 87–105. DOI: 10.1177/1555412012440310

Wood, M. 2002. *Slavery, Empathy, and Pornography*. Oxford: Oxford University Press.

Wowk, K., McKinney, L., Muller-Karger, F., Moll, R., Avery, S., Escobar-Briones, E., Yoskowitz, D., and McLaughlin, R. 2017. 'Evolving Academic Culture to Meet Societal Needs'. *Palgrave Communications* 3, 35. DOI: 10.1057/s41599-017-0040-1

Wright, A., and Zable, A. 2013. 'The Future of Swans'. *Overland* 213, 27–30.

Wynne, B. 1996. 'May the Sheep Safely Graze? A Reflexive View of the Expert-Lay Knowledge Divide'. In S. Lash, B. Szerszynski, and B. Wynne (eds.), *Risk, Environment and Modernity: Towards a New Ecology*, 27–83. London: Sage.

Yearley, S. 2009. 'Sociology and Climate Change After Kyoto: What Roles for Social Science in Understanding Climate Change? *Current Sociology* 57(3), 389–405. DOI: 10.1177/0011392108101589

Zaki, J., and Ochsner, K. 2012. 'The Neuroscience of Empathy: Progress, Pitfalls and Promise'. *Nature Neuroscience* 15, 675–680. DOI: 10.1038/nn.3085

Stories

Amidon, S. 2004. *Human Capital*. New York: Farrar, Straus and Giroux.

Amis, M. 1984. *Money: A Suicide Note*. London: Jonathan Cape.

Anamata Future News. 2015. Youtube [webseries]. https://www.youtube.com/user/AnamataFutureNews/videos.

An Inconvenient Truth. 2006. Directed by Davis Guggenheim. USA: Paramount Classics.

Arrival. 2016. Directed by Denis Villeneuve. USA: Paramount Pictures.

Asimov, I. 1950. 'The Evitable Conflict'. *Astounding Science Fiction* 45(4) (June), 48–68.

Atomic Energy as a Force for Good. 1955. Directed by Robert Stevenson. USA: The Christophers.

Banks, I.M. 1987. *Consider Phlebas*. New York: Macmillan.

Bellamy, E. 1960. *Looking Backward: 2000–1887*. New York: New American Library.

Blish, J. 1969. 'We All Die Naked'. In *Three for Tomorrow: Three Original Novellas of Science Fiction*, 153–204. New York: Meredith Press.

Borges, J.L. 1999. *Collected Fictions*. Translated by Andrew Hurley. London: Penguin Books.

Camus, A. 2002. *The Plague*. Translated by Robin Buss. London: Penguin.

Cartmill, C. 1944. 'Deadline'. *Astounding Science Fiction* 33(1) (March), 154–178.

Chernobyl. 2019. USA: HBO.

Chiang, T. 2015. *Stories of Your Life and Others*. London: Picador.

The Children. 1980. Directed by Max Kalmanowicz. USA: World Northal.

The China Syndrome. 1979. Directed by James Bridges. USA: Columbia Pictures.

Contagion. 2011. Directed by Steven Soderbergh. USA: Warner Bros. Pictures.

Continuum. 2012–2015. USA: Showcase.

Crichton, M. 2004. *State of Fear*. New York: HarperCollins.

Davis, C. 1946. 'Nightmare'. *Astounding Science-Fiction* 37(3) (May), 7–24.

The Day After Tomorrow. 2004. Directed by Roland Emmerich. USA: 20th Century Fox.

DeLillo, D. 1977. *Players*. New York: Alfred A. Knopf.

DeLillo, D. 2003. *Cosmopolis*. New York: Scribner.

Dickens, C. 2003. *Hard Times*. London: Penguin Books.

Eggers, D. 2010. *Zeitoun*. London: Penguin Books.

Ellis, B.E. 1991. *American Psycho*. New York: Vintage.

Ellison, H. 2014. *From the Land of Fear: Stories*. New York: Open Road Media. Kindle DX Edition.

Enron by Lucy Prebble. 2009. Directed by Rupert Goold [Festival Theatre, Chichester, UK, 17 September].

Fairman, P.W. 1968. *I, Machine*. New York: Lancer Books.

First Reformed. 2017. Directed by Paul Schrader. USA: A24.

Forster, E.M. 2011. *The Machine Stops*. London: Penguin.

Game of Thrones. 2011–2019. USA: HBO.

Gee, M. 1998. *The Ice People*. London: Richard Cohen Books.

Gronlund, L. 1890. *Our Destiny: The Influence of Socialism on Morals and Religion; an Essay in Ethics*. London: S. Sonnenschein & Co.

Harper, J. 2018. *The Lost Man*. London: Little, Brown.

Haverty, A. 2007. *The Free and the Easy*. London: Vintage.

Heinlein, R.A. 1966. *The Moon Is a Harsh Mistress*. New York: G. P. Putnam's Sons.

Heinlein, R.A. 1978. 'Solution Unsatisfactory'. *The Worlds of Robert A. Heinlein*. London: New English Library, 92–127. Orig. pub. under the pseudonym Anson MacDonald in *Astounding Science-Fiction* 27(3) (May 1941), 56–86.

Hersey, J. 1946. *Hiroshima*. New York: Alfred A. Knopf.

Herzog, A. 1977. *Heat*. New York: Simon & Schuster.

Hopkinson, N. 2000. *Midnight Robber*. New York: Warner Aspect.

In Time. 2011. Directed by Andrew Niccol. USA: 20th Century Fox.

Incorporated. 2016–2017. USA: Syfy.

Indiana, R. 2018. *Tentacle*. Translated by Achy Obejas. London: And Other Stories.

Jemisin, N.K. 2015. *The Fifth Season*. London: Orbit.

Jemisin, N.K. 2016. *The Obelisk Gate*. London: Orbit.

Jemisin, N.K. 2017. *The Stone Sky*. London: Orbit.

Jemisin, N.K. 2018. *How Long 'Til Black Future Month?* London: Orbit.

Kingsolver, B. 2012. *Flight Behaviour*. London: Faber & Faber.

Koontz, D. 1981. *The Eyes of Darkness*. New York: Pocket Books.

Ladybug, Ladybug. 1963. Directed by Frank Perry. USA: United Artists.

Lanchester, J. 2019. *The Wall*. London: Faber.

Le Guin, U. 1971. *The Lathe of Heaven*. New York: Avon Books.

Le Guin, U. 1974. *The Dispossessed*.

Le Guin, U. 2015. *The Wind's Twelve Quartets & The Compass Rose*. London: Gollancz.

Les Misérables. 2019. Directed by Ladj Ly. France: Le Pacte.

Leviathan. 2013. Directed by Lucien Castaing-Taylor and Verena Paravel. USA: Harvard Sensory Ethnography Lab.

Liu, C. 2015. *The Three-Body Problem*. Translated by Ken Liu. London: Head of Zeus.

Lloyd, S. 2008. *The Carbon Diaries 2015*. London: Hachette Children's Books.

McCaffrey, A. 1968. *Dragonflight*. New York: Ballantine Books.

McCarthy, C. 2006. *The Road*. New York: Alfred A. Knopf.

Microscope Explorer (updated version, 7 April 2020). 2020. Online/PDF [Game]. Lame Mage Productions.

Mitchison, N. 1985. *Memoirs of a Spacewoman*. London: The Women's Press.

Moss, S. 2018. *Ghost Wall*. London: Granta Books.

Moss, S. 2020. *Summerwater*. London: Picador.

Mr. Robot. 2015–2019. USA: USA Network.

Murray, Les. 1993. *Translations from the Natural World*. Manchester: Carcanet Press.

On the Beach. 1959. Directed by Stanley Kramer. USA: United Artists.

Person of Interest. 2011–2016. USA: CBS.

Pohl, F. 1959. 'The Snowmen', *Galaxy Magazine* 18(2), 141–149.

Pohl, F., and Kornbluth, C. *The Space Merchants*. New York: Ballantine Books.

Princess Mononoke. 1997. Directed by Hayao Miyazaki. Japan: Studio Ghibli.

Rand, A. 1943. *The Fountainhead*. Indianapolis, IN: Bobbs Merrill.

Rand, A. 1957. *Atlas Shrugged*. New York: Random House.

Reynold, M. 1968. *Mercenary from Tomorrow*. New York: Ace Books.

Rich, N. 2013. *Odds Against Tomorrow*. New York: Farrar, Straus and Giroux.

Roberts, J.W. 1893. *Looking Within: The Misleading Tendencies of Looking Backward Made Manifest*. New York: A.S. Barnes.

Robinson, K.S. 1992. *Red Mars*. New York: Spectra.

Robinson, K.S. 1993. *Green Mars*. New York: Spectra.

Robinson, K.S. 1996. *Blue Mars*. New York: Spectra.

Robinson, K.S. 2015. *Aurora*. London: Orbit.

Ross, A. 1889. *Speaking of Ellen*. New York: G.W. Dillingham.

Shakespeare, W. 2006. *Hamlet*. Edited by Ann Thompson and Neil Taylor. London: The Arden Shakespeare.

Shute, N. 1957. *On the Beach*. London: Heinemann.

Silko, L.M. 1991. *Almanac of the Dead*. New York: Simon & Schuster.

Solo: A Star Wars Story. 2018. Directed by Ron Howard. USA: Lucasfilm.

Spirited Away. 2011. Directed by Hayao Miyazaki. Japan: Studio Ghibli.

The Terminator. 1984. Directed by James Cameron. USA: Orion Pictures.

Terminator Genisys. 2015. Directed by Alan Taylor. USA: Paramount Pictures.

Terminator Salvation. 2009. Directed by McG. USA: Warner Bros. Pictures.

Testament. 1983. Directed by Lynne Littman. USA: Paramount Pictures.

Threads. 1984. Directed by Mick Jackson. UK: BBC.

Vinge, V. 2016. *True Names and the Opening of the Cyberspace Frontier*. London: Penguin.

Vinton, A.D. 1890. *Looking Further Backward: Being a Series of Lectures Delivered to the Freshman Class at Shawmut College, by Professor Won Lung Li (Successor of Prof. Julian West)*. Albany, NY: Albany Book.

Vizenor, G. 1990. *Bearheart: The Heirship Chronicles*. Minneapolis: University of Minnesota Press.

The War Game. 1965. Directed by Peter Watkins. UK: BBC.

Wells, H.G. 1914. *The World Set Free: A Story of Mankind*. London: Macmillan & Co., Limited.

Wolfe, T. 1987. *The Bonfire of the Vanities*. New York: Farrar Straus Giroux.

Wright, A. 2013. *The Swan Book*. London: Constable.

Wylie, P. 1945. 'The Paradise Crater'. *Blue Book* 81(6) (October).

Wylie, P. 2007. *Triumph*. London: University of Nebraska Press.

INDEX

Note: *Italic* page numbers refer to figures and page numbers followed by 'n' denote endnotes.